├┄├┄├┄├┄├┄├┄├┄├┄├┄├┄

# Managing Human

## ERRATUM

### Managing Human Resource Development
by Leonard Nadler and Garland D. Wiggs

The statements on page 157 that "there is no restriction about selling from the platform" at Lakewood Publications' conferences and that "selling is not only permitted but encouraged" are incorrect. Lakewood Publications gives the following instructions to all faculty members at each of its conferences sponsored by *TRAINING: The Magazine of Human Resources Development,* including the national TRAINING conference in New York City:

> *If you have any "sell," save it for after your session.*
> We are pleased that faculty members find that speaking at a TRAINING conference provides valuable contacts. But equally important is to keep in mind that participants at TRAINING conferences don't want to pay for a session that is company propaganda or product puff. Reaction to this type of sell is often so strongly negative that the faculty member loses credibility rather than gaining new prospects. Use your biography (distributed to each attendee at your session) to describe your products and services. This eliminates any need to "sell" your wares from the podium. If you want to personally sell services or distribute promotional literature, do it *after* your session. Frankly, we feel so strongly about this that we won't invite back faculty members who use their sessions to sell their products.

┅┽┅┽┅┽┅┽┅┽┅┽┅┽┅┽┅┽┥

*Leonard Nadler*

*Garland D. Wiggs*

┅┽┅┽┅┽┥

# Managing Human Resource Development

Jossey-Bass Publishers

San Francisco • London • 1986

MANAGING HUMAN RESOURCE DEVELOPMENT
*A Practical Guide*
by Leonard Nadler and Garland D. Wiggs

Copyright © 1986 by: Jossey-Bass Inc., Publishers
433 California Street
San Francisco, California 94104

&

Jossey-Bass Limited
28 Banner Street
London EC1Y 8QE

**Library of Congress Cataloging-in-Publication Data**

Nadler, Leonard.
  Managing human resource development.

  (The Jossey-Bass management series)
  Bibliography: p. 275
  Includes index.
  1. Personnel management.   I. Wiggs, Garland D.
II. Title.   III. Series..
HF5549.N18     1986          658.3          86-7339
ISBN 1-55542-006-0

Manufactured in the United States of America

The paper in this book meets the guidelines for
permanence and durability of the Committee on
Production Guidelines for Book Longevity of the
Council on Library Resources.

JACKET DESIGN BY WILLI BAUM

FIRST EDITION

*Code 8623*

*The Jossey-Bass*
*Management Series*

Consulting Editors
Human Resources

Leonard Nadler
Zeace Nadler
*College Park, Maryland*

# Preface

This book, which deals with managing the human resource development (HRD) unit within an organization, could not have been written a decade ago. Although there were HRD managers then, managing the HRD unit was not as complicated or as significant as it has become.

In the past, HRD practitioners were rightly concerned with designing and delivering HRD learning programs. That is still the main focus of the HRD unit, but there are new challenges as well. Organizational leaders are asking more questions about how the HRD unit is managed and how it interfaces with all other parts of the organization.

The need for a book focusing on managing the HRD unit became apparent through our consulting work with a variety of organizations, both in the United States and abroad. At George Washington University, where we offer a graduate program in HRD, the students, often HRD practitioners, asked for more work related to managing the HRD unit. We used to send those students to other parts of the university for work in business administration and management science. But they often felt that those courses were too general and did not address the specific concerns of the HRD manager.

Clearly there was a need for a good book that would address these concerns and be of use to our clients and students. There are many books on how to design HRD programs, identify needs, select instructors, and so on. Although some of these books contain a chapter on managing the HRD unit, none contained the depth that we sought in response to the needs of our clients and students.

## Purpose and Audience

Our purpose was to write a book directed specifically to current HRD managers and those aspiring to manage HRD units. Many HRD managers have a background in HRD or have worked in school systems ranging from elementary schools to universities. They were selected by their employers for their knowledge of the HRD function, but they are also expected to know how to manage. Many have not had the experience or training to enable them to fulfill that role.

Sometimes line managers are assigned to head HRD units as part of their career development. Generally, they know little about the HRD function, except that it provides some kind of training. This book is designed to help these managers expand their knowledge of the HRD function, while improving their ability to manage this unique unit within the organization.

There are also those in HRD who are not yet managers, although they aspire to be. Too often they are advised to leave HRD and get some managerial experience. But if this advice is followed, the organization may lose an effective HRD person with management potential. This book will enable an HRD practitioner to make the transition to manager without having to leave the unit.

Thus, the primary audience for *Managing Human Resource Development* includes current and aspiring HRD managers, human resource specialists, and line managers who may be asked to take on HRD responsibilities. This book can also serve as a source for managers throughout the organization, enabling them to understand the HRD unit better and thus improve their interactions with the HRD manager and staff.

At one time, almost all human resource functions (generally called personnel) were to be found in one unit in an organization. As specialization developed, some of those functions spun off into separate units. HRD is one example of this spin-off process. For this reason, there are now people in various human resource units who do not understand HRD and how it should be managed. Such understanding can contribute to the important goal of coordinating, not consolidating, human resource activities within an organization.

Although not primarily intended as a textbook, *Managing Human Resource Development* provides an overview of the field that could prove useful in university programs in HRD. This book could also be used as either a text or a reference in university programs in management, personnel, business administration, and similar areas.

### Scope and Treatment

In Chapter One we discuss HRD as an expression of the philosophy of an organization. We present an overview of the field and define the terms and concepts we will be using in the remainder of the book.

From the general, we move to the specific in Chapter Two as we discuss policy. The involvement of HRD managers in policy development is fairly recent, and there is some research that can help us understand just what HRD policy looks like in some organizations.

There are many ways to organize the HRD unit, and in Chapter Three we discuss the most common patterns we have found. Particular attention is given to the question of whether to provide HRD by using internal resources or by relying on external resources. Attention is also paid to the differences between large and small organizations and to the complexities faced by multisite organizations.

The next two chapters concern finance and budgeting, an area all too often overlooked by HRD managers. In Chapter Four we discuss organizational financial systems. For the reader with a background in business or accounting, the bulk of this chapter will not be new. However, for those who do not clearly understand the differences among corporations, partnerships, and individual proprietorships and how each organizes its particular financial basis, this chapter will be most helpful. Especially useful is a discussion of how these factors relate to HRD. Also explained are the two basic financial statements—the balance sheet and the profit and loss statement.

Chapter Five becomes even more specific as we deal with budgeting for HRD. Here we discuss the three most common ways of organizing the HRD unit: as a budget-item center, as a cost center, and as a profit center. Different types of budgets with specific reference to HRD are also presented.

The size of an HRD unit can vary from a single individual to hundreds. Chapter Six explores research concerning the roles of HRD staff, with particular focus on how that research can be applied to staffing decisions. Attention is paid to using nonprofessionals within the organization as part of the HRD staff.

For those who choose to make their careers in HRD, Chapter Seven explores patterns for the professional growth of the HRD staff. Here, the major emphasis is on the permanent staff, but consideration is also given to those temporary and part-time people who work in the HRD unit.

HRD programs require facilities and equipment, both internal and external. This topic is discussed in Chapter Eight. In recent years there has been an increase in the number of organizations choosing to build their own HRD centers. We explore the pros and cons of that development as well as what is essential in the area of facilities and equipment for HRD.

A frequently overlooked aspect of HRD management is the need to maintain ongoing relations with all departments within the organization. This is the topic of Chapter Nine. We also provide examples of how relations can be promoted and mention some of the benefits of providing for this unique aspect of HRD management.

The need for sound planning has become increasingly apparent. In recent years strategic planning has begun to make an impact on organizations. In Chapter Ten we discuss that type of planning, as well as the more conventional types of long-range and short-range planning, and explore how they relate to HRD.

In small HRD units, the HRD manager also functions as a supervisor. In large units, there may be one or more supervisors who report to the HRD manager. In Chapter Eleven we discuss the various supervisory activities related to HRD.

Finally, in Chapter Twelve, we address other issues and current trends. Given the dynamism in the field of management, we could be considered foolhardy for including material that attempts to look into the future. The issues explored here illustrate the complexity of HRD and demonstrate how that function relates to many different aspects of organizational life.

## Acknowledgments

This book is the result of many years of experience working with a multitude of clients and students. Although to list them all would take many pages, we are grateful for the contributions each of them has made to this project.

Special acknowledgment is due to two people who have contributed in different ways. Patti Wiggs kept Gar to the task and provided a sounding board for his ideas. Zeace Nadler served as editor and had the task of keeping both authors moving along. Many are the times she edited and returned drafts knowing that she had to confront the "pride of authorship." Through it all she maintained her composure, sense of humor, and professional good judgment.

*Washington, D.C.*                                      Leonard Nadler
*June 1986*                                              Garland D. Wiggs

# Contents

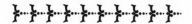

# The Authors

Leonard Nadler is professor of adult education and human resource development in the School of Education and Human Development at the George Washington University. He is also president of Nadler Associates.

Nadler received his B.A. degree (1948) in business administration and his M.A. degree (1950) in business education from the City College of New York. His Ed.D. degree (1962) is in educational administration from Columbia University. He provides assistance in individual and organizational development to a variety of private and public organizations. A major emphasis of his work has been helping organizations improve their human resource development staff and programs. He has worked in thirty different countries.

He is a member of numerous professional societies such as the American Society for Training and Development (ASTD), American Association for Adult and Continuing Education, World Future Society, and the Society for Intercultural Training, Education, and Research. He was a member of the National Board of ASTD for five years. He is the recipient of many awards, including the Gordon Bliss Memorial Award of ASTD, the highest award for an individual member given by ASTD. In 1984 he was selected by the readers of *Training* magazine as one of the ten outstanding trainers. In 1985 he received an award from the Washington, D.C., chapter of ASTD for his contributions to publications in the field of human resource development.

Nadler has published more than 125 articles and chapters in various professional publications. His own books include *Clients and Consultants* (coeditor, 1985), *The Handbook of Human Resource Development* (editor, 1984), *Personal Skills for the Manager* (1983), *Designing Training Programs: The Critical Events Model* (1982), *Corporate Human Resource Development* (1980), *Developing Human Resources* (2nd ed., 1979), and *The Conference Book* (coauthor, 1977). He is the series editor of the Gulf Publishing series entitled Releasing Human Potential, a consultant to the *The Trainer's Resource* (HRD Press), and a consultant to Jossey-Bass Publishers, for their series entitled Human Resources.

Garland D. Wiggs is professor of adult education and human resource development at the George Washington University, Washington, D.C., and president of Association Educational Services, Inc.

Wiggs received his B.B.A. degree (1956) from the University of Cincinnati, his M.A. degree (1960) from Northern Colorado University, and his Ed.D. degree (1971) from the George Washington University. He is a licensed professional counselor in the Commonwealth of Virginia.

He serves as a consultant and learning specialist for numerous private and public organizations throughout the United States. As human resource development practitioner, he has served his clients by assisting in establishing policy; assessing learning requirements; designing and implementing technical skills training and education programs, human resource utilization, and career development programs; conducting course and program evaluations; and developing course materials and job aids.

Wiggs was an associate director of the Educational Service Bureau of the *Wall Street Journal,* education director of the Ohio Petroleum Marketers' Association, education director of the Printing Industry of Ohio, and merchandising specialist and dealer trainer with Texaco, Inc.

Wiggs is a past president (1976) of the Washington, D.C., chapter of the American Society for Training and Development.

He is also a member of numerous professional organizations including the National Society for Performance and Instruction, the American Association for Adult and Continuing Education, and the Commission of Professors of Adult Education.

# Managing Human Resource Development

*A Practical Guide*

# Chapter 1

# Role of HRD in the Organization

$T$his book is about the organization and management of the human resource development unit in all kinds of businesses, industries, and government organizations and agencies in both the for-profit and nonprofit sectors of the economy. This chapter will set the stage for the remainder of the book by establishing the philosophical base for the human resource development (HRD) functions in organizations and will define the terms currently used by HRD practitioners in this ever expanding and diverse professional field.

### Managing for Mission Accomplishment

When asked, "What makes your organization successful?" some managers will respond, "Our service reputation, of course"; others will say, "It's our product lines" or "our extensive member programs"; while still others may say, "Our marketing savvy" or "good, sound financial management!" An even better question to ask these successful managers would be, "Just how did you manage your resources to get your organization to this successful juncture in its business life?" What was it that caused their enterprises (a for-profit business organization, a nonprofit membership association organization, a community health care institution, a government agency, or a military organization) to become successful, while others ended up in bankruptcy court as failed enterprises? There are, of course, numerous reasons why one enterprise is successful while others fail.

However, it should be noted that all organizations, the successful and the unsuccessful alike, began their operations with three major ingredients for success: financial resources (money and securities), physical resources (equipment, tools, facilities), and human resources (people to do the work). The management team had to develop and manage these three critical resources. If an organization's success is equated to goal achievement, as it certainly should be, the enterprise achieves that mission through well-developed and well-managed resources. Hence, the ultimate responsibility for an organization's success rests with its managers.

The management team consists of all the individuals in managerial and supervisory positions, from the chief executive officer to the first-line supervisor. The organization's management team must develop a comprehensive financial management plan to ensure that sufficient funds are generated and managed in such a way as to be available when needed to keep the organization afloat. The team must also see to it that the equipment and facilities needed to produce its products or provide its services are constantly updated to meet the current and anticipated needs of their customers and/or clients. Given the rapid rate of change in modern technology, the management team must also keep abreast of the new materials, equipment, and production processes that may allow it to increase efficiency and lower costs.

For a majority of organizations today, the most difficult resource to manage is its human resources—its people. The effective utilization of an organization's employees is most often *the* critical factor in the successful accomplishment of its mission. Regardless of the amount of computerization that has taken place in offices, or robotization in factories, all companies and organizations require people to perform their work. It is the responsibility of the management team to provide the leadership necessary to recruit, select, orient, manage, and develop the organization's employees, who in turn will carry out their assigned responsibilities to help the enterprise achieve its goals. Managers are successful only if their employees are successful. The truly successful organization accomplishes its mission through development of its human resources to their fullest potential. In many organizations today, managers are accused of not managing and supervisors of not supervising. While executives try to find solutions to the problems associated with poor labor-management relations, low motivation, low morale, and low productivity, labor costs continue to skyrocket. These management problems in U.S. industry have been exacerbated by plant shutdowns and closures, employee layoffs, reductions in the work force, and numerous labor union contract "give backs" during recessions in the economy.

As Nadler (1979) has suggested, three major specialized staff functions have begun to emerge in the human resources management (HRM) field to assist managers and supervisors in carrying out their responsibilities for subordinate employees. These specialized human resource staff functions in an enterprise must always be controlled by line management and viewed as an integrated management process. Ideally, new employee recruitment and selection should always be based on management's assessment of its job placement needs. Each employee should have a clearly defined, mission-oriented description for his or her position. The employee's HRD activity requirements for training, education, or development should be determined only *after* comparing the individual's entry-level competencies (skills, knowledge, and attitudes) with the required job competencies and expected performance standards for the job or task assignments. Effective on-the-job performance is most often a direct result of the mutual efforts of the individual employee and his or her immediate supervisor. Hence, job duties and responsibilities must be clearly defined, and there must be agreement as to job performance expectations. Effective plans for the employee's needs for job performance improvement and personal growth are a necessity, as are good supervisory practices that promote on-the-job coaching and counseling of the employee.

In the well-managed enterprise, each of the human resource functions—management, development, and environment—should be seen as interdependent. For example, the initial selection criteria for the new position should always be based upon its placement need (HRM). The new employee's learning requirements (HRD) will depend to a large degree on how well his or her

| *Development (HRD)* | *Management (HRM)* | *Environment (HRE)* |
| --- | --- | --- |
| Training | Recruitment Selection | Job enrichment |
| Education | Placement Appraisal | Job enlargement |
| Development | Compensation Work force planning | Organizational development |

previous competencies (the skills, knowledge, and attitudes already acquired prior to entry into the position), match those needed for the new job assignment. The HRE activities of the enterprise should be directly related to its management team's perceived need for organizational growth, renewal, and change to meet new environmental challenges (and opportunites).

There are many examples of the effective functioning of human resource development throughout history. There is much historical evidence to suggest that fathers taught their skills to sons, and mothers taught theirs to daughters. Later, apprentices learned craft skills from their guild masters; and, when the industrial revolution began in earnest, factory schools were established to teach new workers their required job skills. The roles and functions of human resource development are directed toward the release of the human potential in individuals, groups, and organizations through *learning* experiences that result from planned and organized training, education, and development activities.

## Roles of the HRD Practitioner in Mission Accomplishment

Nadler (1979) identifies three major subroles of the HRD practitioner: learning specialist, administrator, and consultant. While this book is focused on the HRD administrator role, the learning specialist and consultant roles are equally important for accomplishing the mission of HRD in an organization.

HRD might best be viewed as a comprehensive learning system for the release of the organization's human potentials—a system that includes both vicarious (classroom, mediated, simulated) learning experiences *and* experiential, on-the-job experiences that are keyed to the organization's reason for existence (profit, survival, service, product, and so on). The organization's HRD mission is (1) to maximize the learner's (employee's) effectiveness on the current job, (2) to facilitate the individual's mobility to the next probable assignment, and (3) to increase the employee's (learner's) commitment to the organization by providing stimulating learning opportunities for personal growth and change.

HRD must provide needed learning and growth experiences to both individuals and groups to help them resolve organizational problems and exploit opportunities for organizational change. The individuals and groups served by HRD activities may be employees and nonemployees alike. Many, if not most, large enterprises today accept responsibility for providing for the special learning needs not only of their own employees but also for their customers, clients, and often the general public.

In order to differentiate HRD from "learning" that might be acquired in an ad hoc or haphazard way, we define HRD activities as those that meet the following criteria: "Human resource development—organized learning, over a given period of time, to provide the possibility of performance change" (Nadler, 1984a, xxviii). With such a specific definition, it becomes possible to assign management responsibilities for HRD, to allocate resources for HRD, and to measure the effectiveness of HRD programming in the enterprise.

*Training Defined.* By far the greatest number of HRD activities in all types of organizations are in the area of *training*. Training activities focus on learning the skills, knowledge, and attitudes required to initially perform a job or task or to improve upon the performance of a current job or task. The skills, knowledge, and attitudes to be learned in the training activity must be clearly identified, and there must be opportunities for direct and immediate application of what has been learned.

The costs associated with the design and conduct of training activities should be viewed by management as an expense attributable to the cost of doing business. The results of the learning in this HRD activity are directly measurable, in that the learning is job related and performance based. Training activities, therefore, can be offered at very low risk to their organizational sponsors. One example of an employee training program would be a word-processing skills training course for clerical employees, working in a unit with newly installed word-processing equipment. The skills, knowledge, and attitudes necessary for the word processor position can be specified, and the clerk-trainees can apply their newly learned abilities immediately upon completion of the training.

*Education Defined.* Education focuses on learning new skills, knowledge, and attitudes that will equip an individual to assume a new job or to do a different task at some predetermined *future* time. The applications of the newly learned skills, knowledge, and attitudes will be sometime in the foreseeable future—two years or less, in the majority of cases. The learning to be gained is identified from *known* prerequisites of the future job or task assignment.

Industries that require their employees to have high technological skills and competencies frequently offer more education activities than do organizations having fewer advanced and changing technology requirements. Education activities may well represent a significant amount of the total HRD budget and activity level in certain enterprises today because of the need for their employees to perform new jobs and to become acquainted with emerging technologies. It is often true that a number of individual employees will participate in varied education activities if the enterprise provides tuition reimbursement for their enrollment in courses or programs of study at a technical institute or college. This is especially true if the employees' educational assistance program (EAP) is controlled by an HRD policy that specifies that the course or program of study must be directly job or career related if the tuition is to be reimbursed to the employee.

Education activities are to be viewed as short-term investments in the future. An example of an HRD activity in the education area is the company-sponsored engineering degree program, offered in the firm's classroom facilities by the extension division of a major university. The learners in the university's off-campus engineering degree program are all presently employed by the firm, as engineering technicians. The company needs additional engineers, and the management philosophy has always encouraged a "promotion from within" staffing policy.

The learning gained from educational experiences can be measured; that is, one can test the participant to determine the actual amount of learning gained from the educational experience as such. However, the on-the-job application of the learning is impossible to measure before the learner actually gets the job assignment. Consequently, there is some risk associated with such HRD activities. For example, the individual might eventually not be employed in the proposed future job. An even more likely possibility is that the individual might accept a job offer in another (competing) organization.

*Development Defined.* Development activites are not job related but are oriented to both personal and organizational growth. The focus of such activities is on broadening the learner's conceptual and perceptual base in areas not previously explored or experienced by the individual. Development activities provide "learning" opportunities that encourage such growth.

A major organizational goal for such employee growth is to better equip the employee to cope with *any* future unknown forces of change that may impact on the organization. A secondary, but often an equally important, goal for HRD development activities reflects the concern many managers have regarding the retention of their employees in the organization.

By asking employees to identify their own career plans through the mechanism known as an individual career development plan, the enterprise is better able to provide a variety of learning activities, work experiences, and so on to aid in the achievement of such career goals. Such developmental activities can help individuals qualify for the career of their choice—some moving up the organizational ladder, some moving out of the organization to seek other employment, and still others staying, until retirement, employed in the job cluster of their chosen career.

Development activities can only be viewed by senior management and by the board of directors as long-term, high-risk investments in the ultimate future of the enterprise. But such

activities can help ensure that there will always be a cadre of
employees and managers in the organization who will be able to
cope with whatever future changes may impact on the enterprise.
Generally, only very large business corporations and agencies of
the federal government have *formal* HRD development programs
for all employees or managers. However, many employers have
long recognized the validity of offering temporary work project
assignments (for example, job rotations, vacation replacement
assignments, community service project assignments, and the like)
to selected individuals to help broaden their base of understanding
as well as to provide opportunities for personal and professional
growth in areas not previously explored by them. Such development activities are known to increase the individual's worth to the
enterprise, as well as to provide opportunities for his or her
personal growth and well-being.

### Purpose of HRD

    The ultimate purpose of HRD activities is to "make a
difference" in the real world of costs, quality, quantity, accuracy,
and timeliness. HRD activities, as such, do *not* reduce costs,
improve quality or quantity, or benefit the enterprise in any way.
It is the on-the-job *applications* of learning that ultimately *can*
reduce costs, improve quality, and so forth. Hence, critical
management challenge is, How can the results of training and
education best be applied back on the job?
    *Performance Gap Concept.* HRD is one means of closing a
performance gap between what is and what should be—but only in
instances where skills, knowledge, or attitudes can make the
difference. Performance gaps can occur for reasons having nothing
whatsoever to do with lack of learning. The work may be boring;
the work flow may be inappropriate for handling the materials
needed to do the job; the organization may have "grown like
Topsy," and its structure may no longer be appropriate for the
work units; or there may be poor supervision or management
leadership. Many of these situations are *not* susceptible to
resolution by an HRD activity. However, the professional staff and
the manager of the HRD unit will nevertheless be able to

recommend solutions and show the organization's line managers how to identify and resolve the problems that are causing performance gaps.

We also know that in many cases an individual's competencies (skills, knowledge, and attitudes) make no difference between what is and what should be in the real world of the job. For example, a young sales clerk in a department store may know perfectly well how to ring up a purchase on the computerized cash register. However, when the store's computer system is down because of a software problem, and there are no manual sales forms available at the check-out stand, there is a "performance gap." This "performance gap" is especially noticeable if you are waiting in a long line to purchase a single $5 item, and it takes the young man's supervisor an inordinate amount of time to deliver the missing forms from the far side of the store.

*The Can Do, But Don't Situations.* HRD activities can improve a person's job skills and can also improve his or her sense of motivation. However, good performance on the job can fail to occur for a variety of reasons, having little or nothing to do with ability or motivations. The removal of any roadblocks to transferring learning from the classroom to the job, for example, is a managerial responsibility and a key management support system ingredient. Thus, a shop supervisor might enroll in a course on "Listening" and learn to listen carefully to subordinates' suggestions, complaints, and so on. If, however, the department manager has let it be known, in no uncertain terms, that listening to employees is a gross waste of valuable supervisory time, obviously no one will do any listening.

*Line-Management Tasks.* It is the HRD staff's job to assist the line-management team in carrying out its HRD responsibilities. The line managers, with the assistance of the HRD staff as needed, must (1) identify the "difference" in cost, quality, and quantity expected to result if on-the-job application of the learning takes place; and (2) do whatever is necessary to ensure that the on-the-job application of learning will, in fact, take place. These two tasks are major accountabilities of the line-management team alone—from the first-line supervisors to the chief executive officer of the enterprise. The actual design, implementation, and

management of the HRD programs can be done by the human
resource developers working under the direction of the HRD
manager. Also, whenever necessary, the HRD staff, serving as in-
house consultants to the organization's line managers, can assess
training, education, and development needs to help them determine the causes for the performance gaps within their line or staff
units.

*HRD Manager/Staff Tasks.* The HRD activities are only
"the means to an end" and most certainly not "ends in and of
themselves." The outputs of HRD activities should always be in
terms of their impact on costs, yields, problem solving, exploitation of opportunities, and the like—the real world measures of
success. HRD activities should *not* be measured in terms of how
many hours of training took place or of the number of different
"courses" offered one year versus the previous one. However, the
participants' "happiness factor" is considered by many HRD
managers to be an important criteria in the evaluation of a
successful learning activity. It is important for the participants
(trainees) to "like" the content to be learned, the instructor, and the
learning facility itself—its location and its support services. Do not
ignore those who spread the word about the value of classroom
time to their supervisors, even when such measures are not relevant
to the real mission of the organization. But when only "happiness
factor" measures are used to evaluate the performance of the
organization's HRD unit, it tends to foster the line manager's
belief that the human resource developers are well-meaning but
reactive individuals, "playing at keeping school in the
organization."

In the enterprise where real world measures are applied to
the results of effective HRD activities, the developers are viewed as
a proactive group of human resource specialists (change agents)
who can offer positive help to the line-management team in
resolving organizational, productivity, and personnel problems. In
these organizations, senior managers look to the professional staff
of their HRD unit for assistance in identifying and recommending
resolutions to organizational and customer problems. Lower-level
supervisors and managers in such organizations expect the help of

the HRD unit's staff in identifying appropriate resolutions to their personnel and productivity problems.

***HRD Manager's Dual Roles.*** A HRD manager is called upon to wear two hats when carrying out the responsibilities of directing the HRD function in an organization. The HRD manager is first a line manager of an organizational unit that performs a staff function. Secondly, the HRD manager is a staff specialist who serves as a consultant to the organization's chief executive officer and helps the line-management team resolve its personnel, productivity, and organizational problems.

In their first role, HRD managers are responsible for the same planning, organizing, controlling, budgeting, staffing, and developing functions of management as are the other line managers in the enterprise. In their second role, HRD managers, working toward the resolution of the personnel and organizational problems of the line managers they serve, must rely on their own and their staff's technical HRD skills, knowledge, and competencies to deliver effective and efficient services. But what HRD skills and competencies should HRD managers possess? Are such competencies and skills unique to HRD managers? Some will say, "A good manager can manage any type of unit." Others will emphatically state, "Unless you are qualified to perform the technical HRD skills, how could you manage those individuals who perform them in your unit?" While we will not try to settle that debate here, we do know that there are certain kinds of knowledge that every HRD manager must have in order to be effective in an organization.

### Knowledge Needs of the Effective HRD Manager

***Organizations as Social Systems.*** The effective HRD manager is aware of the fact that organizations, much like human organisms, tend to develop their own "personalities," depending to a large degree on the nature of the enterprise, the founding executive's management style, the type and kinds of employees, and the like. It is also true that organizations, like human beings, will often develop in well-defined stages—birth, growth, and maturity.

When first established, organizations tend to require few HRD activities, since the emphasis is on survival. Most often, new organizations have relatively few employees and tend to hire very few people who have already acquired the skills necessary for their positions. In an organization's next stage, as it begins to grow and becomes profitable (if it is a for-profit firm in the private sector), HRD activities come to be offered on an as-needed basis, serving to "fix" some identified organizational problem. The practice is very much like applying a bandage to an organizational "cut" or "scrape," for the HRD activities are applied *only* when the problem is identified and are continued only as long as the problem exists. Once the organizational "ill" is cured, the HRD activities are not continued on an ongoing, comprehensive, or preventive basis. It is most often the managers of fully mature organizations who recognize the need for continual and comprehensive HRD activities for the successful accomplishment of the mission of their enterprises. Unfortunately, however, even some mature organizations fall victims of organizational senility because their management team fails to encourage employee and organizational renewal through effective training, education, and development activities.

*Operation of the Organizational "Systems."* The effective HRD manager must understand the mission and goals of the enterprise. In addition, "hands on" knowledge about the operations of the enterprise are important to the effective HRD manager. What are the critical HRD variables in the organization? These will be the immediate, make-or-break variables that directly affect the HRD unit's mission accomplishments. For example, is there a need to improve employee productivity, to lower employee turnover rates, to reduce machine downtime due to untrained maintenance personnel, or to develop better supervisory practices within the organization?

What are the performance standards for the critical HRD variables? Does the HRD manager know the performance indicators—the measures of success or failure as set by the organization's senior management team? Does the HRD manager know what is an acceptable deviation from the *stated* standards of performance? Just what assumptions does the organization's leadership make about people and about their productivity and performance standards? What are the key outputs (accomplishments) and key inputs (resources) of the organization? Just how are the management resources needed to accomplish the HRD functions in the organization controlled? What external forces have an impact on the organization, if any? These are all critical problem areas that many managers perceive as being the make-or-break variables affecting an organization's accomplishment of its goals and that consequently should become a focus of its HRD unit's mission.

*Environment Surrounding the Organization.* The HRD manager must be aware of the many forces that have an influence on the organization as it strives to accomplish its mission. The HRD manager should know the competition within the "industry" to which the organization belongs. "Knowing the competition" provides the HRD manager with an important intelligence edge. In addition, the HRD manager must be aware of the many federal, state, and local laws and regulations pertaining to human resource utilization and development; the accreditation policies and regulations of professional associations and societies (as required for individuals employed in the organization); and the general economic, social, and political context in which every organization must operate.

The HRD manager must get to know the key people in the organization whose support will be required for implementation of any successful HRD program. Who are likely to be the supporters, who the resisters? Are there subject matter experts or others who may be neutral to HRD but who are influential in making things happen in the organization? In addition to such internal people, the HRD manager has to establish effective contacts outside the organization. There are a wide variety of people, including supplier-vendors, independent consultants, government officials, representatives of key competitive organizations, and professional peers who can be most helpful to the HRD manager in accomplishing the organization's HRD mission. Knowledgeable HRD managers comprehend the needs and agendas of all those with whom they must interface to accomplish their HRD missions—friend and foe alike!

*Leadership Philosophy of the Organization's Management Team.* The HRD manager must know what senior management expects of its employees and managers and be in agreement with that collective leadership philosophy. The HRD manager's role as in-house consultant to the organization's chief executive officer requires acceptance of the same leadership philosophy if there is to be mutual respect and effectiveness in the HRD consultancy relationship. It is difficult, if not impossible, for HRD managers to be effective in organizations if their personal leadership styles and tendencies are not congruent with those of the organization's senior management group. Unfortunately for some HRD managers, leadership philosophies will sometimes change when a new chief executive officer or other senior-level official is appointed, causing them some very traumatic periods of adjustment (or even requiring a change of employment).

### Characteristics of an Effective HRD Manager

The HRD manager must have the ability to plan for the HRD activities of the organization. Such activities should be developed from identified training, education, and development needs of the employees, customers, and other nonemployees of the organization and from the needs associated with accomplishment of its mission. The HRD activities should also be founded upon sound HRD policies that have been approved and supported by senior management and are codified as part of the organization's operating policies. Such HRD policies should include a statement of the organization's philosophy regarding training, education, and development for its employees, supervisors, managers, and customers or other nonemployees.

The HRD manager should, with inputs from the organization's management team, establish goal priorities for the HRD activities within a one- to five-year time frame. These forecasts for future training, education, and development requirements should always be made in concert with the organization's "business" strategies and with an awareness of issues that may impact on the management team's ability to implement its strategy. The HRD manager must also seek the most appropriate organizational

structure and location for the HRD unit in terms of the enterprise's "business" functions and organizational chart. In this
effort, the HRD manager must clarify and clearly communicate the
relationships among the HRD staff, the organization's operating
elements, and individuals and groups outside the organization
with whom the HRD professional staff must interface. In addition,
the HRD manager should identify and establish appropriate HRD
management information systems to provide good internal and
external data sources and thus ensure overall HRD program
efficiency.

In staffing the HRD unit, the HRD manager should
develop mission-oriented position descriptions for the professional
staff and support personnel that describe the human resource
requirements for the unit. Once the HRD unit is staffed, the
manager should establish and implement ongoing training,
education, and development activities for the HRD employees. Far
too often, HRD staffs, "are just like the cobbler's kids—they go
barefooted." Planned HRD activities for HRD staff members are
just as critical as for any other group of employees if they are to
help accomplish the HRD mission and achieve the organization's
mission and goals.

Effective HRD managers will often use a highly participative approach to their planning and directing efforts, but they will
be decisive as well. The effective HRD manager is usually
perceived as being goal oriented, but is also known to be open-
minded. The successful HRD manager consistently uses forms of
consensual decision making. This kind of decision making is often
said to be used by "weak" leaders. Those in the field of HRD
acknowledge the realities of the organizational environments in
which most HRD managers must function. The effective HRD
manager recognizes the fact that it is not sufficient merely to
tolerate differences of opinion. The key to successful HRD
management is to really want to hear different opinions and beliefs
and to accept them without becoming defensive!

Although the good HRD manager is seen by his or her line-
management peers as being "technically" competent in the HRD
field, they also recognize that the HRD manager is practical and
will be willing to forgo the *ideal* implementation of an HRD

activity when other organizational realities of the situation demand that. The HRD manager is respected for having the technical competencies required for the design and delivery of effective and efficient HRD activities. The HRD manager is also respected for having common sense and being realistic enough to give in when the "greater good"—the needs of the line organizations—demands it.

The most effective HRD managers build confidence in their HRD staffs by accepting the risks associated with delegation. These managers let their staffs solve problems without intervention or interference and provide their advice only when asked or only when absolutely necessary. Individual risk taking on the part of their subordinates is encouraged. They provide the individual staff member the support required to be able to learn from making mistakes.

As a philosophy of organizational management, HRD acknowledges the major contributions that human resources make to the accomplishment of an organization's mission, goals, and objectives. Consequently, once an organization's management team comes to accept the HRD philosophy, it will put a high value on the potential of each individual employee in the organization, will provide opportunities for personal and organizational growth, and will treat each individual with the respect and dignity he or she so richly deserves.

···⁌ *Chapter 2* ⁊···

# Designing and
# Implementing HRD Policy

In this chapter we focus on both the need for and the process of establishing HRD policy within organizations. Managers today recognize that human resources are as important as capital and physical resources to the smooth and efficient operation of the enterprise and to achievement of its mission, goals, and objectives (Drucker, 1974; Nadler, 1980). Just as strategies and policies have been developed for the utilization of nonhuman resources, many managers now recognize the importance of developing policies for guiding managerial decisions in the field of HRD.

The operation of the HRD function has historically been considered the responsibility of the personnel department in the majority of large organizations (Miner and Miner, 1973). The personnel department was responsible not only for policies related to employee training, education, and development (human resource development) but also for policies related to employee recruitment, selection, placement, compensation, and appraisal, record keeping, and work force planning (human resources utilization), as well as for the activities related to job enlargement, organizational development, and the like (human resources environment). It has been only during the past twenty-five years or so that a new organizational structure has evolved in which the three functions of human resource development, utilization, and environment are seen as separate, if equal, activities. They no

17

longer are automatically placed under the umbrella of the
personnel department but instead are overseen by a senior-level
manager of human resources (Nadler, 1980).

## The HRD Manager and Policy Development

The manager of the HRD unit who is responsible for the
organization's HRD program must also be concerned with the
relation between policies for training, education, and development
programs, on the one hand, and the organizational mission and
operations, on the other. The process of developing an organization's HRD policy, as in the case of most other corporate policies,
is predicated on the need for giving focus and legitimacy to a
specific organizational function. The HRD function or program
in an organization will take many forms and utilize many
strategies and techniques in its operation. But no matter what
form it takes, an HRD policy provides the charter necessary for
both line and staff management to conduct the business of human
resource development. An HRD policy statement offers both a
rationale and legitimacy for establishing and implementing the
many and diverse functions of the HRD program and HRD unit
in the organization.

*Policy Defined.* There are numerous definitions of the term
*policy* in use today. For example, *Webster's New World Dictionary*
defines the word *policy* as "a principle, plan, or course of action,
as pursued by a government, organization, individual, etc." In a
study of HRD policies in organizations, Spector (1985, p.5) defines
policy as "an explicit written statement approved by the highest
levels of organizational authority which indicates long-term
direction and the limits within which actions shall be taken, if the
need for action should arise." Some authors describe organizational policies as being "written," "oral," "traditional," or
"cultural." We will give examples of these categories of HRD
policies later in the chapter when we discuss HRD policy.

But whatever definition one chooses, we would argue that
every policy should have the following elements:

1.  Policy should be directly related to the philosophy, goals, and objectives of the organization. Policy tends to be the foundation for all organizational planning. Policy is to an organization as a rudder is to a ship. An organization's board of directors or trustees should provide members of the management team, the employees, and customers the necessary policy to give them focus and direction in operating within and with the organization.
2.  Policy should be clearly written and communicated to all persons who will be affected by its intents and purposes. A policy must be known and understood if it is to be effectively implemented.
3.  Policies prescribe the limits and measures of future organizational and individual behavior and activity. Consequently, a policy must be reasonable and capable of being carried out by the individuals to whom it applies. An unfair or unrealistic policy will either be ignored or be implemented and used to sabotage the organization, just to prove that it was unfair or unrealistic.
4.  Policies must be internally consistent. A policy statement should not set forth conflicting goals.
5.  Policies should allow for application of judgment and individual discretion by those officials who must implement them. A policy should never be a "straitjacket" over the management of an organization, and it should be flexible enough to provide for "judgment calls" by the management team as appropriate to its own situation.
6.  Policies, like an organization's charter (its constitution and bylaws), should be relatively stable, but they should not be written in concrete and difficult to change if and when the need arises.

*Policies as Outputs of the Planning Function.* As Koontz and O'Donnell (1972) suggest, it is within the most basic of all the general managerial functions—the planning function—that the organization's mission, objectives, strategies, policies, and rules must be established. Unless the senior management team (or the owner or board of directors) decides in advance "what to do," "how to do it," "when to do it," and "who is to do it," the remaining management functions of organizing, staffing, directing and leading, and controlling the organization will be in jeopardy. Planning consists of far more than a concern for allocating financial, physical, and human resources or making schedules. Managers of organizations must plan to analyze *why* they are doing what they are doing and *how* it will make the difference in accomplishing their mission.

*Strategic and Tactical Planning.* In most organizations, the relationship of strategic to long-range (and tactical to short-range) planning is a close one in which the actual content of the planning effort is the same and occurs simultaneously. However, there is an important difference. The long-to-short poles in planning represent essentially a *time* perspective, while the strategic-tactical poles relate to organizational needs. Strategic planning takes into consideration the reason for existence of the organization within the context of its total environment, that is, those internal or external forces (resources, opportunities, constraints, pressures, and so on) that affect it. Without strategic planning, an organization runs the risk of organizational stagnation, of loss of creativity and viability, and, ultimately, of failure. One major outcome of effective management planning is organizational *policy*.

*Sources of Policy Direction.* Spector (1985) suggests that there are at least four sources of policy direction within most organizational settings:

1.  Originated—those policies that flow from the organizational mission, goals, and objectives and originate "top down" from senior management officials.
2.  Appealed—those policies that flow from the appeals of lower-level managers for exceptions to existing policies, regulations, or operating procedures.
3.  Implied—those unwritten "policies" that develop from the actions people in the organization have taken in the past and that are commonly believed to constitute policy. Such actions are commonly based on what could be called organizational "common law" or the organization's "culture."

4. Externally imposed—those policies that flow from the actions imposed on the organization by government laws or regulations, union contracts, professional standards, a membership association's code of ethics, and the like.

Broad organizational policy is established by harmonizing the strategic plans of the organization, the philosophical beliefs and values of those who create the policy, and the values held by employees, clients, customers, and the public. These organizational plans, beliefs, and values will be translated into specific policy statements that can then serve as guides for those who direct the organization, as well as for those who have dealings with it. Policy statements will also at times generate the need for new organizational plans. Without established organizational policies, there would be no limits to the kinds of management decisions that could be made and no assurance that future management decisions would be consistent with the organization's mission, goals, and objectives.

*Integration of the Organization's Mission and the HRD Mission.* A well-written and well-promulgated HRD policy can help to ensure the integration of the HRD mission with the organization's mission. Unless the organization's HRD policy gives direction to supervisors and managers and is closely related to the business of the organization, its HRD activities cannot be considered successful.

There are several reasons why an HRD policy should be developed and implemented in organizations. First, an HRD policy is needed to guide management in identifying and implementing the appropriate HRD learning activities for resolving organizational problems or exploiting new business opportunities. Second, an HRD policy is required to ensure that supervisors and managers encourage on-the-job applications of the skills, knowledge, and/or attitudes gained by participants in HRD activities. Third, an HRD policy will help to establish employee career development mechanisms that will continually assess the learning needs required for releasing both the employees' and the organization's growth potentials. Finally, an HRD policy can establish minimums for financial investments in the organization's human resources and provide a self-audit system for its managers.

## Formulation of HRD Policies in Organizations

In the majority of newly created enterprises, employees are recruited and hired who have the specific competencies and educational and/or work experience backgrounds needed for their positions. They learn to perform their assigned jobs and tasks by being told what to do, how to do it, and when to do it by their direct supervisor. Many of these newly hired employees engage in little, if any, formal HRD activity but instead perform their assigned job tasks by doing exactly what they did in their former job, or they learn new job task performances by observing other employees in the present organization and then emulating the standards of performance of those they respect or fear.

It is during the early growth years of a new organization that a variety of learning activities may be offered the employees, clients, or customers on a sporadic, as-needed basis with little or no concern for overall organizational needs or cost effectiveness. But if the organization is to survive and grow, the functions of human resource development must be activated with or without senior management's policy direction or intent. The individual unit, department, or division supervisors and managers will identify their own employees', clients', or customers' specific learning needs and begin to offer a variety of HRD activities designed to meet those needs without the knowledge that other unit managers and supervisors have identified similar learning needs and are offering duplicate HRD activities. The costs of such duplication of efforts within an organization can be enormous. Once senior managers begin to acknowledge the need for more centralized guidance, direction, and control of the organization's duplicated and fragmented HRD activities, an HRD unit is often established and an HRD policy is codified.

Without an HRD policy in place in the organization, there is often a failure to assign specific management responsibility for the various HRD functions in the respective units. Without such organizational policy direction, HRD activities will most often be responsive to short-term, immediate learning needs. The HRD programs in organizations without HRD policies will often have the following characteristics (Spector, 1985, pp. 29–30):

1. HRD programs are largely unplanned.
2. HRD programs are not an integral part of the organization's operations.
3. HRD programs are viewed as being relevant only for a selected group of employees (craft apprentices, supervisory or managerial personnel, clerical staff and the like) or for the firm's customers (equipment maintenance or equipment operating procedures training and the like).
4. There is an organizational or industry cultural bias or management assumption that most employees do not require training, education, or development. ("Most of our employees have earned graduate degrees; they come to the position already educated for their jobs!")
5. HRD activities often are viewed as an event which takes place only at the entry on duty or beginning of a career.
6. HRD is an activity which has a low priority and is considered a peripheral management responsibility (if at all!).
7. HRD activities which do occur are not considered as an official part of the incumbent's job and the HRD learning experiences are often viewed as "rewards" or as "punishments" by the individual participant and the individual's supervisor and peers.
8. Employees consider that any needed updating of their skills and knowledge is their own responsibility and is to be accomplished on their own time.
9. Employee dissatisfaction with the organization and its management is often high due to the lack of career development opportunities.
10. The evaluation of HRD program and activity efforts is done poorly, if at all.

### What Is HRD Policy?

As was stated earlier, policies emanate from the values and beliefs of those who create an organization's strategic plans. There

are three distinct types of organizational "policies" in effect in
most organizations: written policies, oral policies, and traditional
policies.

*Written Policies.* A written policy statement is one that is
recommended by senior management and is approved by the
organization's chief executive officer and board of directors or
trustees. The policy is then codified in the organization's policy
manual and is distributed to all unit supervisors and managers for
implementation in their respective work units. In fact, however,
the majority of organizational policies are predicated on needs first
identified by the lower levels of management—by the first-line
supervisors rather than by the more senior management group of
the organization. This is not to say that senior management
groups and the chief executive officers abdicate their responsibilities for policy making. It means rather that the *need* for "a policy"
is most often first identified by lower-level managers in their
dealings with subordinates. The senior management group and
chief executive officer then respond to the identified need by
establishing "policy." The following illustrates this "bottom-up"
approach to policy development:

> A first-level supervisor called his division
> manager: "Mr. Jones, this is Joe, down in the quality
> control unit. May I contract with the local commun-
> ity college to conduct a writing skills course for my
> people? They really need to learn how to write
> better!" The division manager says, "Well, I really
> don't know if we can enter into a contract agreement
> for such training or not. Let me call the senior vice-
> president for administration, she will know. I'll get
> back to you as soon as I hear."
>
> The division manager calls to say, "Ms. Smith,
> this is Jones in the Widget Division. One of our
> supervisors just called to ask if he can enter into a
> contract with the local community college to do some
> writing skills training for some of his people in the
> quality control unit. Do we have a company policy
> on contracting for training with the school for such

courses?" Ms. Smith replies, "No, we don't have a policy on that as yet. In fact, you are the third manager this month who has asked the same question! I believe it is about time we established a policy regarding contracting for training outside the company. And from what I hear, the community college people are really trying to meet the needs of local business and industry by delivering good training programs in a number of areas. I think we can really save on outside training costs by working with them. I will have a draft of a new policy statement ready for your next month's division managers' meeting, and we can send it up for senior management review by the fifteenth of the month. Once your division managers' group and the senior management team have approved it, I'll get final approval and sign-off on the policy by our president. I think it can be distributed to the department managers for insertion in their copies of the company policy manual by the end of the month if all goes without a hitch. In the meantime, you can tell your supervisor to begin his discussions with the community college people regarding what he thinks his employees need."

The written policy statement is designed to give broad direction to both managers and employees in the enterprise. The policy statement helps to establish management responsibilities. Once an HRD policy has been codified by the senior management team and chief executive officer and promulgated throughout the organization, it will provide guidance and direction for management actions. In the forgoing illustration, a first-level supervisor needed to know his decision-making limits in regard to contracting out with the local community college. Ms. Smith recognized the need for an organizational policy as evidenced by the number of recent calls she had received from several of her managers on the identical matter.

It is also true, however, that many HRD policies will become established from the "top down" in the management hierarchy. For example, in support of an organization's sincere efforts toward accomplishing the goals of affirmative action and upward mobility throughout its work force, its senior management developed and promulgated an HRD policy that included the following statement: "Consistent with the company's goals concerning affirmative action and employee career development, it is the policy of the XYZ Corporation to make every effort to ensure that minorities, women, and the hard-to-spare employees are not overlooked or exempted from participating fully in the corporation's human resource development activities."

In discussing policy formulation, we must point out that the development of policy is not without its pitfalls. For example, one of the authors some years ago had an opportunity to serve as a consultant to a large metropolitan hospital that had been in existence for more than seventy-five years. Over that long period of time, the hospital had accumulated four volumes of written policies and standard operating procedures covering every aspect of the hospital's "business." After analyzing the more than 375 written policy statements in those four volumes, the author found that less than 25 percent of them could be applied in the hospital at the time. Many were so outdated that they might be dangerous to the health and welfare of both the patients and employees if implemented. Some were so blatantly discriminatory that, if enforced, the hospital (and its administrator) would be hauled into court, and still others had been superseded by revised policies and never rescinded. By the conclusion of the consulting project, the hospital had a single-volume policy manual containing only 41 written policy statements.

As external consultants to organizations, we often hear our clients say, "We can't do *that* here! It's against company policy." When we ask them to find the written policy statement in their organization's policy manual, they usually find there is none. It is most true that there are numerous unwritten "policies," both oral and traditional, existing in organizations today.

*Oral Policies.* Unfortunately, many of the oral policies that exist in organizations were never meant to be policies at all. Many such "policies" had their beginnings as a senior manager's oral statement or directive to a few select employees. Over time, the manager's oral statement was adopted throughout the organization as "policy," even though it may not have been considered policy by either the manager who initially made the statement or directive or the other members of the organization's senior management. Also most unfortunately, such policies will often come to form part of the organizational culture, making them difficult, if not impossible, to rescind.

*Traditional Policies.* Nadler (1979, 1982a) makes a clear distinction between an organization's culture, on the one hand, and its written policy, operating procedures, directives, and similar documents, on the other. The term *culture* refers to the kind of behavior that is generally accepted within an organization or a particular unit of an organization, and we must recognize that an organization's culture can often be as powerful an influence over its employees as any written or oral policy. Once a new employee has become acculturated into an organization, he or she begins to share a set of beliefs with the other members of the organization. These shared beliefs lead to a set of expected behaviors. Unlike written policies, which are available to all employees, folkways or cultural norms often become "implicit policy" (French, 1964) within an organization (or a single unit of the organization).

Implicit policies can also be inferred from the particular practices that are in existence at any given moment in time. There have been numerous examples of this phenomenon in organizations where we have served as consultants, including some that were quite humorous: When invited to make a final report on a major consultancy project to an organization's chief executive officer and his senior management group, one of the authors was ushered into the firm's boardroom by the client, the organization's director of human resource development. The room was filled with smoke! All seven men in the room were smoking cigars! They had been meeting for more than two hours prior to our arrival, and the smoke was so heavy that one could hardly breathe. After the twenty-five minute report and a very active fifteen-minute discussion period, the HRD director and the author left the room. When asked about the cigar-smoking group, the HRD director said, "I'll be so pleased when Mr. Smith retires, because I predict that there will be no cigars in the boardroom from then on. Not one of the present six senior vice-presidents smoked cigars until they were promoted to their present jobs."

Many times such individual practices as a chief executive officer's cigar-smoking habit lead to an implicit policy based upon the assumptions of subordinates, that is, based upon what they perceive to be their senior manager's attitudes toward a particular matter or situation.

Such implicit policies can have significant negative or positive consequences on an organization's overall HRD functions, depending on their specific outcomes and direction. The following two actual examples illustrate these diverse effects on an HRD unit's functions:

> The HRD staff and functions of a firm were located as part of its personnel department, a department with a reputation for being most unresponsive to the human resource utilization needs of the company's operating units. Many of the firm's managers followed an implicit policy of not involving the personnel-HRD staff in unit problems because of the department's reputation for saying, "No, it can't be done," rather than trying to help the managers find solutions to their varied "people problems." Operating unit supervisors and managers began avoiding contact with the personnel department's HRD staff by contracting outside the organization for learning activities instead of using the in-house HRD staff to help fill the needs of their units for training, education, and development. The reputation of the personnel department thus caused the organization's implicit policy to prevail, regardless of whether or not the HRD staff and its learning programs could produce the needed results.

Unfortunately, the HRD director in question was unable to overcome the personnel department's poor reputation in the firm and had to move on to another company less than a year after he had joined the first one. But his "story" did have a happy ending:

During his first week on his new job as an HRD manager in another firm, while at lunch with his boss, the vice-president of human resources, he was introduced to one of the more senior managers of a line department in the firm. The department manager suggested they get together to discuss a nagging production problem in one of his units. He said that he felt it was a problem that could readily be resolved by designing and conducting a half-day training program for the unit's employees. The HRD manager met with the department manager the next afternoon. By the end of the following week, the HRD manager had completed a brief but thorough training needs assessment to address the specific production problem with the unit supervisor. He recommended that the unit supervisor develop and post a simple job aid at each of the unit employees' work stations. There was, after all, no need to design and conduct a training program for the unit's employees.

The actual dollar cost for the job aid to the department was less than $500, a savings of more than $15,500, taking into account the wages that would have been paid to employees during the proposed four-hour training program. Needless to say, the department manager was most impressed with the results of the HRD manager's efforts and said so to all in the firm who would listen. Before long, it was acknowledged by a majority of the firm's managers that if they had a personnel or production problem in their department or unit, they should at least check with the HRD manager for advice before deciding what to do. What had taken place in a single unit of a department became the foundation for an implicit policy throughout the organization.

In both of the forgoing examples, the evolved implicit cultural norm became the traditional "policy" in the organization to guide the actions of managers in their decision-making processes relative to the utilization of the organization's HRD staff and functions. Unfortunately, both oral and traditional policies can lead to confusion when interpreted differently by various managers and employees in an organization. It is therefore much safer to develop written HRD policy so that all who are affected will know the rules of the game and will abide by them accordingly.

### Guidelines for Developing HRD Policy

We believe that there are some generic policy components that should be used as guidelines for the development of an organization's written HRD policy:

1.  An HRD mission and purpose statement that establishes a rationale for the varied HRD learning activities (training, education, and development) in the organization.
2.  A statement of organizational (leadership) philosophy related to the HRD mission statement.
3.  A statement of the HRD unit's goals and general objectives related to particular aspects of the organization's mission statement.
4.  Objectives for the HRD unit or function that specify a single result to be achieved within a given period of time.
5.  Establishment of managerial authority through the policy guidelines on learning activity procedures, including scheduling, staffing, directing, evaluating, reviewing, and coordinating within the organization.
6.  Provision for revision and modification of the HRD policy in light of changing needs and conditions.
7.  Criteria for learning facilities and use, maintenance, and purchase of instructional equipment.
8.  Provision for conducting ongoing training needs assessments throughout the organization.
9.  Criteria for costs and finances of the HRD unit or function.
10. Provision for maintaining HRD activity participation records for all employees of the organization.

There seems to be a great deal of variance in different organizations' HRD policy statements regarding content and format. Spector (1985), in a study to identify corporate HRD policy, found that some HRD policies took the form of comprehensive HRD mission, policy, and implementation strategy statements but that other policies were very narrow and limited in their scope and content. Among the written (and unwritten) HRD policy statements that Spector examined (p. 119) were policy to:

1.  State corporate HRD philosophy relative to its investments in human resources and organizational development.
2.  State corporate HRD mission and identification of the employees' and managers' roles in the mission accomplishment.
3.  State role and function of corporate HRD activity.
4.  Establish tuition-aid plan for job-related training.
5.  Establish new employee orientation programs.
6.  Establish learning programs for supervisors.
7.  Submit employee evaluation upon course completion.
8.  Link performance appraisal results to the assessment of employee training needs.
9.  Inform employees about HRD policy, procedures, and opportunities.
10. Inform supervisors about HRD policies, procedures, and opportunities.
11. Reschedule employees' normal work week permitting courses during regular duty hours.
12. Establish learning programs for non-exempt/line employees.
13. Establish learning programs for managers.
14. Establish learning programs for executives.
15. Establish tuition-aid plan for non-job related activities.
16. Provide for selection and assignment of employees to attend professional meetings.
17. Provide for review by HRD unit of training needs identified by supervisors.
18. Establish HRD information system.

In our review of numerous organizations' HRD policy statements, we have found many variations in them. As we stated earlier, some of these statements are very brief, while others are quite comprehensive. In the following example, our readers will identify some, but most certainly not all, of the HRD policy "ingredients" given above.

### A Sample HRD Policy Statement

In recognition of the importance of our people, acknowledging their valued contributions to our mission accomplishments, and consistent with our emphasis on employee and management human resource development throughout an individual's career, it will be the policy of the XYZ Corporation to:

1. Recognize its responsibility to provide appropriate HRD learning opportunities (training, education, and development) to the employees and members of the management team to assist them in gaining and/or updating their technical (subject matter) skills and knowledge and in developing their required managerial skills and knowledge to the highest possible levels of attainment in the search for excellence of performance.
2. Make every effort to ensure that the "hard to spare," minorities, and women employees are not overlooked or exempted from the organization's HRD activities.
3. Acknowledge and emphasize the need for continuous learning opportunities consistent with the organization's long-range mission, goals, and human resource requirements.
4. Encourage active participation in and support of the organization's full range of HRD activities by all employees and members of the management team. It must be emphasized that supervisors and managers at all levels of the management team are ultimately responsible for implementing learning activities that will ensure that their assigned employees perform at their highest levels of competence.
5. Structure and administer the organization's HRD activities by the HRD unit to provide both technical and managerial skills and learning activities for all employees, in close cooperation with and coordination by the management team.

6. Establish priorities for participation in a company HRD activity in such a way as to give special consideration to:

   a. Newly hired employees and/or members of the management team who require new job or task skills, knowledge, and attitudes in the performance of their assigned positions within the company.

   b. Employees and/or members of the management team who need immediate updating and/or increased technical or managerial skills and knowledge to improve their effectiveness in carrying out presently assigned or future responsibilities.

   c. Employees and members of the management team who have established career goals and commitment to the organization and are expected to remain employed in the organization for a sufficient amount of time so as to warrant an investment in their development.

   d. Employees and/or members of the management team who are identified as possessing the greatest long-range potential for advancement to higher-level assignments in the organization.

Members of an organization's management team and its employees should alike recognize that all employee development is essentially self-motivated. Advancement to higher levels of competencies and responsibilities largely depends upon the individual employee's aggressive involvement in updating his or her skills and knowledge; willingness to assume increased responsibilities on the job; active participation in work-related team efforts; and active participation in professional organizations and in public service or community service projects. Self-nomination by individual employees and members of the management team through their immediate superiors is the recommended procedure for applying for participation in the HRD learning activities sponsored by the organization's HRD unit.

As part of the annual individual performance review process with their immediate supervisor, employees and subordinate managers and supervisors should be encouraged to prepare a list of personal career development goals and to identify the learning activities required for the accomplishment of such goals. These individual career development goals should be as specific as possible with respect to the desired learning activity to be accomplished, the recommended approach and resources needed to accomplish the learning goal, and the anticipated target date for completion of the learning effort (not to exceed two years). All managers and supervisors having employees (or subordinate supervisors or managers) under their direct supervision should plan and provide for appropriate technical and supervisory-managerial learning activities for all their subordinates as a basic part of their HRD responsibilities. (This should be done, of course, in cooperation with other human resource units.) Particular emphasis should be given to development work assignments, rotational work assignments, and reassignments both within and outside the employee's own work unit.

The priority factors described in the policy statement should be carefully considered when nominating subordinates for participation in HRD activities sponsored by the HRD unit. The identification of learning needs should be on a continuous basis and should be conducted by the management of each line and staff unit (with the assistance of the HRD unit, if required). This effort will help to ensure that subordinates will increase their competencies and effectiveness on their current jobs. Supervisors should also prepare in collaboration with, and at the initiative of, each employee, an individual career development plan. This action plan should identify the individual's career goals, along with learning objectives that will satisfy, whenever possible, the needs of both the organization and the individual. A periodic follow-up by the supervisor (at least every six months) on the individual's progress toward achieving his or her learning objectives is essential to the success of the HRD program.

Senior managers should offer their personal support to the HRD program and maintain an organizational climate that encourages opportunities for the personal and professional growth of all employees and members of the management team within the organization. All senior managers should be encouraged to facilitate the reassignment and rotation of subordinates as required for their development. In addition, senior and mid-level managers should be encouraged to set an example within the organization by personally participating in HRD activities for their own continuing professional and personal learning needs and goals.

Admittedly, some organizations have set up highly successful HRD programs and activities without establishing formal HRD policy statements. However, many HRD managers have discovered that the adoption of such policy statements has encouraged members of their organization's management team to become far more actively involved in carrying out their human resource development responsibilities. In addition, with an HRD policy in force, HRD managers can better justify the cost effectiveness of HRD programs and activities. HRD budget proposals will be less closely questioned when cost-benefit factors are made evident to the line and staff managers of the units served by the HRD programs and activities.

···{ *Chapter 3* }···

# Organizing the HRD Unit

In this chapter we will discuss the HRD *unit* rather than the HRD function, although we recognize that not all HRD activities in an organization are delivered by the HRD unit. For this chapter, we must also clarify how we are using certain words. Throughout this book, we use the terms *organization* and *company* interchangeably to indicate that the principles and concepts discussed here are applicable to any group of people joined together to accomplish an agreed-upon objective. This includes military as well as civilian, for-profit as well as nonprofit, and public as well as private, groups. However, since this chapter is devoted to the "organization" of the HRD unit, we feel it could be confusing to use the same word with two different meanings. Therefore, in this chapter, we will use the word *company* when referring to groups of people, while *organization* will usually refer to the forming, establishing, arranging, and systematizing of the HRD unit within the company.

At one time, a good deal of a company's HRD was usually provided through a subunit of the personnel department. In recent years, however, the trend has been to set up separate HRD units. This reorganization and placement of the unit are important, for they signify that HRD has a direct relationship to almost every part of the company. We now find that HRD units are "here, there, and everywhere." One of the authors, for example, was serving as a consultant to a large utility, Potomac Electric and Power Company, in helping it plan for its HRD facility needs for the next decade. He was told that the company currently had seven

36

full-time professionals in the HRD unit. By the time the consulta-
-tion was completed, however, he had found forty-four full-time
HRD people in seven different divisions of the company. This is
not an unusual case. Some people see this lack of concentration in
one unit as a negative factor. They keep asking the same question,
"Where should HRD be in the company?" We contend that there
is no single correct answer to this query, but numerous
possibilities.

Some readers might like to have a list of companies and
how they organize their HRD units, but we have found it
impossible to provide such a list, for three reasons. First, many
companies will not readily share this data. This becomes apparent
when one looks at the literature, particularly in publications such
as *Training: The Magazine of Human Resource Development,
Training and Development Journal,* and *Performance and
Instruction Journal.* There are some articles by practitioners who
are in HRD units in companies, but they generally write about
conceptual matters rather than report on the organization of their
units. Some practitioners do write articles about what their
companies are doing or how HRD is evaluated in their companies,
but we seldom find articles telling how HRD is organized within
a company.

Second, some HRD managers apparently do not even know
how HRD is organized within their companies. Perhaps questions
of organization have not been of sufficient interest or importance
in the past. The field of human resources has been very volatile
since the mid 1970s, and there remain many unanswered questions,
such as, Where should HRD be placed, who should the HRD unit
report to, what should its budget be, and how should it be staffed?
As clear answers are not always available, there is a tendency to
avoid discussing these questions in relation to specific
organizations.

Third, the organization of HRD in a company is usually
not static. Indeed, in some companies the HRD unit is constantly
being reorganized as the needs of the companies change. Therefore, when we cite specific companies, you should recognize that
we are reporting how they were organized for HRD at the time this
book was written.

## Organizational Variables

There is no one best way to organize the HRD unit. Therefore, we must look at some of the variables in the situation that will enable the HRD manager to make the necessary decisions. We assume, of course, that the HRD manager has the authority to make those decisions. There are times when the organization of the unit is outside the decision making area of the manager. Still, it is possible for the manager to influence decisions regarding the HRD unit if he or she is sensitive to some of the variables.

*Relation to Company Philosophy and Practice.* It is only in recent years that companies have been encouraged to put their philosophies on paper. Frequently, these philosophies had to be gleaned from statements made by upper-level management, from media interviews, or from the annual company report. It is clear, however, that if company leaders can articulate the philosophy of the company, the rest of the employees at all levels will have some idea of what to expect in terms of policy and practices.

We still have a long way to go to understand the culture of companies—that is, the behavior that is acceptable or expected in a company and the behavior that is deviant or heretical. But we do know that the culture of a company affects the perceptions of those in the company. This applies to all parts of the company, but understanding culture is especially crucial when we look at the organization of the HRD unit. The HRD unit is an unusual part of a company. It is not line, though a major part of its activities take place in that area. It is not staff in the usual sense, for it is directly involved in the day-to-day operations of the company, as well as in the broader functions of forecasting and planning. This leads us to the observation that a company may well have several HRD units, each responsible for different types of HRD activities. This presents a problem for those who wish to have a clear company chart with HRD in one place. Perhaps upper management has to be helped to realize that HRD is unique in the kind of service it provides, and placement in more than one part of the company represents a positive approach rather than a failure to apply good organization principles.

We find companies today that encourage the concept of *intrapreneurship* (Peters and Waterman, 1982). In this approach the company is broken down into small units that are given their own budgets and staffs, along with some identifiable goals. The units are encouraged to operate as separate entities within the larger company and without the usual controls exerted over a department or unit. If that is the philosophy of the company, then we can expect to see HRD in many different places.

An important philosophical question that affects the organization of HRD is, "Who gets HRD?" Is it the philosophy of the company that every employee has the right to expect employer-provided opportunities for learning and growth? Or is the philosophy that all employees should pull themselves up by their own bootstraps? We have purposely dichotomized that philosophical question, but we recognize that there is a continuum. It is important that the philosophy of the company on this point be articulated as specifically as possible. Carrying out these different philosophies requires different forms of organization. If, by policy, every employee is eligible to participate in HRD programs, then the HRD unit must be organized to reach into every part of the company. Where HRD is limited to only certain groups or specified levels of the company, the HRD unit will be organized in a quite different way.

*Company History.* If the company has never had an identifiable HRD unit, then history will play only a minor part in deciding how to organize it. The HRD manager in that situation will have more latitude to organize on the basis of the other factors discussed in this chapter. Where the HRD unit is already in existence, however, a new HRD manager must try to understand its history. It is not always possible to do this before taking the job, as few companies keep written histories.

In one company, for example, a new HRD manager was hired, replacing a person who had been in that position for many years. The new manager found that his behavior was restricted in several areas. When he attended a staff meeting, he had to take the seat of his predecessor. Indeed, for the first

few months he was even frequently addressed by the
name of his predecessor! The policy of that company
was that department heads had to program HRD
funds into their own budgets. Then, as needed, they
would authorize the use of those funds for the HRD
unit. In practice, it was different. The previous
manager had exerted considerable influence and
power, so that at the beginning of each fiscal year
there had been an automatic transfer of all funds
from the department budgets into the HRD unit
budget. The new HRD manager had no way of
knowing about this method of doing things. Given
that history, the department heads had written off
HRD as something over which they had no control
and in which they had little interest. It took a great
deal of work on the part of the new HRD manager to
overcome that piece of history.

An HRD manager who has been in the job for many years
may find that history has created a trap. It becomes difficult to
change what has become tradition. This is not unique to HRD,
but applies to all parts of the company. The difficulty arises when
there is not a clear perception of the contribution that HRD makes
to the company, and just issuing information about HRD may not
do much to alter the situation. It may be necessary to reorganize
the HRD unit so that at least part of it engages in activities that
are highly visible. The HRD manager may want to organize in
such a way that significant parts of the company will get some
special attention, thus giving visibility to what HRD actually does.
It is possible, for example, to get high visibility during a start-up,
that is, when a new plant is being activated or new equipment is
being brought in that will create massive changes. That was not
the purpose in the case of a start-up at Johns Manville, but one
result was that the HRD unit became very visible and involved
(Sisson, 1972).

Another part of the company's history is concerned with
what happened to previous HRD managers. After a period of time
did they leave the company or were they transferred to another unit

within the company? At this point we are not discussing philosophy but the actual events that have taken place. The HRD
manager is an individual working within a company.

The unit may be organized in terms of the future goals and
ideology of the HRD manager. For example, the HRD manager
may choose to highlight programs only for executive levels to
establish some credentials in that area. Or the manager may focus
on international aspects in anticipation of being sent overseas in
his next assignment.

*Selection of the HRD Manager.* Because of the uniqueness
of HRD, it is possible to organize the unit in a variety of ways.
Most often, the way it is organized within a particular company
will represent the interests, competencies, and goals of the HRD
manager. The first question here concerns how the HRD manager
is selected. There are several options. First, the HRD manager can
be selected from those currently in the unit. The person promoted
to that position has the option to continue with the same form of
organization or to make changes. It is certainly not unusual for a
new manager, in any part of the company, to want to put his or
her own stamp on the unit. Sometimes, reorganizing the unit has
little to do with changed needs but a great deal to do with changed
management. It is regrettable, but true, that there are times when
the HRD manager is chosen for negative reasons. There are still
organizations that see the HRD function as less important than
others. Therefore, staffing is accomplished by sending people to
that unit who have not been effective in other parts of the
organization. The HRD manager, then, may be someone who has
not performed well in other management functions. Fortunately,
this tendency is disappearing, though it is by no means extinct.

Second, there are times and reasons for recruiting a new
HRD manager from outside the company. That new individual
will bring to the company experiences from other companies. The
new manager may have been selected specifically because of the
possibility of bringing new ideas, including new ideas about HRD
unit organization, into the company. In any event, it is expected
that the new manager will endeavor to replicate successful HRD
experiences from the past.

Finally, a common practice, discussed more fully in Chapter Six, is to take an employee who has been managing some other unit and assign that individual to manage the HRD unit. This person is usually a general manager in the company who is expected to have the ability to manage any part of the company. That person will often know little, if anything, about HRD functions and operations as the selection has been made on the basis of management ability rather than on that of technical (HRD) competence.

Therefore, there can be at least three different types of managers. As individuals, we can certainly expect that they will differ. They will have different personal goals. Their assessment of their goals, and how this HRD assignment fits into their total career pattern, can be expected to influence their organization of the HRD unit. It is not possible, however, to state exactly how each would organize. Their personal goals are only one of the variables we are discussing.

### Organizational Practices

*Internal or External?* It is possible to provide HRD services to a company by using resources that are internal, external, or a combination of both. There are times when a company may decide that all HRD programs will be contracted out even though it may have an HRD unit. In that situation, the HRD unit is essentially organized to handle contracts. It requires staff members who have the ability to identify the appropriate vendors, negotiate with them, and then monitor the goods and/or services delivered.

It is also possible to decide that all HRD services must be provided within the company. The HRD manager can then choose among several ways to organize. The HRD unit can be a duplicate of the total company, with each major unit of the company being serviced by a subunit of the HRD unit.

Naturally, it is possible to have a combination of both internal and external HRD services, and that in fact is the most common practice. A study completed within the Air Force Systems Command found that the upper-level managers did not expect their HRD unit to provide instructional services (Epstein and

Nadler, 1972). They commented that the unique needs of a research and development organization such as theirs required that their instructional needs be met by utilizing external resources. The nontechnical needs could, of course, be met by the internal HRD unit. Epstein (1971) found that the managers expected the HRD people to devote less than 10 percent of their time to instruction.

Going mainly if not completely external does not mean that the company is not interested in HRD. Quite the contrary. The company may have a strong commitment to HRD, but sees the HRD unit as essentially providing advice and consultation. The company simply thinks that other HRD programs, mainly training programs, are best obtained from external sources. This decision will indicate the need for a small HRD unit, but one that can have significant power within the company. Not all external resources are identical, so the identification and selection of external resources introduce important possibilities of change and growth within a company.

We find that newer, smaller high-tech companies tend toward that form of HRD unit organization. It is not that those companies are not committed to HRD. They recognize that it is essential that they be constantly alert to emerging technologies and up-to-date research. They must keep their people at the cutting edge, through training, if they are to compete with the larger companies who have HRD units and programs. Therefore, those smaller companies usually assign one of their technical people to be the HRD manager. Sometimes this is a full-time position, while at other times it is a collateral duty, usually coupled with another management function. Therefore, there may not be a separate HRD unit, and instead HRD becomes part of some other unit in the company.

The more common practice, in companies with 500 or more employees, is to have at least one person full time in an HRD position. Some of the large, well-established companies appear to believe that they can satisfactorily fill all their own needs. If HRD is needed, there will be a unit—or more than one unit—exclusively devoted to providing HRD. The company will still use some external resources, but the major emphasis will be on the internal

HRD resource and an identifiable HRD unit. There are large companies such as Xerox, PepsiCo., and General Electric that have spent millions to build and operate HRD centers. (The centers are identified by a wide variety of names.) Yet, each of these companies continues to use some external HRD resources to supplement their well-established internal HRD units.

The Xerox International Training Center in Leesburgh, Virginia, uses an interesting practice. It utilizes a number of external HRD people whom it calls "consultants." Actually, most of those external people design, facilitate, or evaluate HRD programs. They are not regular employees, and their contracts can be terminated rather easily by either party. The consultants know this, and therefore some of them engage in outside activities. The usual caution is that they cannot work for a competitor and cannot divulge Xerox secrets. Some of the consultants have been there for years, others only a short time, while still others have become regular employees. This practice allows the center, an HRD unit of the total Xerox company, to maintain some flexibility while retaining control over HRD activities. The consultants are integrated into the regular Xerox HRD units at that installation. In other companies, it has sometimes been the practice to put consultants into separate units.

*Form Follows Function.* This is an old adage, borrowed from the architectural community. As applied to the organization of the HRD unit, it means that the HRD function in the company should first be determined; after that, the form (type of organization) can be determined. As some managers and companies have only a limited vision of HRD, there is the tendency to think that the function of HRD in a company is to run classes—to conduct a school within the company. That is one possibility, but only a very limited one. The main reason for a company to have an HRD unit is that it can help solve current problems and anticipate future ones. This is accomplished through providing learning and/or through consulting. At times these functions overlap, but at other times they are two distinctly different services that the HRD unit can provide.

Where the purpose is essentially focused on performance change through learning, the HRD manager will organize the unit to provide learning activities. The focus should still be on problem solving, but the emphasis will be on providing learning to accomplish that goal. The HRD unit will contain such staff specialists as facilitators of learning (which includes instructors, coaches, and so on), designers of learning programs, and developers of instructional strategies. Where the focus is on consulting, the HRD unit will be staffed with people who have consulting competencies—for example, experts, advocates, stimulators, and change agents. The unit itself may reflect this dual role by having one subunit to provide learning, another to provide consultation. (These various roles and subroles are discussed in detail in Chapter Six.)

The organization of the unit can be expected to change as the focus changes. For example:

> The corporate HRD manager of the Ford Motor Company learned of the model for staffing discussed later in this book and applied it to the corporate HRD unit. He used it initially to look at the unit's operations and determined that it was providing a great many learning programs. This was reflected in the number of facilitators on the corporate staff. It was agreed that this should not be a significant function at the corporate level. Rather, at that level, the unit should be providing consulting services related to HRD. Providing learning programs was assigned to the next lower level, which had eight departments. Accordingly, the staff members who had been performing those functions were reassigned, and the corporate HRD unit was reorganized. It came to consist of eight subunits, each of which was assigned to a specific department, mainly to provide consulting services.

One can begin to discern a new trend emerging among companies in that line managers are becoming aware that they have a responsibility for providing HRD for their employees. Previously, many line managers relied on the HRD unit for almost all their HRD needs. The new trend is for the line managers to become more involved in directly providing HRD for their employees. Thus, in many companies on-the-job training is no longer limited to lower-level employees but instead permeates the entire company.

Line managers are increasingly looking to the HRD unit for assistance in helping them deliver training right at the work site. For education, the situation is a bit more complicated, depending on the company's needs. If the education is for a currently existing job, particularly one within the same managerial unit, there is no difficulty. If it is a question of preparing the employee for a job in another part of the company, the HRD unit can make a significant contribution by being the link between the two parts of the company. The HRD unit can also provide assistance in identifying needed external instructional resources to meet educational needs. Another alternative is for the HRD unit both to plan and to offer the educational program. As for development, managers will continue to look to the HRD unit for help. But some of the topics may be outside the competencies of the manager and even the staff of the HRD unit. At that point, the HRD unit comes to serve as a broker, identifying the relevant external resources and bringing them to the attention of the interested manager.

Line managers, in those situations, will look to the HRD unit for assistance, but in a different way than in the past. Learning activities have been provided to line managers to enable them to acquire the competencies and materials to conduct training at their work sites (Nadler, 1955). More recently, a similar approach has been described and called *synergogy* (Mouton and Blake, 1984).

*Relationships to Other Organizational Activities.* Within all companies there will be some degree of interdependence among the various units. Therefore, the HRD manager must be sure that the organization of the HRD unit does not separate or isolate HRD from the rest of the company. Since the late 1970s there has been an increasing awareness of the importance of human resources within companies. This has produced new ways to organize the various human resource units, including HRD. At one time, it might have been possible to say that HRD should be placed under the personnel function. Indeed, the U.S. government did this, "temporarily," in 1938. At that time, it was probably a wise decision, but, as often happens, temporary became permanent. It was only toward the end of the 1970s that the federal government came to organize HRD units outside of the personnel unit. The leader in this trend was the Internal Revenue Service (IRS), and it actually made the break in the early 1960s.

Some HRD people have a tendency to see this movement as a rejection of the personnel unit. In turn, the personnel people have endeavored to recapture the HRD function. This conflict is present in some companies, but it is seldom written about or openly discussed, so it is difficult to find specific examples. Too often it leads to some form of company guerrilla warfare, resulting in a waste of time and resources. This struggle, conducted so far in a polite fashion, is obvious when one looks at the professional societies. Witness the program of the American Society for Personnel Administration to certify their members with a subspecialty in training. Likewise, the American Society for Training and Development (ASTD) has been broadening its emphasis to include *all* human resources, as evidenced by their national conference program and some proposed mission statements.

There has been too much professional energy lost in dealing with such territorial disputes. Efforts should instead be made to explore the *relationship* among the various human resource functions of which HRD and personnel are only two parts. As we are concerned directly with the HRD unit, rather than the personnel unit, our observations are directed to that area. Historically, when submerged within the personnel unit, the HRD function tended to mirror the personnel function. The HRD subunit was supposed to serve the needs of the personnel unit rather than the needs of the line managers. The needs of line managers were communicated to the HRD subunit through the agency of the personnel unit.

Another area of relationships is concerned with *accountability*. That is, once the HRD manager has been provided with resources by the organization—physical, financial, and human— the organization will want to know what the HRD manager has done with those resources in relation to the goals and mission of the organization. The HRD manager must determine to whom, or to what part of the organization, the HRD unit is accountable. As HRD can be found in many different parts of an organization, it becomes necessary for the HRD manager to determine accountability in that particular company. In turn, accountability can determine how the HRD unit should be organized. All of this relates back to the earlier discussion on the function of the HRD unit. Is it to provide learning programs? If so, the accountability will be in terms of programs conducted, number of learners, or some other quantifiable figure. The HRD unit should then be organized to produce the requisite numbers. This may require staffing it with a large number of facilitator/instructors, and there should perhaps be several subunits with designers and developers of instructional strategies.

If the HRD unit is expected to be involved in problem solving within a company, then the unit should be organized to provide both consulting and learning programs. The difficulty with problem solving is in reporting accountability. While it is the manager who had the problem, he may have solved it with the help of the HRD unit. How, then, should accountability be reported? If the HRD manager takes credit for solving the problem, line managers will shun the HRD unit. If the HRD staff members solve the problem, they may do so at the cost of usurping management prerogatives to which they are not entitled. It is a complicated issue that requires much further study. At this time, HRD managers can only be encouraged to recognize this problem and bring it to the attention of the line managers.

The relationship of HRD to *performance appraisals* is also a problematic area. Many performance appraisals contain questions about the needs of the employee being appraised, but that section too often goes unanswered and unimplemented:

> A new HRD manager in a large oil company
> was given the task of developing a training and/or
> education program for upper-level managers. In
> meeting with the chief executive officer, the HRD
> manager was asked for a program that would cover
> the usual topics, such as leadership, motivation, and

planning. The HRD manager raised the question of performance appraisals. The chief executive officer was only too happy to respond. He brought out the form and the small book that described and illustrated the performance appraisal plan in that company for upper-level management. (Up to this point, the HRD manager had only heard of these materials and had never actually seen them.) The chief executive officer was very proud that this plan had been in existence for three years and that some longitudinal data were therefore available. When the HRD manager asked to see the data, the chief executive officer laughingly remarked that it was too sensitive to be seen by other people. The HRD manager suggested that the chief executive officer prepare the data or delegate the task to someone he trusted. It might be only a general analysis of the combined needs, as names might have to be omitted. The HRD manager pointed out, however, that if the data could be name specific, they would be even more helpful. The chief executive officer rapidly terminated the meeting and the project died.

Unfortunately, that scenario applies to too many companies, even when the appraisal process is not the responsibility of upper management. Making performance appraisals available to the HRD unit can help in the total process of developing the appropriate and competent work force for the company.

We noted earlier that it is important for the HRD unit to clarify its relationships to the other human resource units and functions within the company. Career development is one human resource area to which there must be a very direct relationship. The field and concept of career development have grown significantly since the middle 1970s. This is another example of companies coming to understanding the importance of their human resources. But there has been some confusion about the relationship of career development to HRD. Gutteridge and Hutcheson (1984) make a clear distinction between the two and have developed a model that shows the relationship. They note that a good career development system in a company must relate very strongly and directly to the HRD system. But, although the two intertwine and even overlap, they are distinct systems, and different competencies are needed within the respective units.

### Variations in Organizing the HRD Unit

In the previous section, we discussed some of the factors such as accountability, that influence the organization of the HRD unit. In this section, we will focus on a number of additional factors that must be considered in organizing the HRD unit.

*Geographical.* The organization of the HRD unit will be different if the company is single site, multisite, or multinational. In a single-site company, the HRD unit will of course be located on that site. Included in this category are companies located in one specific community or city, even though they may have several locations within that city. Given the geographical proximity, it is relatively easy for HRD staff to regularly visit the various locations within the city or its immediate environs. The HRD manager need not make any significant provision for travel funds or plan for time lost in travel. The HRD staff is readily accessible to everybody in the company, and this allows for a significant amount of daily contact. Communication will be continuous and, generally, more oral than written.

The multisite designation assumes that the sites are sufficiently distant from each other that overnight travel may be required. This means that the HRD manager must include in the budget sufficient funds for travel and related expenses. It also means a certain amount of "lost" time in travel.

A multisite company requires a significantly different form of organization for the HRD unit than the single-site one. For example, the HRD manager must decide whether to send staff out from one place, usually corporate headquarters, or to locate HRD staff permanently in the various sites. If the HRD people are all located in one place and travel to service the various sites, the HRD manager should consider other alternatives. Should the staff be assigned on a geographical basis? That is, should certain staff members be allotted specific locations and service all the HRD needs in their assigned locations? It can be an advantage for the HRD staff so assigned to get to "know the territory." They can build rapport with the employees at all levels, at the sites assigned to them. The HRD staff member so assigned will also be able to identify appropriate local resources and keep up-to-date on local changes and factors that affect performance in the assigned area.

There are also drawbacks to this method of assignment. It is obvious that a single HRD person may not have the variety of competencies required for the assigned sites. Of course, other HRD staff can be brought in as needed, but that means additional cost. Depending upon the geographical spread of the various sites, it may be difficult for the HRD manager to have sufficient contact with the HRD staff. It may also mean that particular consideration must be given, when recruiting HRD staff, to those who are willing and able to travel. Family responsibilities, professional growth through attending university classes, and other factors may seriously inhibit the availability of a good staff member to travel as needed.

Another alternative is to place the HRD staff in a location away from headquarters. As needed, that staff, actually an HRD subunit, could service one site located away from headquarters or might even serve several sites within a specified geographical area. This is a common pattern. Digital Equipment Corporation assigns people to various areas in the United States, and they are responsible for providing HRD for the assigned area. As with many companies that organize HRD in a similar fashion, there is usually some kind of corporate HRD unit, but that unit does not necessarily have control over the regional HRD unit. Rather, the corporate HRD unit is expected to provide leadership, to clarify policies, and to keep the regional units informed on corporate directions.

When a regional form of HRD unit organization is utilized, it should be clearly established to whom the local HRD staff person is responsible. There is no one best way, but, once again, there are alternatives. The local HRD staff person can be administratively responsible to the line manager at the geographical area or plant site, but professionally responsible to the corporate HRD manager. The tendency, usually, is for the local HRD staff person to become closely identified with the local situation. This can present a problem when it is decided to reassign that person to another HRD unit in a different area. This problem is not peculiar to HRD but is a common personnel problem in any multisite company. The individual being tapped for reassignment may prefer to remain in the same geographical location, even if it means looking for a different job outside the HRD unit or outside the company.

For a multisite operation, it is important that the HRD manager maintain communication with corporate headquarters as well as among HRD staff at the various sites. Steps must also be taken to ensure that all the staff members at the various sites are able to keep in touch with each other. There are many ways to do this. One common practice is to arrange for the entire HRD staff to attend an annual meeting of one of the various HRD professional associations. (The major associations are listed in Chapter Seven.) The HRD manager can coordinate matters so that all company HRD staff who are attending that meeting are available on the same day, usually the day before or the day after the annual meeting itself. During that day, attention can be paid to general concerns, and personal relationships among the HRD staff at the various sites can be reinforced.

Providing HRD for a multinational company, as opposed to a multisite operation, involves significant differences. A major one is to establish the relationship between the headquarters (located in the United States) and the one or more sites in other countries. Within the United States, it is important, but not too difficult, to recognize and provide for the differences that exist in various parts of the country. Internationally, this is a much more complex task to perform.

Consideration must be given to the level of economic development in a country, its political relationships with the United States, the availability of competent HRD staff, the long-term goals of the company within the specific country, and the potential for developing "local" HRD staff. (The term local is generally used in the international field to designate employees who are from the country in which the site is located. This can

apply to local employees at any level of the company.) Each of
these variables will be different in the various countries in the
world where the company has a site. For example, a company may
wish to use a tuition refund program to send some of its local
HRD people to a university in the United States to improve their
competencies. That was the case with some multinationals in
Malaysia during the mid 1970s. The Malaysian government
endorsed this move but required the foreign companies to also
provide "scholarships" for other Malaysians who would come
back and work for Malaysian companies. An HRD manager at
corporate headquarters would have to take this requirement into
account when planning for staff professional growth through
study in the United States.

If the HRD staff members are located in several countries,
the HRD manager has to provide for linkage. This is particularly
important if the HRD staff is composed predominantly of natives
of those countries. The following example goes back several years
but is still appropriate today:

> In the middle 1970s, Esso (now Exxon) had
> many HRD people in its various installations
> throughout South America. Under the leadership of
> Leonard Wetzel, a professional growth experience
> was planned in Florida, and over thirty local HRD
> people were brought to Marcos Island. For the most
> part these staff members from the various Latin
> American countries had never met before. Some had
> been in communication by phone and mail, but this
> was their first face-to-face meeting, and many excit-
> ing things happened! The planners of the event had
> wisely built in an opportunity for the socialization
> that is part of the Latin American culture. Most of
> the sessions were conducted in English, as all the
> staff members were required to speak English. How-
> ever, the small-group sessions and some other activi-
> ties were conducted in Spanish. From this event,
> friendships developed that facilitated the work
> situation when the employees returned home. HRD

staff members in the various countries no longer
hesitated to call each other on the phone. They had
become friends. There was an increase in sharing
across borders that proved beneficial to all concerned,
especially Esso.

It is not always possible to achieve results of this kind. A
multinational hotel chain had HRD people in Israel as well as in
some neighboring countries. When there was tension in that part
of the world, it was very difficult to bring HRD staff together.
They were all part of the same company, but the political
differences of the moment, as could be expected, impacted on the
situation. It is best not to put local employees in positions that are
not fully acceptable to their own governments.

*Subject Matter.* Another variation is to organize the unit to
service employees within some specific subject matter areas. This
can be done in two ways. The first is in terms of levels within the
company. For example, there can be a unit that serves only the
executive level. Such a unit would focus on the needs of that level
and would constantly be searching for the resources to meet those
needs. They would, in fact, become specialists for that level. We
can find this in companies where there is a subunit within the
HRD unit that focuses on "management development." As
supervisors constitute a large and significant part of the work
force, it is not uncommon to find a subunit whose major or only
work is with supervisors. Its efforts will include improving
performance on the job (training), as well as providing learning
experiences for those who have been identified as having potential
to become supervisors (education).

For years, work with "lower" (in status) employees was
usually assigned to the newer or less qualified members of the
HRD staff. It was common to have a person or subunit that
focused on secretarial or office skills. With the advent of technology into the office (word processors, computers, and so on) and the
movement toward office automation, office skills are no longer
considered lower in status. The same applies to the technical area
that at one time encompassed blue-collar workers. Today, the
concept of the technical area is much broader (Barney, 1984).

A second way to organize is through subject matter areas. For example, in a large company there is usually the need for an organized and readily available orientation program. Conceptually, orientation programs should *not* be conducted by the HRD unit but by a combination of the personnel unit and the line supervisors of the new employees. Practically, we find that orientation frequently becomes an HRD program. If so, a small subunit or group of HRD staff might be assigned to study, design, and deliver the orientation program. A similar situation often exists in companies where a significant part of the work force is in the technical area. The HRD unit may have subject matter specialists on the staff who represent designated technical areas in the company. Theoretically, it is best to staff such a unit with those who have the necessary technical skills and are only in the HRD unit for short periods of time. Although this is the tendency, there are still many HRD units that are organized and staffed with permanent HRD staff to reflect the various technical skills in the company.

Sales presents a different picture (Connell, 1984). A mystique has grown up around this area that suggests that only good salespeople can be good sales trainers. One could do all the research necessary to prove that this is not necessarily the case, but the practice has existed for such a long period of time that it is unlikely to change in the near future.

Underlying this organizational structure is a specific concern. There are those who believe that you cannot teach about a job unless you have held that job yourself. If this belief were adhered to, then most instructors involved in any aspect of management programs would be excluded: Most of them have never held jobs as managers! Nevertheless, HRD staff do conduct programs for these levels. It has been suggested that this is one reason why these programs are not as effective as they might be. This contention has yet to be proven, although it is certainly a concern that merits consideration.

***Centralized or Decentralized?*** A question that is frequently asked is, "Should there be one centralized HRD unit or should there be HRD units throughout the company?" The obvious and usual answer is, "It depends." Some companies are organized on a decentralized basis. Where that is the case, the HRD function should also be organized into different units, reflecting the decentralization of the company. (This does not mean that there will not be a "central" HRD unit of some sort, as will be discussed later.) In a decentralized company, identities and allegiances will rest within the decentralized units. When that is the case, there should be an HRD presence within those units, ranging from one person to a sizable HRD subunit. In some of these situations, the lines cannot be expected to flow from the decentralized units into that "big unit in corporate." Each unit must be organized to stand on its own. The "big" (status not size) HRD unit has the responsibility for coordination and will be concerned with many policy and administrative matters, but it will not provide direct services.

In a centralized company, there is more likely to be only one HRD unit. This does not preclude the possibility that there are people spread throughout the company with some HRD responsibilities. But all these different individuals will look to the central HRD unit for services as well as leadership. A problem that can arise is that individuals may abrogate their responsibility for HRD to the central unit. The central unit then becomes a school that offers courses rather than a problem-solving unit. In addition, budgetary responsibility is located in the centralized unit, and, therefore, line units may not consider the financial factors when requesting HRD services.

Note that we are not suggesting which form of organization is best for HRD. Rather, the HRD unit should reflect the philosophy of the company as expressed by its centralizing or decentralizing tendencies. This tends to be ignored when researchers study the HRD function in a company. The traditional questions are asked: How many people are on your HRD staff, how many employees are in the company, and what is the size of your budget? Note that the response to those questions will vary greatly depending upon whether the company is centralized or decentralized. Despite that, we find that researchers combine the data and ignore the fact that in a decentralized company each HRD unit will come up with relatively small numbers when responding to those questions.

A new trend in organizing companies is emerging and is rapidly being reflected in the way HRD is organized. We are beginning to see HRD units being identified at three different levels of the company. The newest place to find a significant HRD unit is at the very top. Such a unit serves essentially in a consulting role to top management in the area of HRD. In the Government Printing Office (GPO), for example, there is a strategic planning group at the top level. It contains one HRD professional. In terms of numbers and budget this is very significant. In terms of influence, it certainly has the potential to outweigh all the other HRD programs being conducted within the GPO.

A second place to find HRD is within department units which are located below the upper managerial levels but above the operating level. This is the traditional place where HRD has been located, along with other staff units. But HRD is no longer automatically assigned to this level. As the concept of HRD has become increasingly accepted, we are finding more companies that have organized special human resource units at department levels.

Finally, in some companies there is now a vice-president for human resources, and all or almost all of the human resource functions have been brought together in that unit. HRD becomes a subunit within human resources but not a subunit in the personnel unit. Such an HRD subunit may at times influence policy, but its major efforts usually go into planning and delivering HRD services.

Another part of this new trend is to provide for the delivery of HRD services within operating units. Traditionally, unit heads (supervisors, department managers, and so on) were expected to see to it that needed HRD was provided for their employees, but they were not expected to actively take part in the process. Delivery was by the HRD unit or outside vendors. The trend now is for supervisors and department heads to become part of the delivery system. The HRD unit is required to provide the supervisors and managers with the necessary competencies and to do the specialized work of designing learning programs and instructional strategies, as needed and asked for. But the supervisors and managers are expected to identify needs and deliver all or part of the program.

Although this section has discussed centralized and décentralized forms of organizing HRD within companies, we do not want to leave you with the impression that these are the only alternatives. There are other variations, including task forces and project groups. These are two of the different ways of bringing people together, from various parts of the company, to work on a specific problem or task requiring inputs outside of the regular reporting channels. Each of these temporary groups makes different demands on the HRD unit. Although these forms of organizing have limited and determinate lives, the HRD unit should stand ready to provide assistance to such groups from the time they are conceived until the time they are dispersed. Obviously, there is the need to provide training to those who will take part in such temporary groups.

If a company makes significant use of task forces and project groups, it is desirable to have an HRD subunit with the responsibility to service those groups. Our own experience has shown the wisdom of having at least one HRD person as part of such a group or readily available to it. Those groups face problems for which HRD might be the correct answer. Not knowing what HRD can do for them, they tend to look elsewhere for help, particularly outside the company. Such a subunit, however, would have to respond much differently to these temporary groups than it would to the permanent units within the company. The evaluation of performance of that subunit would also have to be different from the usual evaluation measures applied to the other HRD subunits in the company.

## Problems and Opportunities

The discussion, up to this time, has essentially focused on the physical factors within companies and how they relate to organizing the HRD function. Of equal importance are the personal relationships between the staff of the HRD unit and the staffs of the other units in the company. These relationships can present both problems and opportunities.

*Dual Nature of the HRD Manager's Role.* Being a manager means dealing with conflict. Recognize that we are not using the term *conflict* to mean a fight or in a negative sense, for conflict is present in all organizations. A good deal depends on how a manager copes with the situation, and coping starts with recognition.

HRD is essentially a staff function. At one time, in most companies, there was an absolute dichotomy between staff and line. We can recall when staff was labeled "nonproductive" in the sense that it was not expected to produce the goods or services that the company sold or offered to others. Another concept of staff was, and in some cases still is, that staff is part of the "overhead." It is something that the line must live with and pay for. It is only in fairly recent years that there has been a recognition of the interdependency between line and staff. Each is necessary, and each has a contribution to make to the success of the company. In certain forms of organization (such as the matrix form), the lines between line and staff blur and become almost insignificant.

It is common to find that the manager of HRD, now in a staff position, previously filled a position as a line manager. The move from line manager to staff manager requires a significant shift in thinking. One distinction is that a line manager is expected to solve day-to-day problems and facilitate the operations of the company. But a staff manager is generally concerned with short- and long-range problem solving and only rarely becomes involved in the immediate situation. An HRD manager coming from a line management position must recognize this significant difference. If not, that HRD manager may do a good job on a day-by-day basis but will not be able to relate the HRD unit to the short-range and long-range goals of the company. With only an immediate focus, the manager will not be involved in strategic planning in the company and will not try to determine how HRD relates to such planning. The organization of the HRD unit must reflect the attention given to long-range activities by having a person or subunit that focuses on those issues.

If the HRD manager has come from the line, he or she will probably still have strong ties to other line managers. This can represent an opportunity, for the HRD manager will have a good understanding of the line situation and what the line expects from a staff function like HRD. It can also be harmful, if the HRD manager retains strong ties with line management and therefore does not fully appreciate the differences between line and staff functions (Nadler, 1983). This tends to happen when the HRD manager is looking forward to returning to a line position. To such a manager, building a forward-looking, long-range HRD unit is not important. The HRD manager will not be in the position long enough to bring that about or to receive recognition for a successful effort.

If the HRD manager is a professional HRD person (that is, has a long-term commitment to the HRD field), there are other factors to be considered. The HRD unit is usually composed of individuals with varying degrees of identification with HRD. For some, HRD is merely another step on the way to a higher management position. To others, it may be a temporary assignment for a particular project, lasting for several months or perhaps for as much as a year. Given the differing degrees of identification with the field of HRD, the HRD manager faces the challenge of organizing the unit in such a way that will enable each member to achieve a measure of satisfaction, though each may have a different goal during the time that he or she is assigned to the HRD unit.

*"We" and "They."* It is quite common to find staff and line units creating artificial gulfs between them. More than almost any other staff unit, the HRD unit must have a strong identification with both the line and other staff units. It should not be a matter of "we and they" but "us." There is no one means that the HRD manager can employ to close that gap. It can be done, however, through careful organization of the HRD unit to reflect the needs of the different groups and subgroups within the company. The HRD unit, for example, must be able to relate to *all* levels of the company. Therefore, the unit must be organized in a way that encourages those relationships. The HRD manager must be able to identify the expectations of the various levels and groups in the company and staff the unit accordingly. If there is a union in the company, it may be possible for a subunit within the HRD unit to service employees covered by the union contract. This requires that the HRD staff in that subunit be completely familiar with the

contract, the history of labor-management negotiations in the company, and the people involved on both sides. This managerial subunit should focus on the learning needs of the managers and should be aware of the criticism regarding inadequacies in the M.B.A. programs of the past decade.

Within companies there is an ongoing competition for limited resources. No company has unlimited resources, and therefore such competition is normal. The HRD manager usually finds himself with too few resources for all the demands placed upon his unit. This can be one reason for placing HRD subunits within the various operating units, as this allows the subunits to draw upon the resources of particular operating units. However, locating small subunits outside the main HRD unit can be a blow to the ego of the HRD manager. In the past, moreover, the idea was that "big is better." The goal was to create a large unit in terms of financial and human resources or, in plainer words, to build an empire.

Some years ago, however, Schumacher (1975) told us that "small is beautiful." While companies may not look for beauty, his writings started a quest for alternatives, and one result has been *downsizing*. That is not a tactic for dealing with poor economic conditions. Rather it is a concept that suggests that it may be better to set up small companies within companies rather than to use the traditional hierarchial method of organization. Peters and Waterman (1982) lent some weight to this view in their analysis of the "best-run companies" in America.

What should be the size of an HRD unit? One is reminded of the story told about Abraham Lincoln: Mr. Lincoln's long legs were one of the targets of his critics. The story is told that, at a party one evening, one of his critics sought to embarrass Mr. Lincoln by asking, "Tell us, Mr. Lincoln, how long should a man's legs be?" After a pause, Mr. Lincoln replied, "Long enough to reach the floor." How big should an HRD unit be? Big enough to accomplish the goals that have been agreed upon within the company. The important question about an HRD unit, as about any other unit in a company, is not its size but its effectiveness. We are not suggesting that the HRD unit should be "lean and mean," unless that criteria is applied to other parts of the company. The

HRD manager must be able to justify the size of the unit against some agreed-upon criteria within the company. He must always, however, recognize that there will be continuous competition for limited resources.

*Company Expectations.* What does the company expect of the HRD unit? If the HRD unit is only to conduct courses, to be a school within the company, the expectations and organization of the HRD unit will be much different than if the expectation is that the HRD unit is there to help managers solve problems. In both situations, learning is involved, and the end result may well be organized group learning in classroom situations. That, however, is the observable result. The more important question is, what is the purpose of learning in the two cases?

Where the expectation is that the HRD unit will simply offer a list or catalogue of courses from which managers and/or employees can choose, then the unit can be organized like a school faculty. The HRD manager will, in essence, be the principal. The HRD staff, like faculty members, will have subject matter specialties, and the various subunits will be organized around those specialties. Where the expectation is that the HRD unit will focus on problem solving, the HRD unit will be organized in a way that more closely resembles the overall organization of the company, which may have operating units such as manufacturing (with many subunits), purchasing, sales, shipping, office services, and so on. The HRD unit will have subunits for each of these operating units or groups of operating units.

Generally speaking, the expectation is that the HRD unit will service the learning needs of the employees of the company. In some situations, the unit may also be expected to serve nonemployees. This is common in franchise operations. The Southland Corporation, which among other things franchises 7-Eleven stores (Lee, 1984), offers extensive programs for its nonemployees—that is, for the individuals who purchase franchises from the company.

Like other parts of a company, the HRD unit is susceptible to changes in the economy and other external factors. We have heard the saying that, "When economic conditions get bad, training is the first thing cut." There is very little specific evidence of that, but perhaps it serves as a comforting explanation to those

HRD managers who find their budgets cut when there is an economic decline. However, we will concede that "training" gets cut, if by "training" the HRD unit means training, education, and development. If the HRD unit distinguishes among these three learning programs and prepares separate reports for each, the impact of a declining economy on the HRD unit is frequently much different (Nadler, 1976). At any rate, under poor enough economic conditions, everybody's budget gets cut. The HRD manager must try to take a broad view of such situations and look at what is happening throughout the entire company.

Even in good economic times, moreover, there may be events or conditions within a company that cause it to become unsettled—for example, a merger, a divestiture, a rapid change in product lines, or new government regulations, and so on. The HRD manager must remain sensitive to these forces for change within the company and be prepared to reorganize the HRD unit to reflect them.

Since change in companies is a constant, what is the role of the HRD unit in change? The HRD unit can probably be of most help by providing stimulators and change agents. This requires that the HRD unit has people who possess those competencies. It also requires that the HRD manager build up, over a period of time, the recognition that the HRD unit can make a crucial contribution during periods of change within the company.

Change involves a period of transition (Nadler and Nadler, 1985). There is a contribution the HRD unit can make while the company is in its present state, preparing for transition. By focusing essentially on training and education, HRD can prepare people in the company for the new behaviors that will be expected of them. Once the transition has started, there will again be the need for HRD, as employees try to cope with the anxiety and stress produced by change. This requires that the HRD manager organize the HRD unit so that it can service a company in transition as well as in its current state. As change and transitions are constant in companies, the HRD unit may contain a specific subunit with competencies in dealing with the learning related to change and transition.

···{ *Chapter 4* }···

# Organizational Finance: Guidelines for HRD Managers

$\text{A}$ll managers are expected to have some competency in areas of finance. The HRD manager is no exception. To move from the role of learning specialist or consultant into that of HRD manager requires that the manager receive some training or education in finance. The HRD manager has too often left the financial side of the job in the hands of others, even while, recognizing that control of the budget can also mean control of the function. The budget will be discussed in the next chapter. In this chapter, we will focus on financial systems and how HRD relates to them.

## Internal Financial Policies and Practices

There is no one financial system that is common to all companies. Rather, there are a variety of legal alternatives.

*Form of Organization.* The accounting and financial system selected by an organization will relate to the form of that organization. In the United States, there are three common forms: corporations, partnerships, and individual proprietors. We will not deal with the numerous variations within these forms but instead concentrate on those that are most frequently used.

The *corporation* represents a very common form of legal entity in the business world. A corporation has a life of its own, independent of its members. For example, all the leading executives and managers could leave, but the corporation would continue to exist. An organization is incorporated in a specific state, and each state has slightly different regulations. This explains, for example, the numerous organizations incorporated in Delaware, where the corporate laws are more advantageous than they are in some other states. The HRD manager should know in which state the organization is incorporated and whether there are any special regulations that might have an impact on HRD. Corporations utilize attorneys, either as regular employees or on retainer, and they should be able to respond effectively to such a query.

But why, in practice, should HRD managers be concerned about the laws of their particular states? One issue relates to what has been termed *bonding* or *payback*. For example, the corporation may enroll an employee in a lengthy education program, with the understanding that the employee will return to a different and higher-level job in the organization. The agreement, frequently in writing, states that the employee *must* return to the organization. If not, the organization expects the employee to pay back the expenses incurred by the company, which can include tuition, travel, fringe benefits, and salary during the education period. This can be a significant amount of money. The actual enforcement of such contracts varies among states, and so the HRD manager would have to be aware of the specific regulations within his or her state. This is just one example of an HRD activity that could raise legal questions or even involve litigation.

If a corporation is listed on a stock exchange, it will be subject to the regulations of the Securities and Exchange Commission (SEC). This means that certain financial statements must be made available to the general public. It also means that the financial statements can be used in HRD programs. During the 1950s a series of programs called "How Our Business System Operates" (HOBSO) was developed. Those particular programs have disappeared, but similar programs do exist today under other names. Since a public corporation must make its financial statements available to the public, the astute HRD manager should consider using the corporation's financial statements in updated HOBSO programs rather than simply using general material about the economic system. There are, in fact, many ways to use a corporation's own financial statements in training and education situations. For example, consider a program for managers about the impact of depreciation on their planned purchases. After a general discussion of the concept of depreciation and its various forms, the instructor could use specific examples from the company's financial statements rather than those from some outside source.

Large corporations have sophisticated accounting systems, which are usually managed by a financial officer called the comptroller. The forms of accounts, titles, and so forth are set up by that office. The HRD manager must be familiar with the accounts, particularly those that relate directly to the HRD function. Unless the HRD manager conforms to the accounting system of the corporation, the HRD unit may find itself unable to gain access to budgeted funds.

A second form of business organization is the *partnership*. While corporations can be either large or small, partnerships tend to be small in size, capital investment, and operations. As a partnership grows, it can "go public" by incorporating and selling shares to the general public, either on the New York or American stock exchanges or over the counter. Partnerships produce financial statements, but these are generally not made available to the public, though they may be made available to some levels of management. If so, the HRD manager should endeavor to gain access to them. Managers who are privy to the financial statements have more power in the organization than those who are not.

Partnerships are set up under state jurisdictions, but the laws pertaining to them are generally not as detailed as those for corporations. The size of the partnership, its level of activity, scope of operation, and so on will be the determining factors in the kind of financial structure it maintains. Although the partnership accounting system may be much less complicated than that of a corporation, the HRD manager must still be familiar with it in order to ensure that the HRD operation is in the financial loop.

The third form of business organization is the *individual proprietorship*. Individual proprietorships are usually small companies, and few of them have HRD units. If anything, they will have a personnel or human resources office staffed by one person who is responsible for the HRD operation as a collateral duty. Generally, a single owner controls an individual proprietorship. Financial statements are retained by the individual proprietor, and little information is shared with anybody else in the organization.

A variation occurs in some of the high-tech companies that have emerged since the late 1970s, particularly in the computer field. They were started by single individuals as individual proprietorships. Subsequently, they were "bought out" by a corporation. Although the former individual proprietorship may retain its own identity within the corporation, it is now subject to the financial policies and practices of the corporation as a whole. Another alternative that individual proprietorships, like partnerships, have found attractive is to incorporate and "go public."

*Time Elements.* All organizations run on some kind of financial time schedule, but these schedules are not all the same. Hence, the HRD manager must determine the internal clock of his or her own specific organization. The most common time element is the *year,* but this twelve-month period can be viewed in two ways. First, there is the *calendar* year, which starts on January 1 and ends on December 31. Second, there is the *fiscal* year. These are twelve months that can start at any time. It is not even necessary for a fiscal year to start on the first day of a month. In using the term *fiscal,* however, it is important to clarify what is meant. When an organization uses a calendar year, it may sometimes also be called a fiscal year if it is identical with the business operating period of the organization. The noncalendar year may also have other names, though it is still a fiscal year. In universities, it is common to refer to the "academic year," which generally starts on July 1.

Usually, the financial period selected is important to the organization but to few other people. In the retail trade, the fiscal year usually ends on January 31 so that it will include the special inventory sales that occur after the holiday season. These sales usually come just prior to closing the books for the year. It is thought advisable to sell off as much inventory as possible so as to reduce the labor cost of taking inventory. This also produces an increased cash balance and a lower inventory figure, both of which contribute to a healthy-looking financial statement.

Understanding the twelve-month period is necessary if one is to understand the yearly life cycle of an organization. Within clusters of the same type of industry or business, we find similar financial periods, which may reflect high sales periods (as in retailing) or the seasons (as in construction). If the financial statements are published, it is possible to make comparisons among organizations. The financial period is generally divided into four equal quarters of three months each. Although there may be monthly financial reports, the general practice in U.S. companies is to report quarterly. The three months to be covered will depend on whether the calendar or fiscal financial year is used and how those three months periods relate to cycles within the organization. For the calendar year, the quarters end in March, June, September, and December. For the fiscal year, the quarters will end at three-, six-, nine-, and twelve-month intervals after the start of that year.

The HRD manager must know the financial periods and recognize their impact on HRD planning. As with other managers, the HRD manager should be able to compare current HRD data with data from "the same period last year." The flow of HRD activities, as with most organization activities, tends to be repetitive. Where it is not, explanations by the HRD manager are helpful to those to whom the manager is accountable. Moreover, goals and missions change, and these changes will be reflected in some different HRD activities. When reporting the changes, the HRD manager can include comment along with the financial statement. This is an acceptable practice by all managers.

*Accounting Systems.* Every organization has some kind of accounting system. A corporation generally has a large and fairly sophisticated accounting staff, depending upon the nature of its business. Since public corporations are required to file a variety of financial statements, they may even employ outside accounting firms. Their financial statements and other information are made available to all the stockholders through regular reports and at the annual stockholders' meeting. The accounting systems utilized by a partnership can vary, depending upon factors such as size, complexity, and number of partners. It can range from a system as simple as that generally found in the individual proprietorship to a system as sophisticated as that found in large corporations. The individual proprietorship may rely on a very simple system, consisting essentially of a cash receipts and a cash payments journal. These records can then be analyzed on a regular basis by an external accountant. That accountant may also perform such related functions as preparing financial statements for the owner. ·But whatever the form of the organization, the HRD manager must be familiar with its accounting system and follow its accounting procedures if he or she is to have access to the financial resources of the organization.

*Return on Investment.* In evaluating HRD, there is frequent reference to such financial data as return on investment, cost-benefit ratio, profit enhancement, and so forth. In the literature, the term *return on investment* is frequently used but its meaning is not always understood. For example, in accounting terms, the profit or return on investment is the difference between income and expenses. The economist, however, takes another point of view and sees the profit as the difference between what the investment has returned from company operations as compared to what that investment would have returned in some other financial activity. This has been a critical difference in the years when we were plagued with high inflation and high interest rates. The HRD manager does not need to be overly concerned with that distinction except for using "investment" as the basis for calculating a return. Usually, when HRD managers speak of return on investment, they are referring to return on cost or expenses. But since the words are used with different meanings in different organizations, it is essential that HRD managers determine exactly what is meant by them in their own particular organization.

*Cash and Accrual.* Accounting systems can be set up on a cash basis or an accrual basis. The first is familiar to most of us. It is similar to our own personal accounting or financial system. We do not have income until we receive cash or an equivalent negotiable instrument, such as a check. We work for an organization and that organization owes us money, but there is nothing we can do with that money until we actually get it. True, we can incur some debts against it, but if we do not get the money in time to discharge our debts, we will be in trouble. Likewise, an expense occurs when we pay out some of our cash. Although we may have the obligation to pay, it does not become an expense until we actually pay it.

Using the cash system, it is fairly easy to know our financial status at almost any time. It is the difference between our cash income and our cash expenses. Of course, we must also keep in mind expected income and anticipated expenses. These, however, are not reflected by entries into our accounting system. We may make some notations about them, but they are not part of our financial system until they actually occur. This may explain why some companies, particularly small ones that use the cash system, find themselves with cash flow problems. They usually have not developed a system to track expected income and expenses, since these items are not reflected in the accounting system until actually received or paid.

To be more accurate and to avoid some of the financial problems of the cash system, large organizations generally use the accrual system. Under this system, the company lists income on its books when it has finished a job or provided a service, even though the transfer of funds may not occur until a later time. To avoid confusion and misrepresentation, the accrual system provides for accounts receivable. These are moneys owed but not yet paid to the organization for work performed. When the money is received, the accounting system transfers the paper amount from accounts receivable to cash received.

A similar series of transactions takes place for expense items. The expense becomes the company's obligation when it is incurred, though the actual payment may not be made until a later time. The HRD manager may sign a contract, for example, to use a conference site for a program. The signed contract is an obligation and will be listed in the company records as an account payable. The actual payment for that site, however, may not be made until the end of the program. At that time the accounting system will pay out the money, thereby increasing the cash paid account and reducing the accounts payable. As you can see, the accrual accounting system is preferred because it more accurately reflects the continuing operations of the company than does the cash system.

The HRD manager must know which accounting system is being used in order to know how to plan for expenditures. (The HRD function usually does not generate income.) The type of system being used can also influence the form of reporting by the HRD manager. Under a cash system, it may be necessary to provide a great deal of explanation, for the expenses reported in a particular financial period may not really reflect the operations. For example, the HRD unit may purchase materials for programs that will continue to be used beyond the reporting period. Under the cash system, the expense for those materials will be reflected in the period paid. Under the accrual system, it is possible to make provision for those expenses over the period during which the materials will actually be used.

*Depreciation.* This item is the cost of major or capital purchases of equipment, spread over the life of those items. Generally, depreciation is not reflected in the cash system, although the IRS allows depreciation for some taxpayers on the cash system. In contrast, the very nature of the accrual system makes depreciation mandatory.

Let us look at the situation in which an HRD manager purchases several stand-alone computers during a particular fiscal period. If the cash system is used, the total cost of those computers is reflected in the statement for that fiscal period despite the fact that the computers will be utilized over a longer period of time. The accepted practice is to depreciate the cost of the computers over their useful life. The IRS publishes tables of useful life that can be used for this purpose. Putting figures on this transaction, let us say that the computers cost $5,000 each, and the HRD manager has purchased twenty computers for a total cost of $100,000. Under the cash system, there will be a bulge in the financial report for that period—suddenly, there is a charge to HRD for $100,000. From an overall cost-benefit picture this would be disastrous. It would also not present a true picture of the situation.

Using the accrual system presents a picture that is less startling and more accurate. Let us assume a life of five years for the computers. That means that the HRD unit will show an expense of only $20,000 per year. If the organization issues quarterly financial statements, the difference between the figures produced by the cash and accrual systems will become even more obvious. For a particular quarter, the depreciated cost would not exceed $5,000. This is certainly a more accurate picture for that quarter than $100,000!

        To summarize, the comparison would look as follows:

|                                   | Cash | Accrual |
|-----------------------------------|---------|----------|
| Initial cost                      | $100,000 | $100,000 |
| Annual depreciation (for five years) | none | 20,000 |
| Quarterly depreciation            | 100,000* | 5,000** |

        * = One time charge.
        ** = Charge to each quarter for five years.

Of course, good accounting practice, as well as IRS regulations, would probably require the company to depreciate over the useful life of the computers and not use the cash method. The HRD manager needs to understand and apply this to be in line with the financial practices in the organization.

        If the HRD manager does not understand the accounting system and how it applies to HRD, the result will be confusion and an incorrect reflection of the finances of the HRD operation. The HRD manager should not leave this entire transaction in the hands of the accounting people. They, for their part, are not experts on HRD and might very easily report HRD expenditures incorrectly, to the detriment of the HRD function. They would not do so because they wanted to make the HRD operation look bad. Rather, they would expect the HRD manager, like the other managers, to be familiar with the accounting system and to know how the financial operations of the unit should be reported.

        *Locus of Control.* There are, of course, many ways to organize the actual accounting system. Each of these will reflect the way the total company is organized. Companies usually set up a *centralized* accounting system, and all accounting actions pass through one designated unit. This unit is usually staffed by special personnel familiar with bookkeeping and accounting systems and is sometimes headed by an accountant. At one time we might have said that only large corporations use computerized systems. With the spread of reasonably priced small computers and the necessary software, it is safe to say that most organizations now have some kind of computerized accounting system. When that is true, the HRD manager must be familiar enough with the system to know how to input data. A computer, for better or worse, provides a very controlled system. For example, it can accept only specified inputs. If the HRD manager cannot make the appropriate inputs, somebody else will do it for him. This could involve a modification of the original data and, consequently, a loss of control on the part of the manager.

The same situation applies to outputs. The HRD manager must know how to utilize the variety of reports available from the system. It is not necessary to know the technology of the computer, but it is essential to know its capabilities. We are past the stage where computer printouts can be viewed with disdain or suspicion, and an increasing number of managers have become accustomed to computer-produced reports. If the HRD manager chooses to ignore that reporting system, it is probable that his or her HRD reports will also be ignored by those to whom they are distributed.

Under a *decentralized* system, each organizational unit handles its own accounting functions, with just some general direction from a central source. That central source is necessary for preparing the financial reports required by government agencies, banks, and so forth. The decentralized system does present a drawback when one tries to obtain HRD financial information for the entire company. "In a large, decentralized organization like Honeywell, individual divisions budget for and track their own training and development expenditures. As a result, the corporation's *total* outlay for human resource development (HRD) is nearly impossible to determine with any degree of accuracy" ("Honeywell: Management Development at . . .," 1983, p. 20).

As a result of the development of desk top computers, it is possible to have a centralized system yet also provide for decentralization. With desk top computers that hook into the mainframe computer, managers can make inputs of financial activities directly into the company's computer system at any time. Data can be updated constantly, not only at quarterly periods. Managers can receive reports very quickly and easily through the computer on a variety of activities within the organization. Of course, some computer files will be locked, access only being possible to those who have the password for those files.

At the same time, the people who look at organizational systems tell us that the better organizations will come to adopt smaller working units (Peters and Waterman, 1982; Scobel, 1981). The emphasis will be on small decentralized units to encourage the concept of intrapreneurship. If that trend continues, we can anticipate some changes in accounting systems. These will not be evident until there is substantial experience with a great number of small organizational units, and there will still be need for some kind of centralized information unit. It is possible to set up a company's computer system so that it will reinforce some decentralized accounting procedures, while still retaining the ability to meet the needs for centrally produced financial statements. It is also possible to have stand-alone computers, not just terminals, within decentralized units, where they can maintain the data files for their own operation. The technology currently exists to allow a small work unit to have its own stand-alone computer that can be turned into a dumb terminal and become part of the organization's mainframe computer.

### Financial Statements

Every organization prepares financial statements. They can be as simple as a one-page statement of income and expense, or as complex as a twenty-page brochure with color photographs, mountains of financial data, and a message from the president. It is not necessary for HRD managers to be familiar with all aspects of financial statements, but they should have some understanding of the balance sheet and the profit and loss statement.

The intent of this section is to familiarize the HRD manager with the terminology and concepts used in these financial statements. We do not intend to make accountants or financial experts of HRD managers, but all managers have a responsibility to be able to communicate using the same financial language so that they can work with each other as well as with the accounting staff within their organization.

   ***Balance Sheet.*** The balance sheet can take many forms. Exhibit 1 presents the essentials of a balance sheet for a company using the accrual accounting system. Before examining the balance sheet in detail, however, we should review the nature and purpose of that financial statement.

**Exhibit 1.**
**The ABC Company**
**Balance Sheet**
**(December 31, 1985).**

Assets

| | | |
|---|---|---|
| Current assets | | |
| Cash | | $ 1,000 |
| Accounts receivable | | 5,000 |
| Inventory | | 4,000 |
| Fixed assets | 8,000 | |
| Less: Depreciation | 3,000 | |
| Depreciated value | | 5,000 |
| Prepaid expenses | | 500 |
| Total assets | | $ 15,500 |

Liabilities and Net Worth

| | | |
|---|---|---|
| Current liabilities | | |
| Accounts payable | 2,000 | |
| Total liabilities | | 2,000 |
| Net worth | | |
| Stock | 10,000 | |
| Surplus | 3,500 | |
| Total net worth | | 13,500 |
| Total liabilities and net worth | | $ 15,500 |

   The balance sheet is essentially a photograph. It is a picture of the financial status of the company at a given point in time. A balance sheet is issued at least once a year, and it covers a specified period of time. For the ABC Company, the period covered is from January 1, 1985, to December 31, 1985. It takes time to prepare this basic financial statement. Sometimes, as much as three months can elapse between the close of the fiscal year (the date of the balance sheet) and its issuance. Therefore, it is necessary to note the period that a balance sheet covers. If it is the annual statement, it usually lists only the balance in each account at the close of the period. If it is an interim statement, it will list the period being covered. It is not customary to issue a balance sheet more frequently than once a quarter.

The balance sheet has three major parts, and the term *balance* represents the concept expressed in the formula:

$$assets = liabilities + net\ worth$$

The term *assets* refers to what the company owns. There are several categories of assets. Current assets include cash or other items that are expected to be converted into cash in the near future through normal business operations. Accounts receivable represent sales that have been made, or services provided, for which the cash has not yet been received. Inventory represents what the company has available for sale. If it is a service company, there will not be any inventory.

Fixed assets include such items as land, buildings, machinery, and equipment. As noted earlier, depreciation is a factor when discussing most fixed assets. For the HRD manager, this category is important, because computers, projectors, and similar items of equipment can be carried as fixed assets. Whether they are so carried will depend in part on the accounting policies followed in a particular organization. In order to do any financial calculations and projections, the HRD manager must know exactly how those items are handled, the rate of depreciation, and the organization's financial policies relating to fixed assets.

If a balance sheet has an entry for prepaid expenses, it means that the company has paid cash for some goods or services that it has not yet received. Since it has been paid, the amount has already been deducted from the cash available to the company.

The HRD manager must be aware of this account, and how it is used within the organization. The time periods of HRD programs will generally not coincide with the time period of the balance sheet. A program may start in one period but not be completed until the next period. Let us assume that the HRD manager has contracted for a facility to be used for several programs over a period of six months but that the next balance sheet will cover only the first three months of that period. In order to get the facility, the HRD manager may have had to pay the full sum for the entire six months, but only one-half of the sum will be a charge to the period covered by the balance sheet. The other half of the sum (for the second three months) will be entered on the line for prepaid expenses.

Those items the company is obligated to pay, but has not yet paid, are termed *liabilities*. There are many kinds of liabilities, and only the most common—current liabilities—will be discussed here. Accounts payable are those obligations that will be due in the near future. Using our earlier example, let us assume that the HRD manager has negotiated with the facility to pay half the money at the end of three months and the balance at the end of six months. As the HRD manager has obligated the company to use the facility for the next six months, the company must make provision to pay that invoice when it comes due three months after the balance sheet has been closed. This is done by entering the obligation to the facility in accounts payable.

In Exhibit 1, only accounts payable are shown, for that is the liability that is of most direct concern to the HRD manager. What the HRD manager does has a direct effect on that account. There are other liabilities such as notes payable, wages accrued, and bond interest accrued. Although the HRD manager should know something of these, they will not be of direct concern to him.

The difference between the assets and liabilities of a company is its *net worth*. In Exhibit 1 this is reflected in the item called *stock*. This immediately indicates that we are dealing with a corporation, as partnerships and individual proprietorships do not issue stock. In these last two forms of organization, this item will bear titles such as partnership interest, partner's holdings, owner worth, proprietorship equity, and so on. The item *surplus* represents the worth of the organization over and above the stock. It is actually the sum of all the profit since the organization began that has not been paid out in the form of dividends or similar transactions.

In financial analysis of a company, it is customary to compare two balance sheets for like periods. The shifts in the various accounts can provide a good picture of how the organization is developing and whether it is growing or whether it is facing financial difficulties. The HRD manager may require help from the appropriate financial members of the organization to interpret these data. Asking for such help may indicate a lack of some competency on the part of the HRD manager; but, on the positive side, it will communicate the interest of the HRD manager in understanding the financial picture of the organization.

*Profit and Loss Statement.* How often have you heard the question, "What is the bottom line?" The term *bottom line* is often used, but it is less often understood. In basic terms, the bottom line is the last line of the profit and loss statement as seen in Exhibit 2. The bottom line represents the result of many activities in the organization. The profit and loss statement in Exhibit 2 is vastly oversimplified, as it must be for this discussion. From it, however, we can draw some significant points that are crucial for the HRD manager.

Like the balance sheet, the profit and loss statement is a photograph. It tells us what happened in the past for a specified period of time. When you read the profit and loss statement, you must always remember that it is past history but history from which a great deal can be learned. The time period is important. The general practice is to start each profit and loss statement at the beginning of the financial year of the company. Then it becomes cumulative. Sometimes the statement will be set up to show the current month as well as the cumulative figure for the period. The profit and loss statement is often used for comparison purposes; that is, July of this year is compared with July of last year. Most organizations have cycles, and it is important for management to be able to make these comparisons. Very seldom does the comparison go back farther than one year unless there are some significant problems. Another important relationship can be identified by comparing the profit and loss statement to the budget for the year. Of course, the budget is for a twelve-month period, so it may be necessary to arbitrarily divide it into twelve monthly aggregates. If this is done, special footnotes may be required to reflect the cyclical nature of company operations.

During this discussion of the profit and loss statement, there will be frequent references to training but not to education or development. The reason is that the statement reflects current, not future, operations. Training can influence current events, while education and development look to the future. Although education and development will be reflected on the statement if funds have been paid or obligated for those activities, they are not expected to have the impact on profit and loss that training does.

The general form of the profit and loss statement is presented in Exhibit 2.

**Exhibit 2.**
**The ABC Company**
**Profit and Loss Statement**
**Year ended December 31, 1985.**

| | | |
|---|---:|---:|
| Gross sales | | $ 20,000 |
| Less: Returned sales and allowances | | 1,000 |
| Net sales | | 19,000 |
| Less: Cost of goods sold | | 8,000 |
| Gross profit on sales | | 11,000 |
| Expenses | | |
| Selling | 2,000 | |
| General and administrative | 6,000 | |
| Total expenses | | 8,000 |
| Net profit or (loss) | | $ 3,000 |

Most such statements are much more detailed than this one and are accompanied by schedules that provide even more detail for selected items. Although there is agreement on the flow of the profit and loss statement, there can be variations from one company to another, as long as accepted accounting practices are followed.

The first part of the profit and loss statement is concerned with gross profit on sales. The term *sales* is generally used, although the company may be selling a service rather than a product. This is one place where HRD can have an impact on the profit and loss statement, although there may not be an absolute, direct relationship between sales and HRD. Thus, one possible way for a company to increase sales is to improve the performance of its salespeople. A good sales training program can contribute to this, but only if it is the performance of the salespeople that has been the problem. If the low sales figure is due to aggressive pricing by competitors or if other companies have better products or better delivery and servicing systems, then the training program for the salespeople cannot be expected to have any significant effect on the sales figure. Moreover, even if the training is appropriate, the results of the improved performance may take quite a while to be reflected on the profit and loss statement and may not even show up until the next fiscal period.

The gross sales figure is modified and reduced by a variety of factors. It is expected that companies that manufacture a product as well as retail companies will have returned sales and allowances. When management thinks that figure is too high, action must be taken. Possibly, there is the need for improved quality control, and training might be one answer to that. The gross sales figure must also be modified by the cost of goods sold, that is, by the cost to manufacture the goods. This is where productivity becomes important, though it is usually not directly reflected on the profit and loss statement. It might be included in one of the numerous schedules that generally accompany that statement. Although training is not the complete answer to productivity, it is certainly one of the important factors (Nadler, 1983; "The Human Factor," 1984). This is where training affects the profit and loss statement and produces benefits that will ultimately be reflected in the bottom line.

This brings us to the gross profit on sales figure that must then be reduced by applying various kinds of expenses such as selling, general, and administrative that are not directly concerned with the manufacture of the goods. These expenses are needed to keep the company operating. As sales are a crucial element, some companies list their selling expenses as a separate item which in turn includes such items as salaries, sales expenses, and advertising. Another category of expense is general and administrative, which includes salaries, office supplies, telephone and telegraph charges, postage, and rent. These are the basic expenses required to keep the company going and are sometimes called the overhead.

We are now at the *bottom line*, that is, net profit or (loss). The parentheses around "loss" are one way of showing a negative figure. A traditional way, in the past, was to put this figure in red ink, as compared to the black ink normally used on the statement. The use of those colors has led us to say that a company is "in the black" or "in the red." As most financial statements are now produced by computers, we will have to wait and see if those terms are replaced by being "out of the parentheses" or "in the parentheses"! At any rate, when we come to the bottom line, we know whether there was a profit or loss.

But where is HRD on this statement? The answer depends on how the HRD function is organized within the company, but some general distinctions can be made. If HRD is considered part of overhead, as with other staff functions, it will appear under general and administrative expenses. But it is also possible for HRD expenses to appear as part of the cost of goods sold. The criteria for making this decision are discussed in Chapter Five.

## Tax Considerations

We cannot leave this discussion of financial factors without discussing the IRS, since that government agency oversees a good many of the financial operations of organizations. Organizations generally develop their financial policies and establish their practices in conformity with what they and their accountants think the IRS expects. These expectations are not always clear, hence the mounting case load in the tax courts.

At one time, IRS rules and regulations had little impact on HRD, but this began to change in the late 1970s. For example, the IRS has generally taken the position that learning related to an individual's current job (training) is a deductible expense for an employer. Even here, however, the IRS has sometimes raised questions about that deduction and, Congress has so far not taken the necessary steps to clarify this issue. Members of the executive branch have tried to argue that learning of any kind provided by employers (training, education, and development) is essentially a fringe benefit. Such being the case, withholding tax should be deducted and the employee should pay tax when HRD has been provided by an employer. Given this confusion, Congress passed a law in 1981, in an attempt to establish some ground rules. Known as section 127 of the Internal Revenue Code, it had a sunset life of two years. The intent was to give the executive branch sufficient time to explore the issue and report its findings and recommendations to Congress. This was to have been done prior to December 31, 1983, so that Congress could take appropriate action.

That did not happen, and the law lapsed at the end of 1983. This meant that the IRS was free to tax all HRD to the individual. One implication of this was that employers would have to withhold tax from employees for the amounts that would be taxable. Employers who did not do this would be subject to paying the tax, plus interest and penalties. This would produce an intolerable situation and make HRD extremely expensive for employers and employees.

Finally, toward the close of 1984, Congress passed a new law. It was only for a year—once again to give the executive branch and Congress an opportunity to act in less haste. The law was very limited in that it did not cover all of HRD but only tuition refunds—the money that an employer reimburses to an employee or pays on the employee's behalf for learning outside the company. Congress also wisely backdated the law to cover the period from January 1, 1984.

## Conclusion

HRD managers, particularly those without line experience, have tended to shy away from exploring the financial system of the organization. That behavior isolates the HRD manager from other managers and from the financial operations of the organization. In the United States, organizations are formed in one of three ways: as a corporation, a partnership, or an individual proprietorship. The organizational form influences the way the organization handles its financial activities. The corporation, and sometimes the partnership, produce financial statements that are important for the HRD manager in his or her role as manager. These statements can also be used in a variety of HRD programs for employees at various levels.

Companies have different accounting systems and the HRD manager must be completely familiar with the system of his or her specific organization. A general knowledge of accounting is also helpful. For accounting purposes, an organization will use either the calendar year or the fiscal year. The choice affects the financial statements and the financial cycles of the organization. Organizations can use either a cash or an accrual basis for their accounting records. Centralized and decentralized financial operations may not replicate the organizational hierarchy, but the form of financial control can indicate power centers in the organization.

A company can produce many different kinds of financial statements, but there are two essential statements that all must have: a balance sheet and a profit and loss statement. The balance sheet reflects the current position of an organization at a specific moment in time. It lists the various assets and liabilities; the difference between these two items is the net worth. When the liabilities exceed the assets, there is a negative net worth that indicates impending or actual bankruptcy. The profit and loss statement is a performance record for a given period, not to exceed twelve months. It is cumulative during that period, though it can also show the current month's operations. An examination of the various factors can help identify the sources that produced the net effect.

In addition to the internal picture, the HRD manager should also know the tax considerations that are related to HRD operations; the major area of concern is the deductibility of some HRD expenses. When the laws or the IRS's interpretation of those laws change, the HRD manager needs to communicate these changes to higher levels of the organization for decisions.

···⊰ *Chapter 5* ⊱···

# Budgeting Tools and Processes

There is an adage that "the person who controls the budget controls the function." This applies to HRD as well as to all other units in organizations. As indicated in the previous chapter, it is important for the HRD manager to know the principles of financial management. It is also important for him or her to understand budgeting and to have competency in that area. Otherwise, control of the HRD function may pass into the hands of those who do know how to prepare and manage a budget, a financial instrument that Finney has defined as "an operating and financial program for a future period, based on results attained in prior periods and on data obtained by research and analysis" (1946, p. 473). But, as we shall see, preparation of the budget is only one part of the HRD manager's broader financial management responsibilities.

The organization of the HRD unit as a financial center in an organization should be the result of policies and practices that have been carefully planned by the HRD manager and the organization's senior management. In this chapter, we will identify and discuss three different forms of financial management units for HRD: the budget item center, the cost center, and the profit center. You may find that your HRD unit is organized in one of these ways but that the label is different in your organization. Look behind the label to determine how the organization expects your HRD unit to function financially. As far as possible, the financial management form of the HRD unit should be similar to that for other units within the organization. The HRD unit should not be organized in some unusual form that is alien to the organization. To do that would be to erect a barrier and signal that the HRD unit is different from the regular units within the organization.

## Budget Item Center

One of the most common ways to organize the HRD unit is through the budget item center. At the beginning of each fiscal year, the unit is allocated a budget, which is based on the plan presented by the HRD manager during the budgeting development process. Under this system, the HRD unit does not charge the other units in the organization for its services and serves only those units that are part of the organization. The unit is expected to expend its entire budget during the course of the year in providing services to the various organizational units. The concept underlying this form of organization is that the HRD unit provides a service to the various organizational units and should therefore be treated in the same way as other staff services, such as personnel, purchasing, and general administration. These units are also considered part of overhead rather than part of regular line operations.

Under this service concept, the HRD unit uses a variety of techniques to determine the HRD needs of the organization. Usually, the emphasis is on ongoing needs that can be programmed for during budget preparation. The HRD manager provides for identifying these needs by building needs assessment activities into the budget. Additionally, a wise HRD manager always builds in some extra funds (perhaps hidden) with which to respond to organizational needs that were unforeseen but that could surface during the fiscal year. For some generic programs, such as supervisory training, the various units in the organization are assigned quotas. The HRD unit usually develops catalogues or other forms of announcements so that everybody in the organization will know what programs will be offered during the fiscal year.

There are *advantages* to the budget item center format. At the beginning of the year, the HRD manager knows exactly what financial resources will be available to use, barring any unforeseen economic crisis that might affect the entire organization. This format encourages individual units to send people to the HRD programs since the cost does not come out of the operating budgets of the sending units. The funds for HRD programs come from the general administrative budget of the organization. Put another way, each operating unit in the organization is charged for administrative overhead, which includes HRD. One way for a unit manager to recover some of that charge is to send people to the HRD programs. Reporting for a budget item center is straightforward since it is usually a matter of counting courses, enrollments, certificates issued, and so on. These lend themselves to charts, graphs, and statistical manipulations in the quarterly or annual reports and make it simple to compare the current year with prior years.

Among the *disadvantages* of the budget item center is that it places no real pressure on the HRD unit to relate to the real learning needs of the organization. Of course, a good HRD manager will try to focus on those real needs, but he or she may be faced with a lack of interest by line managers. For specific problems, moreover, the line managers may seek HRD help outside the organization. When questioned about this, such line managers may respond, "The HRD unit is running a school and is looking for large registrations. It is not interested in my problems unless I can send them a large number of bodies. Right now I have only two people who need that kind of training. The HRD unit tells me it may be offering that training three months from now. My people can't wait. They need it now!"

This is not just a line manager's perception. The HRD manager must consider the economics of the situation and must report in a financial formula that usually goes:

$$\text{cost of program} \div \text{number of participants} = \text{unit cost}$$

This type of reporting encourages HRD managers to set up large classes so as to reduce unit costs. This may not produce the best instructional environment, but it is the one most frequently used when unit cost becomes the critical factor.

As large numbers of learners are important to the budget item center operation, the HRD manager will lean toward those methods that will produce the largest number. For example, the Office of Personnel Management of the federal government issued a regulation that every supervisor must have forty hours of training in supervision. In the private sector, the HRD units of some organizations, with approval from above, issue bulletins requiring all supervisors to go through a specified series of courses, whether they need the courses or not.

Generally, these required courses will bear little or no relation to the needs of the units or the line managers or to actual problem solving. Rather, employees attend them with the false expectation that they will lead to advancement or rewards. Such courses, however, usually cannot be evaluated in terms of performance change on the present job. Highly motivated learners are desirable, but not if their motivations are not consonant with the needs of the organization. Employees may take courses for education, presumably to prepare themselves for promotions. But their selection of learning experiences may not be based on prior consultation with their supervisors or career counselors, even if such consultation is available within the organization. The result may be that they can implement the education opportunity provided by the HRD unit only by taking jobs outside the organization. In such situations, HRD has actually contributed to increasing employee turnover. This will not appear on the budget in any discernible form, but it will certainly be a revealing piece of data for budget reviewers at higher management levels.

Another possibility is that employees will take courses for personal development or simply because they want to learn. There is nothing wrong with individuals wanting to learn for the pure joy of learning, but it can create problems when the organization is paying for what it thinks is training (learning provided to improve performance on the present job of the employee). This situation becomes apparent when the HRD manager is asked to relate the budget expenditure to job performance.

Another disadvantage of the budget item center is that the results of the program are almost impossible to evaluate in terms of performance change. Of course, the HRD manager can always arrange for evaluation of the learning that took place. But unless there has been a careful exploration of mutual expectations (between the supervisor and the learner) before the learner comes to the program, it is usually not possible to evaluate for performance change.

## Cost Center

The core of the cost center concept is that the HRD unit charges for all its services. These charges are made directly to the organizational units involved, so that the HRD unit can recover all its costs by the end of the fiscal year. At the end of the year, the report of the HRD unit's budget performance will show that it has broken even—no surplus, no loss. Cost centers have existed within organizations for many years. Peters and Waterman noted that "the core management practices of IBM, HP, 3M, TI, McDonald's, Delta, Frito, Tupperware, Fluor, J&J, Digital, and Bloomingdale's bear strongly on the point that markets of all kinds work well inside" (1982, p. 114). For HRD, the practice of charging internally became more prevalent during the 1970s. This was a partial response to the question, How much does HRD cost?

Under the cost center concept, the HRD unit starts each fiscal year with little in the way of a budget allocation. Provision is made for some administrative and start-up costs, as no programming funds are carried forward from the previous year. In some situations, however, even these initial costs must be recovered by charges to users during the year. At Lutheran General Hospital, for example, the HRD unit's budget is completely recovered since other departments are billed internally for its services ("Lutheran General Hospital," 1983).

The cost center approach necessitates that line managers include budget items related to HRD in their own unit budgets. It is not always possible for line managers to anticipate all HRD needs a year in advance, when the budget is being prepared, but this approach forces them to think about HRD for their employees as they plan for the next fiscal year. The budget development process is a bit more complicated with cost centers than with budget item centers. The HRD unit still has responsibility for delivery of its off-the-shelf programs, such as those for supervisors, managers, orientation, and so on. But the HRD unit in addition will have to respond to other HRD needs of operating units needs as they arise during the fiscal year.

The *advantages* of this approach are many. Primarily, it forces the HRD unit to make sure that its activities are directly related to the needs of the units and their employees. If the needs that are identified are not relevant, line managers will not want to release funds from their budgets to the HRD unit. This forces the HRD unit to be very specific in offering programs. So-called buckshot programs (those that are expected to meet a broad range of needs) will be offered less frequently. The consumer, that is, the line manager, will want to be satisfied that there will be some return to his unit before agreeing to pay for the program. Payment for HRD activities is only a transfer of funds on the books of the organization; no actual cash is exchanged. As discussed in Chapter Four, the HRD manager must understand how this transfer is accomplished and must know when funds will actually be made available for utilization by the HRD unit. Using the cost center approach requires a higher level of understanding of the budgeting process in the organization than is necessary when using the budget item center approach.

The cost center approach enables all concerned to have a fairly accurate picture of the costs of HRD. The degree of exactness will depend on how the organization maintains its books, how overhead is charged, and similar financial decisions. There is also the need to know the organization's fiscal policy on salaries and wages while employees are attending an HRD program, on travel expenses, and so forth. The policy on these items should be firmly established and consistent throughout the organization. This policy allows for comparisons of costs among units and eliminates the need to make budget decisions each time an HRD program is offered. If the HRD unit is going to charge for a program, the HRD manager must know the exact cost of that program. The cost center approach forces the HRD manager to be cost conscious, as any manager should be. As a result, the HRD manager frequently cuts down on such fringe benefits as needlessly plush surroundings or overly expensive food and beverage service.

Among the *disadvantages* of the cost center approach is one that was discussed earlier as an advantage. This approach requires that line managers plan ahead for HRD, which can be difficult for a variety of reasons. Many line managers do not want to make decisions about HRD planning for it is not one of their usual functions. In most MBA programs, as well as in many company programs for managers, very little, if anything, is said about HRD. Although it would be advantageous to raise line managers' levels of consciousness about their responsibilities for HRD, too many line managers would prefer to leave HRD to the HRD manager.

There are, however, a variety of activities available to increase a line manager's awareness of HRD. The basic one is that the line manager must be made to see the obvious financial benefits of some of the programs. As it is not possible to show financial benefits for all programs, the HRD manager should initially focus on those programs that can be shown to have obvious and direct cost-benefit implications. Then, in all candor, the HRD manager should acknowledge that there are some programs for which a direct return cannot be shown. This does not mean that those programs should not be funded from the line manager's budget but rather that the HRD manager will find it more difficult to get the line manager to pay for them.

From the viewpoint of the HRD manager, the cost center approach can discourage risk taking. If all the expenses of the HRD unit must be recovered, it can be anticipated that the HRD manager will tend to offer those programs that will produce the greatest revenue for the HRD unit. These may well be good and necessary programs, but the HRD manager will be less likely to reach out to identify other organizational problems that might not have mass appeal.

In addition to planning, line managers must provide for some flexibility in their budgets in order to meet new problems for which HRD is the appropriate response. Specific performance problems cannot be identified a year in advance, but it should be obvious to all line managers that problems will arise during the course of the year that can be solved by HRD. Line managers must learn how to budget for these eventualities.

Recall the period of the late 1960s and the programs for the hard-core unemployed or the disadvantaged. Many chief executive officers supported those programs and directed their companies to become involved in them. It soon became obvious that there was a need for an HRD component (Nadler, 1979). More recently, we have seen this same situation with regard to quality circles. Upper levels of management became enamored of the concept, without exploring it in much detail, and ordered that quality circles be installed within their organizations. However, for quality circles to work, training is required. The line managers agreed, but they had not foreseen the need to provide for this in their budgets and consequently had to scrounge for funds to implement a decision made at a higher level. They had to take funds they had allocated for other purposes and use them for training.

A budget item center would be able to handle this problem very easily with an allocation of special funds from the chief executive officer. It would be more difficult for a cost-centered HRD unit to respond. It would require that the line managers fund the HRD activity from their own budgets. Obviously, they would be reluctant to do so. However, an alert HRD manager could point out this problem and arrange for the chief executive officer to make special discretionary funds available for the program, so that the line manager's budget would not be taxed.

As it can be expected that similar problems will continue to arise, let us look at two other ways to cope with this dilemma. One way is to provide research and development funds in the cost center budget. That is, the HRD manager is provided with some discretionary funds (seed money) that can be used for developing new programs that had not been anticipated. Generally, such funds should also be available so that the HRD unit can do the research and development required for experimental programs that need significant design work before they can be offered.

A second approach is more difficult but does have some added benefits. The HRD manager explores, with selected line managers, their willingness to contribute to an HRD research and development fund for setting up special programs. Of course, these managers would expect to send people to the programs and to receive some benefits from them. The HRD manager places these

earmarked funds into a special account (assuming the organizational accounting system allows for this) to be drawn on for a
particular program. When the program is ready to be offered, the
cost for the program includes provision for payback to the
"investors."

There is another element of the cost center approach, and it
can be viewed as either an advantage or a disadvantage. The cost
center approach encourages external competition from HRD
vendors (often erroneously called consultants). Under the cost
center approach, the principle is usually established that if the
same program can be obtained from outside the company, for a
lower cost, the line manager is free to negotiate for the external
program, including purchased programs that are conducted either
on the company premises or elsewhere.

Some HRD managers see the use of outside sources as a
threat to the existence of their units, but it need not be. If the
internal HRD cost is out of line with the external, the HRD
manager should be looking more closely at how to cut his or her
costs. Moreover, the HRD manager has a built-in advantage over
the competition by being on the inside, knowing the organization
and its decision makers. This position within the organization will
be enhanced if the HRD manager has a good track record in
servicing line managers. It is true that external competitors can
sometimes offer a program at a lower cost since they spread their
development cost over a much larger organizational base. In
addition, if it is a program that has been in use for a long period
of time, the development cost may already have been recovered.

Rather than a threat, then, external resources should be
considered a positive element and an additional resource for the
HRD manager. The HRD manager can often sponsor selected
programs internally. Through careful negotiation, the vendor can
be helped to understand that the cost should be kept at a level that
makes it attractive when offered through the HRD unit.

## Profit Center

The profit center concept is very much like that of the cost
center, with two significant differences. The charges include not

only recovery of cost but some element of profit. Also, the profit center unit can sell its programs externally as well as internally. The profit center concept is not new, though it did not become prevalent until the mid 1960s. However, one early practitioner of the profit center was DuPont. DuPont marketed cleaning compounds and found that many of its customers needed help in learning how to use those compounds effectively. The company had good in-house programs for its own maintenance people, and it decided to sell them externally.

The big thrust toward profit centers came in the middle of the 1960s and it brought about some interesting organizational relationships. Sometimes the HRD unit remained internal and intact as in the case of Lockheed Corporation. As a result of a cutback in the aerospace industry, Lockheed found itself with an excellent HRD unit but without enough work to keep its staff employed. The company began to explore external alternatives, one of which was to provide training for the police in various California localities. Using its excellent HRD staff, Lockheed was able to offer quality programs that put the company into a profit center operation.

Other companies, however, spun off their HRD units. This produced profit centers such as Litton Educational, Xerox Learning, and Westinghouse Learning. Although this trend slowed down a bit during the 1970s, there was still interest in this approach. AT&T, before divestiture in the early 1980s, began to offer, externally, some of the organization effectiveness programs that it had previously used only internally. Control Data converted its HRD operation into a profit center with emphasis on providing services outside the company (Noer, 1985).

Like the cost center, the profit center starts with a small budget. The difference is that the amount it charges to users includes a profit whether the user is internal or external. This is not a departure from common practice in other areas of organizational life. In some industrial organizations it has long been the practice to charge for internally manufactured goods as they move from one department to another within the same organization. Each department is expected to "sell" its product to the next department with a profit figure included. Then, at the end of the fiscal year, each line manager is required to return a stipulated profit on operations to the company. If this approach is to be used, the HRD manager must ascertain the percent or level of profit expected of other managers. It is not unusual to find that the HRD unit charges a higher rate to external than to internal users. There can be many reasons for this. When selling a product or service internally, there would probably not be a cost for advertising or marketing. There may also be a psychological basis for charging less, though this will not appear on the profit and loss statement of the HRD unit.

Some of the *advantages* of the profit center are similar to those of the cost center. Obviously, since line managers are expected to pay for HRD services, they tend to be more demanding than they otherwise would be. This is an advantage, for it forces the HRD unit to be more assiduous in meeting the actual needs of individuals and the organization. The actual cost of HRD to both the HRD unit and the line manager can be clearly determined. In fact, the cost must be ascertained or there cannot be any calculation of profit to the HRD unit. The line managers will have to budget for HRD services, and this will make them more aware of the need for HRD. It also requires that the HRD unit be able to provide financial data on costs to enable the line managers to budget effectively and, afterwards, to determine if the HRD service has been worth the cost.

Likewise, the *disadvantages* are similar to those discussed for the cost center, the greatest one being that the profit center approach might make the HRD manager unwilling to take any risks. The HRD manager might seek out the programs that can be sold, and he or she might even pay more attention to external customers than to those within the organization. There is a larger market in the world outside than can ever exist within one organization. Further, the focus can easily become one of identifying programs to sell rather than helping the organization to solve problems through HRD. In time, the HRD unit can become almost irrelevant to the internal HRD needs of the organization. The HRD manager should not be surprised if line managers begin to purchase HRD programs from external sources. The internal HRD unit is no longer "theirs," part of the company, but is a vendor like anybody else.

## Combinations of Centers

Up to this point the three types of budget or financial centers have been discussed separately. But various combinations of the three types can be developed to make maximum use of the advantages of each one and also to reduce some of their disadvantages. Let us look at some of the factors that must be considered when these types are combined.

Each organization is different, and the *policy* of the organization must be considered very carefully. For example, if there is no policy to allow departments to charge each other, then the cost center and profit center methods would not be acceptable. Conversely, if there is a policy to charge, then the HRD unit should certainly find out how to implement that policy.

This leads to the question of the *organizational placement* of the HRD unit. In earlier years, the HRD unit was usually under the personnel department. The tendency since the mid 1970s has been for the HRD unit to be placed in other parts of the organization. That placement can also influence the budget arrangement.

Centralized HRD units are usually found in some administrative part of the organization. The specific placement varies from one organization to another, but it has become common to find HRD units in such diverse places as administration, human resources, human resource management, and personnel. When so placed, they may be considered part of the general overhead and this almost forces the units to be organized as budget item centers. In looking at other units at the same level, one would find it difficult to identify any that charge out for their services. In most organizations such units are not considered profit centers. There is a variation to this. As some HRD units have moved in the direction of providing consulting rather than learning programs, they have adopted the practice of charging on an hourly or daily basis. If that is the policy and/or practice in the organization, the HRD unit can certainly charge as a cost center.

HRD can also be decentralized; that is, various operating units may have their own HRD units that function independently of any corporate HRD unit. In such cases, the HRD budget is part of the decentralized unit budget. There is no HRD activity that crosses lines to another department, so the budget item center would be the most appropriate form to use.

After having said that, we recognize that newer forms of organizations have emerged (for example, flat, matrix, and project) and that there will probably be even more variations in the future. The placement and form of centers for HRD should be part of this change. Given new organizational structures and relationships, we can expect that other forms of HRD centers will emerge.

Within the limits of company policy and organizational placement, the HRD unit may be organized on the basis of *individual preference*. HRD managers may have expectations and beliefs that influence the kind of center selected. Some of these will be based on their previous experiences as line managers, as well as their expectations and future goals as HRD managers. There is no way we can explore the numerous variations based on individual preference, but we can emphasize that this is a significant factor to be considered.

Externally, the *state of the economy* will have an effect on the selection of the internal combination. If the economy is depressed, it is less likely that the HRD unit would opt for a profit center operation, as it would be at the mercy of economic factors over which it had no control. During such a time, the external HRD field becomes very competitive and profits decline. Perhaps a part of the profit center will be retained, but the bulk of the efforts will be concentrated on internal operations through the budget item center. If a particular segment of the economy has declined, an organization may find it to its advantage to move its budget item center operations into more fertile fields outside the organization through profit center operations.

As can be seen, it is possible to have more than one center within the same HRD unit. The permutations are fairly obvious:

1.   Budget item center/cost center
2.   Budget item center/profit center
3.   Cost center/profit center
4.   Budget item center/cost center/profit center

The HRD manager should not hesitate to explore all possible alternatives. Above all, the HRD manager should avoid being trapped into the patterns of the past, which may no longer be desirable, given the constant changes in organizations, individuals, and external factors such as the state of the economy.

There are two additional factors to which the HRD manager must be sensitive. If combinations are used, then the staff in the HRD unit may all be working together but with much different goals. Those who are in the profit center operation may be critical of the budget item center people and comment that "those budget item people have a free ride! They do not have to sell or make a profit. Everything is handed to them." The budget item center staff may retort with, "The profit center is where the action is. It can be evaluated on a dollars and cents basis, and that is what this organization wants."

These conflicts can be partially overcome by not designating centers, but rather identifying programs as budget item, cost, or profit operations. Staff are permitted, perhaps even encouraged, to work across those lines. However, such an arrangement can prove very difficult to administer and can be disruptive to staff. A different psychological orientation is required for working in each of those centers, and some of the staff may not be able to move freely among the three types.

Despite the limitations of some of the combinations, the HRD manager should feel free to explore them and then staff them as the situation demands. Appraisal of staff should be related to factors that do not, for example, reward those who are working in the profit center at the expense of those in one of the other centers.

## Budgeting Process

Each organization has its own forms and processes for budgeting. The HRD manager must clearly understand those forms and attempt to structure the budgeting process for his or her department to be as congruent as possible with the budgeting process in the organization as a whole. Although HRD is a unique activity that may need special handling in some respects, the HRD manager must reconfigure the HRD operation to accommodate the organization's budgeting process. If the manager fails to do this, the HRD unit can expect difficulty in obtaining the necessary financial resources.

Before we examine budgetary forms, processes, and policies in HRD, one of the first things we must do is to agree on terminology. Terms vary from one organization to another. Sometimes these differences are only semantic, such as using the term *transportation* for *travel*. Sometimes they are more substantive in nature. In some organizations the terms *transportation* or *travel* mean only the actual cost of the mode of transportation. In the case of air travel, it may or may not include ground travel at either or both ends of the trip. In other organizations, those terms, particularly *travel*, also include the cost of food and lodging, which are reimbursed. At still other organizations those terms include payment of a flat per diem, with the traveler responsible for living within that rate or absorbing the difference. Before budgeting can begin, these terms and the subcategories they include should be clearly understood.

*Forms of the Budget.* No one budget form is accepted by all organizations. In this section, we will discuss three different forms currently in use. As line managers become more comfortable with the rapid retrieval of data, including budgetary data, that is possible through the use of a computer, we can expect the present forms and information-gathering procedures to be modified. With regard to computer processing of budgetary data, it is important to remember that if the data is not prepared according to the data processor's instructions, the final budget document may not resemble the HRD manager's intentions. It may not be desirable, but form does define function in these instances.

Let us look at the three most prevalent types of budgets. The most common budgetary form is the *line item* budget. The sources of funds will be listed under "income." Funds may be allocated from the general revenue of the organization, as is the case with the budget item center. For the cost or profit center, there is usually a breakdown of expected income from various sources.

Under expenses, each item is listed separately. Frequently, the accounting department will determine which line items are to be included; the HRD manager need only enter the appropriate amount on the line provided. For each line item that requires an explanation, a supplementary schedule is attached. For example, there will be a line for salaries. A supplementary schedule will list each employee by name, job or functional title, and salary, including any anticipated raises, increments, or other changes. The supplementary schedule should also indicate any anticipated increases in staff.

Another budgetary form is the *program* budget. This approach, called the "Program Performance and Budgeting System" (PPBS), was introduced by McNamara when he moved from Ford to the Pentagon. During his tenure, it was in general use in the federal government. After McNamara left the Pentagon this budgetary form slowly fell into disuse. In the private sector it never gained general acceptance, although variations of it remain.

As the name indicates, this budget lists the various programs and the performance or change expected for each. The HRD budget lists the programs according to participants: supervisors, salespeople, pipefitters, and so on. The cost for each program is estimated and entered into the budget. A statement of goals accompanies each program listed. For example, for supervisor programs the goal might be for every supervisor to have at least five days of training during the fiscal year. A supplementary schedule lists the costs that account for the total figure in the budget.

One of the values of the program budget is that it can be reviewed in terms of each department's contributions to organizational goals. Let us consider what must occur if there is to be a 10 percent cut in all budgets. The program concept does not allow for just reducing costs by 10 percent. Instead, a decision must be made regarding the objectives of the program. Let us return to our supervisor training program: Does a 10 percent cut mean that the number of supervisors to be trained will be reduced by 10 percent, or that total training time will be reduced by 10 percent? If training time is to be cut, what goals must be changed so that the material to be covered can be reduced by 10 percent?

Similarly, if the decision is made to increase income by 10 percent, the program budget helps to focus on that goal. For the budget item center this is an impossibility since it does not generate income. For the cost center, this means charging 10 percent more internally, but what does this do to the budgets of the other departments? For a profit center such as the HRD unit, this goal requires identifying new external sources of income or determining ways of deriving additional income from existing external sources.

The budgetary form known as *zero-based budgeting* (ZBB) was introduced during the Carter administration. When its exponents left, it disappeared from government use as did PPBS, but it remains in use in some areas of the private sector.

ZBB is based on the concept that each year starts completely new. You cannot take last year's budget and simply adjust for inflation or other variables. Instead, each item in the budget must be justified anew each year. Implicit within ZBB is the concept of the "sunset" clause: the sun sets on every budget item, and it may cease to exist. If the item is not judged to be making a contribution to a current or future goal of the organization, it does not appear in the final budget. This budgetary form puts major emphasis on the justification of items, as well as on the level of funding.

***Budget Cycles and Policies.*** Each organization has a budgetary cycle. The HRD manager must be well acquainted with that cycle. Even a reasonable request to meet a clearly defined need can encounter budget difficulties if it is not congruent with the organization's budgetary cycle.

The final budget of an organization is the end result of a great deal of work. It is not uncommon to find that an organization requires two years lead time from the start of the budget process to adoption. The proposed budgets of the various organizational units will go through many iterations. Not all of these steps are designed to cut the budget, although that very often happens. Instead, there may be reallocations or other internal adjustments.

Every organization has some kind of budget policy. When this is a written policy, with regulations and guidelines to which the HRD manager must adhere, it is easy for the manager to be completely familiar with this policy.

When the policy is not written, the task is much more difficult. To ascertain an unwritten policy, the HRD manager must effectively communicate with the other managers in the organization.

*Budget and Organizational Structure.* The organizational form of the HRD unit is also a budgetary consideration. If it is a centralized unit, budget preparation may be fairly easy. When HRD is decentralized, budgeting will take place at many levels. Indeed, it may very well be that the entire HRD budget is brought together only in the final stages of budgeting.

The different kinds of organizational structures also influence the budget process as well as the items contained in the budget. If the HRD unit is a budget item center, the manager may have few decisions to make with regard to the annual budget, unless major organizational changes are proposed. Since they are not expected to generate income, funds are usually allocated from general income, and budgets for these centers may only list expenses.

If the HRD unit is a cost center, the budget should include anticipated charges or billings to other units of the organization. To do this, the HRD manager should have some idea of how the different parts of the organization might change. Internal shifts in products, sites, and so on can significantly affect the budget-planning process. When the HRD unit is a profit center, both internal and external charges should be carefully documented. Consideration should also be given to the possible state of the economy in the future. Understanding external forces and economic trends are crucial to a successful profit center operation.

*Budgeting and Planning.* Most organizations use their annual budgets as their short-range plans. Long-range plans are commonly thought of in terms of five years. Some aspects of the long-range plans are reflected in the annual HRD budget; for example, the provision for purchasing or replacing equipment. Particularly with the ongoing impact of technology on the HRD field, the HRD manager must include the financial provision to keep the equipment as up-to-date as possible.

A new type of planning emerged in the early 1980s: *strategic planning.* Essentially a reaction to the lack of long-range planning during the 1970s, this controversial type of planning is a process that enables an organization to look to the future and at what it wants to be. The strategic-planning process involves both short-range and long-range plans.

*The Budgetary Process.* The process of preparing the budget reflects the management style of the HRD manager. Too many HRD managers sit in their offices, with papers spread all around the room, the door locked, and everybody warned to stay away. Even though it vitally affects the professional lives of all those in the HRD unit, the budget may become a secret document. Such secrecy gives rise to a variety of rumors, overloads the grapevine, and generally produces negative reactions.

The budget process is one area in which the HRD manager should utilize the participative management approach. Everybody at all levels in the HRD unit should be involved in the process. This is the time to examine those ideas that were previously discarded because "they were not in the budget" to see whether they might appropriately be included in the budget that is now being prepared.

When preparing a new budget, the HRD manager should review the budget for the previous year, both planned and actual. In part, it is a learning experience, for this comparison provides a way of assessing one's budgeting abilities, but it is also a refresher on the thinking that must be involved in preparing the budget. At the same time, however, the HRD manager should avoid being trapped by the past. It is all too easy to bring out last year's budget, adjust it for inflation and similar economic factors, and resubmit it as the new budget. Such a process does not take into account changes in organizational goals, planning by other managers, or all the other nonfinancial items that must be considered when preparing the budget.

In addition to reviewing the previous budget for the HRD unit, the HRD manager should also look at the financial statements of the organization. (Samples are shown in Exhibits 3 and 4.) These have been discussed in Chapter Four. The purpose of this review is to get a general feel for how the organization is doing financially as well as to understand the organization's history as reflected in those financial statements.

Let us assume that the budget has been prepared and is ready for submission. The date for submission must be strictly

**Exhibit 3. HRD Department Budget for Fiscal Year 19——.**

| | | |
|---|---:|---:|
| Sources of funds | | |
| Budget allocation | | 600,000.00 |
| Other | | |
| External (grants) | 5,000.00 | |
| Internal: | | |
| Other departments | 32,000.00 | |
| Special allocations | 20,000.00 | |
| Total other | | 57,000.00 |
| Total funds | | 657,000.00 |
| Fixed expenses | | |
| Administrative: | | |
| Salaries | 175,000.00 | |
| Fringe benefits | 35,000.00 | |
| Office expense | 3,000.00 | |
| Tel & tel | 4,000.00 | |
| Postage | 2,000.00 | |
| Travel | 15,000.00 | |
| Professional development | 10,000.00 | |
| Overhead charge | 10,000.00 | |
| Equipment—purchase | 30,000.00 | |
| Equipment—depreciation | 10,000.00 | |
| Equipment—maintenance | 2,000.00 | |
| Total fixed expense | | 296,000.00 |
| Variable expenses | | |
| Instructors—external | 100,000.00 | |
| Developers—external | 100,000.00 | |
| Consultants | 100,000.00 | |
| Equipment—rental | 10,000.00 | |
| Materials | 15,000.00 | |
| Travel | 20,000.00 | |
| Facility rental | 16,000.00 | |
| Total variable expense | | 361,000.00 |
| Total expenses | | 657,000.00 |
| Net | | 0 |

observed. When a submission is late, the budget may encounter difficulties in the adoption process. Even though the HRD manager may not enjoy the financial and arithmetical exercises involved in budgeting, the budget must be submitted on time, in the form and manner prescribed.

**Exhibit 4. HRD Department Comparison of Budget to Actual for Fiscal Year 19——.**

Statement as of January 31, 19——

| | Budgeted for Year | Budgeted to Date | Actual to Date | Difference |
|---|---|---|---|---|
| **Sources of funds** | | | | |
| Budget allocation | 600,000.00 | 50,000.00 | 50,000.00 | .00 |
| Other | | | | |
| External | 5,000.00 | 416.67 | .00 | 416.67 |
| Internal | | | | |
| Other departments | 32,000.00 | 2,666.67 | 500.00 | 2,166.67 |
| Special allocations | 20,000.00 | 1,666.67 | .00 | 1,666.67 |
| Total funds | 657,000.00 | 54,750.01 | 50,500.00 | 4,250.01 |
| **Expenses** | | | | |
| Fixed expenses: | | | | |
| Administrative: | | | | |
| Salaries | 175,000.00 | 14,583.33 | 14,583.33 | .00 |
| Fringe benefits | 35,000.00 | 2,916.67 | 2,916.67 | .00 |
| Office expense | 3,000.00 | 250.00 | 300.00 | -50.00 |
| Tel & tel | 4,000.00 | 333.33 | 250.00 | 83.33 |
| Postage | 2,000.00 | 166.67 | 150.00 | 16.67 |

| | | | | |
|---|---|---|---|---|
| Travel | 15,000.00 | 1,250.00 | 1,000.00 | 250.00 |
| Professional dev. | 10,000.00 | 833.33 | 500.00 | 333.33 |
| Overhead charge | 10,000.00 | 833.33 | 833.33 | .00 |
| Equipment—purchase | 30,000.00 | 2,500.00 | .00 | 2,500.00 |
| Equipment—depreciation | 10,000.00 | 833.33 | 833.33 | .00 |
| Equipment—maintenance | 2,000.00 | 166.67 | .00 | 166.67 |
| Total fixed expense | 296,000.00 | 24,666.66 | 21,366.66 | 3,300.00 |
| Variable expenses: | | | | |
| Instructors—external | 100,000.00 | 8,333.33 | 4,000.00 | 4,333.33 |
| Developers—external | 100,000.00 | 8,333.33 | 9,000.00 | -666.67 |
| Consultants | 100,000.00 | 8,333.33 | 500.00 | 7,833.33 |
| Equipment—rental | 10,000.00 | 833.33 | 500.00 | 333.33 |
| Materials | 15,000.00 | 1,250.00 | 1,000.00 | 250.00 |
| Travel | 20,000.00 | 1,666.67 | 1,500.00 | 166.67 |
| Facility rental | 16,000.00 | 1,333.33 | 1,500.00 | -166.67 |
| Total variable expense | 361,000.00 | 30,083.32 | 18,000.00 | 12,083.32 |
| Total expenses | 657,000.00 | 54,749.98 | 39,366.66 | 15,383.32 |
| Net | .00 | .03 | 11,133.34 | -11,133.31 |

*Note:* Differences are arithmetical.

## Implementing the Budget

It is important to remember that the HRD manager cannot spend funds purely on the basis of the budget. The *cash flow* of the organization must also be considered. In essence, the budget merely says that certain funds will be made available to the HRD manager—if the cash is there. This does not apply to salaries or other recurring expenses. An important factor that must be considered here is the time of year. It is obvious that some organizations have periodic highs and lows in cash. A retail organization that does a high volume of business during the pre-Christmas period will limit the use of its cash to purchasing merchandise prior to that season. During that season the cash flow goes up, but management wants to have sufficient cash available to meet its obligations without needing to resort to factoring or other discount practices that can be costly. During that time, expenditures for HRD will have a low priority, even though they are stipulated in the budget.

There are other flows that must be considered. For example, consider the case of agencies of the federal government. Their practice is to try to "obligate" (similar to commit) the funds that are in the budget before the end of the fiscal year on September 30, so that they will not be lost. Therefore, a great deal of purchasing takes place near the end of the fiscal year, although actual payment may not be made for several months. HRD managers in the federal government stay alert to the availability of unobligated budget funds at that time. (We should not fault the federal government on this—many private-sector organizations do exactly the same. The difference is that the practice of the federal government is public knowledge.)

The HRD manager must also know the *procedures* for implementing the budget. Each organization has specific forms, approvals, and so on regarding purchasing. If the HRD manager does not follow the accepted procedures, purchases may be delayed or, worse, disallowed. It can be anticipated that an HRD manager who comes from a background in education or the behavioral sciences will not be overjoyed about the paperwork involved in the budget process. After having done the work required by the budget process, that HRD manager may feel that it is a waste of time to have to do all the little chores related to implementing the budget. But if this feeling influences the HRD manager's behavior, then all the previous work will have been for nought. The procedures have to be followed. One alternative for the HRD manager is to delegate the work (Engel, 1983). Somebody else in the HRD unit can be delegated to follow through on the required procedures. This is an excellent practice, but the HRD manager must build in controls so that the results of the delegation can be appraised.

The HRD manager is accountable for the efficient and effective use of the financial resources provided to him or her, as reflected on the budget and operating statements. This accountability can take several forms, all of which require some kind of reporting by the HRD manager to the higher levels that approved the budget. The most familiar form of reporting is the body count; that is, how many student hours were involved, how many programs were conducted, and so on. If the mission of the HRD unit is to provide those hours or programs, then this quantitative approach is required. It does not tell of changes brought about as a result of HRD programs, only what HRD provided.

An emerging technique is to identify *indicators*. Here, it may not be possible to quantify all the data. In this mode, the questions are, What problems were solved by providing HRD, what changes took place? The HRD manager, in conjunction with those served, develops indicators prior to the start of the program. It then becomes possible to report the results in terms of those indicators. Some of the results can be quantified, as when the indicator relates to increased production, decreased downtime of equipment, increased sales, or decreased overtime. Other indicators, such as those relating to quality of work life, morale, and job satisfaction, would be qualitative.

The difficulty with some of these measurements is that the results may not be completely attributable to HRD. An increase in sales might be the result of a competitor's leaving the market rather than the result of a training program for salespeople that occurred at just the same time. Then, again, when the HRD unit helps a line manager solve a problem, there is no agreement, generally, as to how this should be reported. The line manager probably wants to report that he solved a problem by using the appropriate resources, but in this case the resources took the form of the internal HRD unit. If the HRD unit takes credit for the success, the line manager might feel that this puts the credit in the wrong place. One reaction might be to avoid calling on the HRD unit again for problem solving. This is an area that has, so far, received too little attention.

Each type of HRD center has to report differently. The budget item center reports in terms of how close it came to the budget submitted. Those to whom such reports are made will be looking for places where the budget was exceeded or significantly underspent. The bottom line is looked at to determine whether the net result was zero. The cost center operation will focus on whether all the costs have been recovered. For a profit center HRD unit, it is necessary to report in terms of the profit earned as compared to the profit expected.

## Conclusion

As can be seen from this chapter, the HRD manager must recognize the importance of the budget as a management tool. It is essential that the HRD manager be able to prepare a budget in the form required and within the time parameters established by the organization. Through an understanding of the HRD budget, the HRD manager comes to understand the budgets of other units of the organization. This enhances the ability of the HRD manager to relate to other managers in the financial terms that are essential in any organization. Constant review of the budget is necessary and provides the HRD manager with one approach to reviewing the operations of the HRD unit. The budget helps the HRD manager establish the accountability of the HRD unit and its contribution to the organization and individuals.

For budgetary purposes, there are three different ways to organize: budget item center, cost center, and profit center. Each has its own advantages and limitations. It is also possible to use a combination of these centers within the same HRD unit.

The budget item approach is used when the organization allots the HRD unit a fixed amount from the organizational budget. All expenditures for HRD will come out of that allotment. In a cost center approach, the HRD unit does not get a substantial allotment but must charge its activities to the users within the organization. They recover their costs through those charges. In a profit center, the HRD unit does not get a substantial allotment and must recover its costs, plus a profit. It can usually sell its services outside the organization, although it should focus on servicing the organization. At the end of the fiscal year, it is expected to meet its goal of a certain percentage of profit.

To be effective, HRD managers need to be completely familiar with the entire budgeting process. This process varies among organizations, but some basic components will be found in all. Each organization, for example, has its own terminology for some of the items. It is not enough to go to the textbooks on the subject, it is also necessary to go to the comptroller's office or wherever the organization's code of accounts is maintained. Budgetary forms will also vary. The HRD manager must be able to submit the budget in the form required by the organization. And the budgetary cycle and stated deadlines must be observed. Finally, the budget must reflect the different planning aspects of the organization: strategic, long-term, and short-term.

## ··{ *Chapter 6* }···

# Staffing the HRD Function

The staffing of the HRD function is extremely significant for the HRD manager. The decisions that an organization makes about staffing will determine what kind of manager the HRD unit will get, and the kind of manager selected will determine the staffing of the remainder of the unit. Later in this chapter we will differentiate between an HRD unit that is just starting up and one that is already operating, since the approaches to staffing will be different in the two cases. In this chapter the focus will not be on selecting an HRD manager but rather on the options that an HRD manager has for staffing the other positions in the HRD unit.

Staffing is the result of the policy decisions, practices, and inclinations of various individuals within an organization. In this chapter we will be exploring a variety of staffing possibilities, but we cannot offer an exact schema or set of rules. For example, there is absolutely no formula to determine the best ratio between the number of employees in the organization and the number of staff needed in the HRD unit. Number of employees is only one of the variables that contribute to the staffing pattern and is probably one of the least useful. We can, however, identify some of the opportunities and challenges that face organizations when staffing for HRD.

Staffing decisions should be made with the realization that, as internal and external forces impact on the organization, there may be a need to make changes in staffing. One of the most predictable conditions in organizational life is that management will change. Incumbent managers may change jobs, reach retire-

110

ment age, or be fired. New managers may emerge from within the organization or may be brought in from the outside. Depending on the philosophy and value system of the new management group, it may make decisions that have a significant impact on HRD. For example, it may decide that the organization will not provide any learning activities for its employees and therefore does not need an HRD unit. Or it may decide that the work of the organization should be kept as an internal "secret" and that there is thus the need to build a larger HRD unit to serve the special needs of the organization.

## Organization of Human Resources

The field of human resources is so dynamic that it is almost impossible to make any statements without appending the qualification "at this time." This should not be taken as criticism of the field but rather as a reflection of the growing interest in people in the workplace. The period from 1960 to the mid 1970s saw a dramatic increase in the utilization of technology. Indeed, there were those who saw technology as the answer to every problem: "If we can get a man on the moon, why can we not get a man out of the ghetto?". This question reflected the belief that technology could be used to solve every problem, including human problems. There is no doubt that technology has much to offer us, but it has its limits. In the foreseeable future we will still have to work, and humans will have to do much of that work (Levitan and Johnson, 1982).

In the decade of the 1980s, in fact, we are seeing increased attention being given to people in the workplace. Expanding memberships in organizations related to human resources are only one reflection of that interest. In 1970, the American Society for Training and Development (ASTD) had about 4,000 members. By 1980 that figure had grown to 20,000. Of course, a change of direction and focus by ASTD contributed to that growth, but it was undoubtedly assisted by an increasing interest in people in the workplace and by the fact that more organizations had begun to offer in-house HRD. We have seen the emergence, in many organizations, of a vice-president for human resources. This all-encompassing position is usually responsible for areas such as human resource management (HRM), HRD, labor relations, employee benefits, equal opportunity, human resource planning, and so on. This trend differs from one organization to another, depending on the individuals involved and the particular interest that an organization has in its human resources.

The overriding organizational concern is that the various human resource units should work together. It is not essential that all such units be located in one department in the organization. It is helpful, but not essential, to have a vice-president or someone of equal rank responsible for the human resource functions. But if the HRD unit is buried within another human resource unit, the tendency will be to staff for the larger unit rather than to consider the roles and functions that are applicable to HRD.

In the past, the staffing of the HRD function was frequently planned with the goal of eventually moving some of the HRD people into other HRM functions. The HRM unit included people who focused on such areas as recruiting, compensation, classification, appraisal, testing, and HRD. What was ignored was the multiplicity of roles performed by HRD people. It also meant that the HRD staff had to develop skills in those other HRM areas in order to be available for promotion within the HRM unit. There were few, if any, promotional opportunities within the HRD unit. Fortunately, this situation has changed considerably. The HRD unit should always take care not to isolate itself from the other human resource functions. It is essential that the HRD unit have very close ties and relationships with the other human resource activities in the organization. But this must be done without losing the HRD identity and its unique contribution to the organization.

Later in this chapter we will discuss in more depth some of the types of HRD people there are—for example, full or part time, permanent or temporary, and so on. Each organization has its own policies and practices for assigning staff. The HRD manager must know how the other human resource units in the organization are staffed in relation to the aforementioned factors. This does not mean that the HRD unit should be staffed the same way as other human resource units; but the HRD manager should at least be familiar with the expected staffing patterns and be prepared to explain any deviations from those patterns in his or her unit.

## Roles of HRD Staff

A basic consideration in staffing the HRD function is the *role concept*. That is, the HRD manager must look at what HRD people do, as seen by themselves and others. A role is essentially a collection of related functions and tasks. A crucial element is that one cannot be in a role unless others perceive that person to actually be filling that role. A corollary is that one cannot change one's role unless others accept that change.

Some of the original work on role concepts was done by Nadler (1962), Lippitt and Nadler (1967), and Nadler (1979). Three major roles were identified: learning specialist, administrator (later changed to manager), and consultant. There were also eleven subroles. There has been other research using that model (Blank, 1982; Brewster, 1972; Cavallaro, 1984; Glazer, 1983; Epstein, 1971; Herold, 1973; Theodore, 1977). A study was conducted in 1983 (*Models for Excellence*) under the auspices of ASTD, using the role concept, but the major roles and subroles were combined to yield fifteen roles. For the most part, the differences introduced by ASTD were not significant.

In this chapter we will discuss only the learning specialist and the consultant. The administrator/manager is discussed throughout the book.

A role can be specified by a title, but that title may not be understood in the same way by everyone. It is essential that the title be made clear to all concerned through discussion and examples. A good deal of this section of the chapter will deal with roles that have been researched and defined in a variety of settings. That does not mean that the labels will apply to all organizations, but the role model will. Indeed, one very significant activity of the HRD manager is to continually clarify the roles of the HRD staff, both within the HRD unit and in other parts of the organization. Even now, too few people in organizations understand the unique contribution of HRD, and role clarification is one way of informing others of that contribution.

Among the questions that are frequently asked are, In an HRD unit, how many people should be in each role? Should every HRD unit contain people to fill all the roles? The answers to these questions are complex, as there are so many variables to be considered. A major variable lies in the policy area. Does the organization want its own HRD unit, or does it prefer to purchase services from external sources? An organization can have a unit that consists essentially of a manager with a budget. In such a situation, the HRD manager is expected to identify needs but to meet them by purchasing external resources. This is frequently found in organizations that focus on research and development. When we questioned this practice in one organization, the response was: "Our field is changing so rapidly that we need constant training to keep up with it. We do not see the HRD unit as having the staff who can do that. We need to bring in outside people, from universities and other organizations conducting research in our field, to help us stay relevant." Therefore, the policy in that kind of organization will be to have an HRD manager who is essentially a learning broker.

Some organizations, particularly large and well-established ones, feel that nobody can or should try to tell them their business. If they need HRD, they prefer to have it provided by their own people. It is also, perhaps, a form of protectionism. That is, the organization is saying that it does not want to share its internal problems with external people. It may purchase a few external resources, but it will limit such purchases to services that are *au courant*. It may also purchase packaged materials and modify those packages for internal consumption.

Not all the roles and subroles discussed below need to be filled by the HRD staff. The HRD manager may choose to limit the operations of the HRD unit by, for example, deciding that the subrole of facilitator should be filled by line people rather than by HRD staff.

### Learning Specialist

Historically, this is one of the earliest and the most visible of the HRD roles, although it is not necessarily the most significant of the roles. It includes the subroles of facilitator of learning, designer of learning programs, and developer of instructional strategies.

*Facilitator of Learning.* The facilitator role includes the activities usually included under instructor, teacher, and similar positions. There is no distinction in this subrole as to the kind of facilitation. It includes facilitators who do stand-up instruction (the pedagogic approach) and facilitators who work with groups and supervise self-directed learning (the andragogical approach), as well as the peer-mediated learning that is part of the synergogy approach described by Mouton and Blake (1984). There is also the machine-mediated approach that uses the computer (Reynolds, 1984a).

What kind of facilitators should the HRD manager be looking for? From the preceding paragraph it is obvious that the manager must first determine the learning concepts of the HRD unit, which must be tempered by the needs of the organization and the problems to be solved. In sales training, it is common to have a human presenter, although it is also possible to utilize self-study material. For most skill areas, live instructors are used, but they may function more as facilitator/coaches than as facilitator/presenters. For executives and managers, facilitators are frequently chosen because of the reputation they have or the image they project.

In the past, facilitator was the usual entry-level position in HRD. This is still sometimes the case, but not as frequently as it was in the past. Actually, the HRD manager may find that it is more economical to contract for facilitators on an as-needed basis. If the HRD unit relies on its own facilitators only, the HRD manager is faced with two difficulties. First, there will be a tendency to continually run "classes" to keep the facilitators busy and cost effective. Second, there will be a tendency to offer only those learning opportunities that are within the competencies of the facilitators on staff.

There is also the possibility of assigning internal people to function as facilitators on a full-time, part-time, or temporary basis. It is the responsibility of the HRD manager to ascertain the competency level of such personnel. Generally, they will know the subject matter very well, for that was why they were chosen. They may, however, need assistance to enable them to function effectively as facilitators. One example of how this can operate took place with various departments in the New York State government (Nadler, 1955). The problem was how to provide supervisory training to a large number of supervisors at various sites, which is a common problem in any multisite organization. The approach developed was to select people in each department who could conduct supervisory training programs within their own departments. The plan was for the HRD staff to provide these selected supervisors with one week of instruction. The supervisors then returned to their own units and conducted the program for two hours a day, for fifteen weeks, with materials provided by the central HRD unit. This system worked successfully for many years. In general, then, the HRD manager must look for the appropriate mix of internal and external facilitators, depending on the policy of the organization, the types of programs, and the budget.

*Designer of Learning Programs.* Another subrole is that of the designer. The term *learning programs* is used to include training, education, and development. The designer should have competencies in all three areas, but the greatest demand is for training and education. There are times when the facilitator may also design, and it is possible for the designer to also function as a facilitator. However, if that is what is desired, the HRD manager must search for people who have both sets of competencies.

Essentially, the designer must know a variety of models for designing (Davies, 1981; Goldstein, 1974; Goad, 1982; Nadler, 1982a) and must be able to determine the relative advantages and limitations of each. This also means having a good knowledge of various learning theories and concepts. It is very unusual to find such a person in the organization except in the HRD unit.

It is very important that the designer be able to work with people outside the HRD unit. A good learning program is based on sound needs assessment. Such assessment requires that the designer maintain direct contact with the supervisors, who are faced with the problems for which learning may be a response. It means that the designer cannot just sit in an office and design learning programs, but must move out onto the factory floor, go where the learners are, speak to the supervisors, and, generally, have the interpersonal skills to relate to a variety of different people on their own home ground. The designer must be able to work with a wide variety of subject matter experts, both internal and external, who contribute to the design of the learning program.

The designer should work with the HRD manager when decisions are needed in the make-buy area (see Chapter Eight). The HRD manager is usually not limited to in-house resources. There has been a proliferation of packaged programs such as those listed in *The Trainer's Resource* (1985). Some of these have been around for many years, such as the managerial grid (Blake and Mouton, 1984). Others are newer, and of course many simply come and go. The designer should be able to advise the HRD manager about the relevancy of these external learning resources.

*Developer of Instructional Strategies (DIS).* The proliferation of technology has greatly expanded this third subrole. There are some DIS who deal only with those instructional strategies that employ electronics, others who specialize in the printed word, and still others who have their own particular specialties. They bear many different titles within their own organizations, and it is impossible to list them all. Emerging technologies will bring us even more titles. Therefore, for this role model, we are using the general designation DIS.

The term *instructional strategies,* as used in discussing this subrole, includes the variety of learning possibilities often referred to as methods, techniques, and devices. Instructional strategies should be seen as the various ways that learning can be enhanced. (For a listing of some of the more common instructional strategies see Nadler, 1982a, chap. 8.)

Before 1960, the DIS was a fairly insignificant subrole. There were many reasons for this. At that time, most of the strategies utilized only an instructor-mediated approach. But the early 1960s witnessed the introduction, on a significant scale, of machine-mediated instruction. Since that time, there has been decided growth of such instruction. This has served to increase the need for a high degree of competency on the part of the DIS.

It is essential that the DIS have a good relationship with the designer before anything is done about strategies. It is a case of form following function. The designer will have determined the objectives and the curriculum, and it then becomes a question of ways in which that curriculum can best be presented to the learner. Let us assume that the designer feels that a case study should be used at a particular point. The designer has essentially two options. One is to go to an external source, but how is a designer to keep up-to-date on what is available and perhaps even develop some criteria for selection? A competent DIS should be able to provide the designer with a list of such sources and some criteria for evaluation. The DIS might suggest one of the Harvard case-study books or could provide a list of vendors who sell case studies.

The second option, depending on the specific objective, might be for the designer to develop an in-house case. The designer may not be capable of writing a case study, since this is more difficult to do than some realize (Engel, 1973), but the DIS should have the competency to write the case or to identify external resources who have that competency. The same approach would apply to almost any instructional strategy. It is very unlikely that any one DIS would be competent in all the instructional strategies, given the large number of them. The HRD manager must make some decisions as to the range of competencies required for the specific HRD unit. For example, the HRD manager may select a DIS who is very competent in machine-mediated or machine-supported learning, which can range from the use of simple audiocassettes to the use of very sophisticated strategies involving computers and videodisks.

When programmed instruction first became a significant strategy in the early 1960s, some designers wrote their own programs. It took almost a decade before it became apparent that writing a program required a very high level of competency and was more than a matter of just putting short paragraphs together. Indeed, one factor that thwarted the efforts of those people expounding programmed instruction was that designers lacked the competency to write good programs. At that time, few DIS were involved in the process.

With the introduction of the personal computer, in the late 1970s, the same condition arose. Computer-assisted instruction had not been used much as a learning strategy before that time. There were those who had developed competency in writing programs, as an extension of programmed instruction, but the instructional delivery equipment was cumbersome and costly. The personal computer changed that, and a good DIS now must have the competency to write programs for computer-assisted instruction. Some designers persisted in doing their own programming until they realized that learning how to write programs for computer-assisted programs was much more complicated than they had thought. This does not mean that a designer cannot write such programs but that it is a different competency than is normally expected of him or her. Of course, technology will once again impact on this subrole. As computer authoring systems become more available, it will be possible for the designer to produce computer-assisted programs without using the DIS.

The designer must be willing to admit that knowing about the existence of strategies and how to use them is not the same as knowing how to develop them. Lacking this knowledge is not a reflection on the competency of the designer. For this part, the DIS must recognize that the designer knows what is to be learned and how. The DIS should be able to provide those strategies that will complement the work of the designer. The HRD manager is faced with the challenge of helping the people who fill these two subroles to work together. Both are important, but too often the DIS has been limited to making overhead transparencies or keeping a record of the 16-mm films that have been rented. Let us look at an example of the developmental work of the DIS:

> A major oil company wanted to improve the performance of its service station managers. The designer developed a curriculum that directly addressed the problem—increasing sales. There were several choices of how to deliver the learning. The company could send instructors (facilitators) around to the various service stations, but that would obviously prove very costly. Instructors could be hired

locally, in the vicinity of a group of service stations,
but that would require that station managers leave
their stations to go to a central learning facility—
perhaps a hotel or motel—which would also be
expensive. The designer, working with the DIS,
decided to provide an individual learning experience
for each station manager. The guideline was that
each station manager should be able to use the
learning package without leaving the site. Also, the
learning experience had to be in small units, or
modules, as station managers could not free themselves up to devote an uninterrupted hour solely for
learning.

　　　　The product that was developed was a self-
instructional multistrategy program that used
printed material, audiotapes (on the assumption that
a tape recorder would be available to each manager),
and slides. For the last item, the DIS recommended a
handheld slide viewer that proved to be very effective.
And, in sum, this training program for station
managers resulted in increased sales without the cost
of a group learning situation.

Another example of the work of the DIS can be found in a
medical supply company:

　　　　The problem here was that the salespeople on
the road, called medical detailers, needed constant
training to keep up with the large and varied product
line of the company. The designer worked with the
DIS to develop a very simple but effective program.
The medical detailers used company-owned cars, or
were reimbursed for the use of their own cars. Each
car was provided with a tape recorder, either one that
was built into the car as a tape deck or one that could
be plugged into the cigaret lighter. The designer,
working with the DIS, developed a series of cassette
tapes that provided the necessary individualized

training. The tapes also included learning material related to sales techniques. This material was developed in conjunction with the sales manager.

The HRD manager obtained the itinerary of each detailer from the sales manager. Then, the HRD unit would send the tape ahead to the hotel where the detailer would be stopping next. When the detailer arrived, the tape would be waiting. The detailer could either play it in the hotel or listen to it while driving to the next customer. Periodically, the tapes were sent back to the HRD unit to be revised as needed. In addition, the detailers were encouraged to make a tape asking questions or suggesting improvements in the system. The HRD manager and the sales manager would listen to these feedback tapes, as would the designer and DIS, and they would make changes as needed.

In addition to developing instructional strategies, the DIS should also keep current on what is available from outside resources. Suppliers are only too happy to place a DIS on their mailing lists, and such lists are sold and traded back and forth. Actually, in a short time, a DIS could be faced with the problem of having to develop a retrieval system to help the designer make the best selection from among the available material. The DIS works with the designer not only on individual learning but also on group learning. In group situations, there may need to be provision for both projected materials (such as films, slides, transparencies) and nonprojected ones (such as flip charts, writing boards, posters, handouts). There has been an increase in the use of computers and instructional television, and we now find that the DIS is often called an instructional technologist or media specialist.

### Consultant

An HRD person functioning as a consultant works on two levels: with the organization and with individuals. When working in this latter role, the consultant is sometimes referred to as a counselor (Blake and Mouton, 1976). The major focus here will be on the organizational consultant, that is, on the consultant who works to help others solve organizational problems that require competency in the HRD area.

Some seem to believe that when one asks questions, one is a consultant. As will be discussed below, a consultant can also provide answers. It is not the asking of questions that makes one a consultant but rather the reasoning that precedes the questioning.

Many books have been written about consulting and consultants (Gallessich, 1982; Kubr, 1983; Lippitt and Lippitt, 1978; Steele, 1982), and some of these make for exciting reading. The job of consultant seems attractive to many people, perhaps because consultants tend to work with upper levels of management rather than with people at lower levels in the organization. It is not possible to make any sweeping statements about consulting, as it is defined very differently by different people. As we said at the opening of this chapter, a crucial element is that one cannot truly fill a role unless others perceive that person to be filling that role. To call oneself a consultant is not enough. Those who are seeking help must also see the individual as a consultant.

The model proposed here for the HRD consultant is built on the four major subroles or types of consulting—expert, advocate, stimulator, and change agent—that are common in HRD. There are many other kinds of consulting, but they are relevant to other topic areas. For HRD there is no one subrole that is better or worse, more important or less important. However, it is necessary for the HRD manager to be familiar with the subroles and to know the consulting competencies of his or her staff. Some consultants on the HRD staff will function better in one subrole than in another, and the HRD manager must be aware of this if he or she is to assign appropriate personnel to a task.

*Content Consulting.* The first two subroles we will discuss focus on the consultant as a content person. For many years, in the field of HRD and allied behavioral sciences, the emphasis was on the consultant as a process person. Unfortunately, this gave rise to thoughts and to practices that were the basis for many jokes about consultants. (A consultant is somebody who borrows your watch to tell you what time it is—and then keeps the watch!)

The *expert-consultant* is expected to have a broad background in research and practice in the field of HRD. The expert-consultant is called on when a manager has a problem and wants to be given the information about sources, resources, and options that will be needed to make an informed decision.

The expert-consultant can be involved in a variety of situations. In one case, a large corporation had been cited by the courts for failing to provide adequate opportunities for female employees to move into management. The internal HRD unit was asked to provide consultation on this problem. After diagnosing the situation, the internal HRD consultant proposed to management that the HRD unit develop a plan involving learning experiences that would enable some women to move into the management track. The HRD manager assigned an HRD staff member, as an internal consultant, to develop the plan. Recognizing that he needed help, the internal consultant in turn called upon an external expert-consultant to find out what had been done in other situations. The external expert-consultant provided published material, described the experiences of others that had been discussed during professional conferences and meetings, and outlined experiences of other organizations with similar problems. From this, the internal expert-consultant was able to provide a set of alternatives for management to consider. This effort received accolades from management for its comprehensive look at the problem and for enabling management to select an appropriate course of action from the various alternatives.

The *advocate-consultant* has a somewhat narrower role than the expert-consultant. It is appropriate to call on an advocate-consultant when a manager wants just enough information to make a particular decision. The manager may already have made a decision about what needs to be done but is not fully aware of the resources available. Here, the manager is seeking a specific response to a specific problem, not a list of alternatives. The advocate-consultant has come to play an important role in response to problems related to the introduction of new technology. It is obviously important to provide the appropriate learning to prepare people for using computers, robots, and other forms of technology.

However, the HRD manager must observe caution about the advocate-consultants in the HRD unit, as such people may tend to have one-track minds. Many years ago, when "brainstorming" was coming into vogue, an HRD practitioner became very much involved with that learning strategy. When he functioned as an instructor, his use of brainstorming was constrained by the work of the designer of learning programs. When functioning as an advocate-consultant, however, he tended to recommend brainstorming as the response to almost any problem. It did not take long before the HRD manager began receiving negative feedback from other managers. After exploring the situation, the HRD manager came to see that this particular employee could not function satisfactorily as an advocate-consultant since he always recommended the same response to problems. After counseling with that employee, it was agreed that he was more suited to instructing than to consulting.

These two subroles, that of expert and advocate, belong to the reactive mode of consulting. A manager needs "specific content" and looks to the HRD consultant to provide that content; that is, the consultant is expected to respond to a manager's need, not to take the initiative him- or herself. There are times when being reactive is entirely appropriate, and the HRD consultant should not be apologetic about taking the stance of the advocate or the expert.

*Process Consulting.* During the emergence of consulting in HRD in the 1960s, however, the emphasis was on serving clients in a proactive mode, in which the consultant was more concerned with process than with content. Indeed, consultants who provided content during consulting were looked down upon by many of their colleagues. Fortunately, this is generally no longer the case. It is as appropriate to be a content consultant as it is to be a process consultant, depending on the need of the client.

The process consultant (Schein, 1978) must have competencies in the various forms of process, which includes working with small groups as well as understanding the organizations within which the groups function. A subrole of the process consultant is that of *stimulator.* The emphasis here is on helping the manager identify a problem, its causes, and possible solutions. In this subrole, there is little or no need for content. The emphasis is on the process. The stimulator-consultant must be highly competent in asking questions, listening, and summarizing, and he must act as gatekeeper in bringing all concerned into the discussion (where groups are involved). This kind of consultant must also occasionally stop the group and have it take a look at the process that it is using to try to solve a problem.

When a stimulator-consultant is needed, the HRD manager must determine whether somebody on the HRD staff has that competency. Otherwise, it may be necessary to use an external consultant in that subrole. Sometimes, for political reasons, it might even be desirable for the HRD manager to look for a stimulator-consultant from outside the organization. For example, one of the authors was called into an organization that was in the process of "downsizing"; that is, it was reducing the size and extent of its operations but not spinning off its smaller units. The author was asked to serve as a stimulator-consultant to the managerial group as it tried to determine which activities should be reduced or eliminated, as well as what should happen to the personnel associated with those activities.

The external stimulator-consultant knew very little about the business of the organization. Indeed, that was one criteria for his being selected, so that he could concentrate on the process of downsizing rather than on content. After several meetings during which the stimulator-consultant was called on extensively, the members of the group all agreed that his assignment had been completed, and it was at this point that the group began arriving at specific decisions. It now felt that it could function effectively and no longer needed the consultant.

The other process consultant subrole is that of *change agent.* The focus is on the word *agent,* as the change should be brought about by the organization's own manager. The change agent should assist the manager in identifying the goals for the future state and in determining how to function effectively in the transition state (Beckhard and Harris, 1977). This is, perhaps, the most difficult of the consultant subroles. It requires competency in helping others plan for change but then moving out of the picture so that the managers can proceed to do their job and actually bring about the needed change. It is too easy, in this subrole, for the change agent to create a dependency situation wherein the line manager comes to rely on the consultant to actually bring about the change.

### Staffing Alternatives

In staffing any unit, an organization must recognize and deal with numerous variables. In the case of HRD, there may be more variables than in some of the other units in the organization.

One of the basic decisions that must be made is whether to have an internal HRD unit or to "buy" HRD services from external sources.

The essential focus in this chapter is on staffing HRD with internal people. We are not saying that this is always the best or the most desirable way for all organizations to proceed. It is, however, the most common method of providing HRD for organizations. As a general rule, the learning specialist and consultant roles can be filled by external resources; and an organization may also choose to fill the position of manager through external resources, although this is not very common. It is sometimes done when there is need for a quick start-up and there are no internal people who have the required competencies. In such cases, the organization generally contracts with an external HRD professional to provide part-time or full-time management service. The danger to avoid is allowing that way of filling the position to become the pattern.

Of course, if the policy of the organization is to rely on an external manager of HRD, it will probably be an indication that the organization does not consider HRD to be particularly significant. When an external HRD manager is used, HRD activities can always be halted abruptly merely by not renewing or canceling the contract for that service. There are some limited situations, however, in which the entire HRD function might be staffed externally. If the organization has never had an HRD unit, it might want to use an external manager to start the operation before it makes too big an investment in establishing its own unit. Also, during periods of transition, an external HRD manager might be contracted for until decisions have been made about the future of HRD in the organization.

There are a variety of factors that influence the decision whether to provide HRD internally or to purchase HRD services from outside the organization. One major consideration is the size of the organization, although there is, as yet, insufficient data to be specific about a cutoff point. Before 1975, organizations of fewer than 1,000 employees usually did not have HRD units, nor did they employ even one person whose sole function was HRD. This appears to be changing. There are now high-tech organizations having fewer than 500 employees that do require HRD programs in order to keep up with technological changes. We are beginning to find that even some small organizations have well-defined HRD units and have designated individuals to manage the HRD function.

This discussion will be limited to those who are considered "professional" HRD practitioners and will not include those who provide clerical support. The staffing of support positions is usually subject to general organizational policies and practices. Moreover, there is nothing unique about clerical work in the HRD unit, as compared with other service units in the organization, with one possible exception. Some organizations have established a position called HRD aide (the title varies). This position is filled by a person who does not have the qualifications for a regular HRD position but who is interested in doing HRD work. The competencies required of the HRD aide are above those required at the usual clerical level. It is frequently understood that, with appropriate education, an aide could qualify for an entry-level HRD professional position. The practice can be either positive or negative, depending on the intent of those who establish such a position. Too often it is a reflection of the organizational perception of HRD—any reasonable person can do the job. It ignores the special education that is required to be an effective HRD person.

## Types of Personnel

The HRD unit must be staffed by a variety of personnel. We will first divide these staff members into three broad "categories," and we will then break them down into full-time and part-time personnel, on the one hand, and permanent and temporary personnel, on the other.

### *Categories*

The concept of employment categories, as applied to HRD staff members, is fairly new and is just beginning to be the subject of research. But applied in the field, this concept has been of significant help to HRD managers. In part, it is based on research (Gouldner, 1957) that produced the concept of "locals" and "cosmopolitans." We have modified and expanded the categories as follows:

Category I:    Professionally identified (identifies personally with HRD as a professional field)

Category II:   Organizationally identified (identifies with the organization and will work wherever assigned)

Category III:  Collateral duties (has other major duties in the organization but is expected to have some involvement in HRD)

There is no intent to suggest that any one of these categories is better than another. Each has a significant contribution to make to the HRD function. It is important, however, for the HRD manager to differentiate among the three categories and to assist the organization in clarifying the status of people who are involved in the HRD operation.

A difficulty we have found is that very few organizations identify these categories as such, even though the categories may be reflected in the way they organize many units, including HRD.

When working with organizations, we have sometimes gone through extensive consulting with them to help them recognize their HRD staffing practices. Too often, there is no written policy regarding the employment of staff by categories. Personnel practices in this area are often preceded by the statement "everybody knows." Whenever that statement is used, it is a signal that we are into organizational cultural behavior that is generally not reflected in policy statements.

*Category I.* Individuals in Category I see HRD as their profession or vocation (Wiggs, 1971). There are no absolute criteria for such identification, but experience has shown that Category I people will respond in the affirmative to the following questions:

1.   Are you currently in a full-time HRD position?
2.   Have you been in such a position for more than three years?
3.   Do you intend to stay in HRD for the next three years?

The six-year parameter is based on our finding that in many organizations five years is the maximum HRD assignment for those who do not belong to Category I. The Category I person is interested in long-range planning for the HRD operation in the organization. Increasingly, the Category I person will have a graduate degree in HRD or in some field allied to it. If given the choice of transferring out of HRD or leaving the organization, the Category I person will generally prefer to leave the organization and seek an HRD position in another organization.

*Category II.* Someone in Category II is a permanent employee of the organization and is only temporarily in an HRD position. That employee's career is with the organization, and the HRD unit is only one of numerous consecutive assignments that will be completed as one rotates through the organization. There are many ways to use Category II people. For example, in the early 1970s, the Ford Motor Company adopted the following pattern for staffing HRD:

Plant level—primarily staffed by management interns or technical and engineering personnel. Assignment's were from six months to one year.
Department level—primarily staffed by management interns and industrial relations personnel. Assignments were from one to three years.

Corporate level—primarily staffed by industrial relations personnel. Assignments were from three to five years.

It is interesting to note that this pattern was seriously disrupted by the oil crisis in 1973—a crisis that had a strongly negative effect on the auto industry. The mobility of those in Category II was reduced, as jobs were eliminated and opportunities for rotation dwindled. Ford employed some Category I people at all levels, but they composed a very small group. Unfortunately, as in some other organizations, people who preferred to stay in HRD rather than move on were considered to be less effective employees. This was a value judgment made by Category II staff members. who expected to continue moving through the organization as they progressed to higher levels. A Category II employee had difficulty understanding the motivation of a Category I employee who enjoyed HRD and wanted to work in that area rather than move on to something else.

This example, of course, is from a production environment. Usually, in a company such as Ford, there is a definite time to move on, even though it may not be written policy. In sales organizations, the situation tends to be different. When a good salesperson is assigned to the HRD function (Connell, 1984), there is the assumption that he or she is also competent to instruct. If the salesperson demonstrates that competency, there is the strong possibility that he or she will be assigned as a sales manager at some later time.

*Category III.* Persons belonging to this category are found throughout the organization. There is the assumption, not always stated, that each manager and supervisor should spend some time instructing subordinates. Some of this instruction is done as on-the-job training that may not require any overt assistance from the HRD unit. In more formal situations, supervisors and managers may conduct sessions or contribute to the design of learning for employees other than their own. There are other people, also Category III's, who have a major position outside the HRD unit but use HRD to accomplish their objectives. Examples are the safety director who uses HRD in conducting sessions on safety, the equal employment opportunity director who uses HRD in conducting sessions on supervising minority or disadvantaged employees, and the human resource management (personnel) director who uses HRD in conducting orientation sessions.

In any organization that has an HRD unit, one can expect to find a variety of combinations of Categories I and II. We are constantly asked for a formula for arriving at the best combination, but it is impossible to provide one. A basic policy decision that must be made is, Who will be the manager of the HRD unit? Some organizations choose to use a Category II person, since that person is already thought of as a manager and it is assumed that he or she should therefore be able to handle an HRD unit. A limitation is that such a Category II HRD manager will tend to focus on short-term planning. The emphasis will be on good current performance of the HRD unit, so that there will be positive consideration of the next managerial assignment.

While working with a manufacturing organization as an external consultant, one of the authors was invited by an internal HRD staff member to have lunch in the executive dining room. He was told that a new manager had just been appointed to the HRD unit and that the entire staff had been invited to this luncheon to hear the new policies for the unit. He questioned whether, as an external consultant, he should attend. He was told that this had been cleared with the manager, who wanted everybody connected with HRD to know the new policy.

After lunch, the new HRD manager rose and, in essence, said the following: "You all know me. I have been with this organization for many years. My goal, after this assignment, is to become a vice-president. Therefore, I need visibility at the highest levels of the organization. From now on, all our efforts will be devoted toward the executives and upper-level managers. I want them to understand that I know their problems and am prepared to help them solve those problems. Of course, when I get promoted to that position, I will not forget those of you who have helped me reach that objective."

In effect, that new HRD manager wanted to wipe out all the supervisory and technical HRD programs in a manufacturing organization! Although he was fired within six months, it took the organization several years to rebuild and make up for the losses he had caused by being so shortsighted.

This may be an unusual example, but we have seen many others that were, if not as dramatic, equally devastating. This is not to suggest that every Category II HRD manager will behave in the same way; but, given the reward systems in some organizations, it would not be surprising to find such behavior. If the organization chooses to name a Category II person as the HRD manager, that organization must also build in pertinent rewards, so that the manager will plan for the future of the unit—even though he or she may have moved on to another unit by the time the plans are implemented.

The tendency has been to staff many positions in the HRD unit with Category II persons. A reflection of this can be seen in the membership data from ASTD. In the late 1970s it reported a membership turnover of 33 percent a year. That seems unusually high for a professional society until one realizes that many Category II's join ASTD while in the HRD unit. When they leave their HRD assignment, they naturally leave ASTD.

Very often, the Category I staff members in the unit are resentful of the II's, who are seen as just "passing through" and as using the HRD assignment as a stepping-stone to further their own careers in the organization. While these accusations may sometimes be true, the Category I's miss a great opportunity by thinking this way. It would be to the advantage of the Category I persons to make the temporary HRD assignments of the Category II's positive and rewarding ones, since, after their assignments in HRD are completed, the Category II's frequently go on to higher-level positions in the organization. Here, then, is an opportunity to make friends in high places and to make upper levels of management aware of the help and support that the HRD unit can offer.

### Full time or Part time

The Category I staff member will almost always be full time with the HRD unit. The Category II staff member will also usually be full time except in the limited situations discussed

below. The full-time HRD practitioner must be considered part of
the professional staff and identified as such. He or she may be
given responsibility for functions not normally considered HRD.
One of the most common is recruiting. An argument can be made
for including recruiting in HRD, since employees who are
recruited must then be trained or educated. But the HRM people
can argue that they know the staffing patterns and the needs of the
organization and that therefore recruiting lies in their area of
operations. In addition, recruiting has become more complicated,
as a result of various government regulations, and the recruiter
must know the legal as well as the human aspects of recruiting.

On a much lower level, we sometimes find that other tasks
are assigned to the HRD unit. These can include planning the
annual picnic, collecting for the United Way or a similar charity,
or issuing the company newsletter. All these tasks require time and
must be planned for when deciding on the number and types of
full-time personnel required in the unit.

Once again, it is not possible to say what the optimum
percentage of full-time personnel is. The tendency, in recent years,
has been to move away from large, full-time HRD staffs into some
of the alternatives that will be discussed later. This should not be
seen as diminishing the importance of the HRD unit. It is simply
to recognize that there are many ways to organize the HRD
function. Being large or small does not make a unit more or less
important. Reductions in the size of units often reflect the trend
toward decentralization.

The HRD unit will also use part-time people. They will be
full time in the organization but assigned to an HRD operation on
a part-time basis and only for a limited period of time. That does
not mean that these people are not important, and they should not
be treated casually. In fact, we have here an example of the matrix
type of organization in which people come from different parts of
the organization to devote some of their time and energy to a
particular task. The part-timers have regular jobs in other parts of
the organization but may work with the HRD unit to perform
defined and time-limited tasks.

Thus, it is common for supervisors to be assigned on a part-
time basis to instruct in programs of supervisory training and

education. There are various patterns for this. One approach is to run the program for two hours a week over a ten-week period. During those two hours, the supervisor so assigned is part time with the HRD unit. That unit has the responsibility for assisting the supervisor to instruct through the use of appropriate adult learning methodology. In addition, the HRD unit provides the outline of the program, the necessary materials, and other logistic support. There are various other time patterns, but all of them are based on the limited time that the supervisor or those delegated by the supervisor have available for instructing. The same applies to other subject matter experts who are utilized in HRD programs. These could be managers or skilled personnel who are called upon to instruct outside of their own work units. (Within a particular work unit, it would be on-the-job training, which is generally not offered by the HRD unit.)

The HRD unit cannot and should not try to staff every area of operation in the organization with full-time subject matter experts. This is too costly and quite impractical. At the same time, if the HRD manager does not make use of subject matter experts from the various operating units of the organization, the scope of the HRD unit will be limited to the very few areas of expertise possessed by the full-time staff. Therefore, in order to fill the gap, it is essential that the HRD unit utilize part-timers from as many parts of the organization as needed.

The placement of the HRD unit within the organization is also a factor to be considered when deciding whether to staff with full- or part-time personnel. As noted, the trend has been toward decentralization—placing HRD units in various parts of the organization. At the upper level, the HRD unit can bring together part-timers from many units of the organization to work on problems that are companywide. The manager of this kind of unit seldom offers programs but rather provides leadership in HRD for the organization and consulting on HRD to upper levels of management. An HRD unit at that level will be staffed by full-time personnel.

An example of the use of part-time subject matter experts can be found in the urban mass transportation industry. Most of the urban transportation companies do not contain identifiable

HRD units; in cases where HRD units do exist, they are usually in charge of general programs, such as orientation or supervisory programs. One such company, in a major city, developed another system. After studying the situation, the company found that each of the operating units had its own HRD operation, usually staffed by one person or at the most two. They were all Category II persons who knew the technical side of the operation but had little understanding of how to organize and deliver the needed learning. A study group was formed that identified the commonalities of the various kinds of technical training required. The HRD unit then brought together selected people from the various operating units and held a series of meeting to develop a core curriculum for technical training. The different people functioned as part-time subject matter experts, and the training they provided resulted in improved performance and reduced costs. Through this approach, the HRD manager capitalized on the internal competencies of the technical people and reduced redundancy in programs.

### *Permanent or Temporary*

Another way to approach the question of staffing the HRD unit is in terms of the duration of the assignment. Here we are *not* discussing the many permanent staff members of the HRD unit, who may belong to Category I or Category II, but in either case are full-timers. A Category I person can anticipate a long, permanent HRD assignment. Aside from brief rotation assignments, this individual expects to carve out his or her career in the organization within the HRD unit.

By contrast, the Category II employee who is "permanent" will be in the HRD unit for a period ranging from one to five years, and the HRD manager must plan assignments accordingly. Long-range assignments should not be given to Category II's, since they might leave the unit before their assignments are completed. There are many other worthwhile and necessary assignments that can be made to coincide with the expected duration of the Category II person's assignment to the HRD unit.

The Category II permanent employee will usually not return to the same position that he filled before working in the

HRD unit. The HRD assignment is usually part of a general rotation pattern for that employee. By working closely with those who make such career assignments, the HRD manager will be able to make more effective use of that employee and even help prepare him for his next assignment. This can reduce the ambiguity of the situation and the anxiety of the employee. And after all, if an individual knows that his present assignment is limited and he is worried about how his next job will relate to his present performance, the effect can be to diminish that person's effectiveness in his present assignment.

The temporary employee is one who is assigned full-time to the HRD unit but for only a limited amount of time. Thus, it is expected that the temporary person will return to his or her original work unit. The temporary assignment is usually for up to a month or so and generally involves working on a specific task or project.

From our discussion, it can be seen that the HRD manager works with a variety of different types of employees. This is much different from the managerial function in an operating unit, where almost all the employees will tend to be full time and permanent. The HRD manager must recognize and identify the differences and be prepared to manage the unit accordingly. Since there are various kinds of employees, there will be different levels of commitment to the unit, and that is perfectly normal.

It is important that the HRD manager make sure that all the individuals in the HRD unit know their status: which category they belong to and whether they are permanent or temporary. The variations do exist and can be very confusing unless they are made clear and all concerned concur. Depending upon the variables, being moved out of the HRD unit is not a matter of reward or punishment, nor is staying with the HRD unit. These are just different ways the organization meets the needs of individuals and units.

### Selecting the HRD Staff

We can now explore the factors involved in selecting the appropriate staff to fill the roles and subroles already discussed.

Naturally, the personnel policies of the organization must be adhered to. Since these policies vary from organization to organization, we cannot provide ironclad rules, but we can suggest some of the factors that should be considered by HRD managers when selecting staff.

*New HRD Units.* Let us first take the case of an HRD manager who is hired from the outside and asked to set up an HRD unit and staff it. The new HRD manager may have to get answers to such questions as, What are the HRD policies of the organization? Who provided HRD before the unit was established? What have been the practices in the past in providing for HRD? Why was the decision made to develop an HRD unit at this time? The manager of a new HRD unit must seek to become visible very quickly and to provide obvious success experiences, because the leaders of the organization will be looking for specific evidence that there really was a need for the HRD unit. Indeed, they were probably the ones who decided to establish the HRD unit and will be looking for early and concrete confirmation of the correctness of their decision.

This must be an important consideration when the new HRD manager selects staff, but it also presents him with a dilemma. He may be thinking of how to build the unit in long-range terms. For example, he may conclude that there is a need for consulting, but he also knows that consulting only rarely brings immediate results. The manager might then look for some generally acknowledged problem and identify those aspects of it that might be amenable to an HRD response. For example, a problem common to many organizations is employee turnover, and this is sometimes related to poor orientation or to the absence of an orientation program (Shea, 1981). Although that may not be the most exciting activity for an HRD manager, it could well be the one that first gets attention and acceptance for the HRD function. Therefore, the HRD manager may have to find staff members who can design such a program and be instructors for it.

*Existing HRD Units.* The HRD manager will have different concerns about staffing an already existing unit. As the organization changes its goals and missions, the need may arise for a different kind of staffing. Those currently in the unit may not have the competencies needed for different subroles or for new areas of activity. The HRD manager has several options. One is to provide for the growth of those in the unit, so that they can achieve the needed competencies. Another approach is to utilize attrition. As HRD staff members leave the unit or the organization, the HRD manager is given the opportunity to replace them with persons who have the needed skills.

The HRD unit itself may have to change, if the organization goes in new directions, but the HRD manager should never lose sight of the basic purpose of the HRD unit—to improve the present and future performance of employees through *learning*. Organizations are constantly changing, and some of those changes can be expected to impact on the work of the HRD unit and how it should be staffed. Obviously, the HRD manager must remain sensitive to both subtle and overt changes in the organization. But he or she must never forget its main function.

Other functions, not directly within the HRD area, may be assigned to the HRD unit. Among such functions are recruitment, performance appraisal, human resource planning, and collecting for the United Way or a similar agency. The last function is obviously not within the scope of the HRD unit but may be placed there because nobody else wants it. The other functions are *related* to HRD but are *not* HRD as defined in this book. Of course, there is nothing to prevent an HRD manager from developing a broader definition of HRD to encompass other functions. If she does so, however, she must then staff the unit with people who have competencies in those areas. Generally, they are not competencies one would expect of people in HRD.

## Organizational Policies

Every organization has a certain number of policies, whether they are written, oral, or traditional. A major policy area for HRD managers relates to the use of resources. Some organizations have a policy that no external HRD resources can be used until all internal resources have been exhausted. The application of this policy will determine the staff size of the HRD unit. A very small unit may not be able to meet many of the needs of the organization without resorting to external help. (This assumes that funds will be made available for utilizing external resources.)

The general personnel policies of the organization will also govern how the HRD manager staffs. Although it may not be written policy, some organizations almost always select people who have grown up within the organization. In fact, this has been one of the major problems in HRD staffing in many organizations. For example, let us look at the urban mass transportation area. Traditionally, everybody starts at the bottom, cleaning the trains or buses, and then moves up in the organization. Very little is done in the way of education, as it is assumed that if a worker has done the lower-level job satisfactorily, he or she is therefore qualified to handle the upper-level position.

There are many organizations, effective ones, where assigning from within is the policy. Organizations such as IBM, Procter & Gamble, and Honeywell (Peters and Waterman, 1982) have for years encouraged long-term employment. Therefore, internal mobility is an important part of policy, and it is expected that individuals will rotate through different parts of the organization. When applied to the HRD unit, as part of the organization, this policy means that the HRD manager must first look internally when staffing.

Another organizational policy can dictate that the HRD unit, like other staff units, include representatives of some of the different groups within the organization. This is frequently found in engineering and high-tech organizations. There are good reasons for this. If the HRD unit is to do more than contract for outside resources, there must be people on the HRD staff who have backgrounds and experiences similar to those of the population being served. This policy may also reflect the feeling that "If you have not walked in our shoes, you do not know our problems." It is easy to prove that this need not be the case, but proof is of no avail if that is the policy of the organization and the HRD unit wants to be considered an integral part of that organization.

*Categories and Staffing.* Earlier in this chapter there was a discussion of employment categories. Even organizations not familiar with this taxonomy have applied it. This is usually found in organizations whose philosophy or culture requires that all employees identify with the organization rather than with a specific field or profession. These are the organizations that encourage long-term employment. In fact, the staffing of those organizations is based almost entirely on Category II qualifications.

Since that system works, it would be meaningless to argue against it, even if one wished to. Looking more closely, however, it will be discovered that there are core groups of Category I persons spread throughout such organizations. For example, there will be at least one accountant who has a degree in the field and who belongs to the apposite professional organizations. The same can probably be said for at least one person in other staff units such as purchasing, marketing, and legal. So too with HRD. There is the need for at least one person who belongs to Category I. But if that person is the HRD manager, he must exercise caution to avoid overstaffing with too many Category I people. This could create a gap between the HRD unit and the operating.units. When the HRD manager belongs to Category II, the HRD unit may contain all Category II's. When this happens, one can expect to see a great deal of contracting out for learning specialists and consultants. In the absence of any policy or generally accepted practice, it is important to create a balance between the two categories. To have only Category I's can be just as ineffective as having all Category II's.

*Use of Roles.* The roles of HRD people were discussed earlier in this chapter. Those roles can be utilized for staffing. It is not essential that all the learning specialist or consultant roles be represented by staff within the HRD unit. Rather, the roles can serve as a checklist in terms of functions and staffing. In some organizations, the HRD manager may be the only permanent person, with all the other roles being filled by temporary or part-time Category II's or by persons from the outside. At the other end of the spectrum, there are organizations that have entire units made up of many people that fill one subrole. The military has very large units whose sole purpose is to design learning programs. This practice is also followed by the IRS. Exxon has used this form of organization, as have other large multisite organizations. With the increasing use of various learning technologies, it is not uncommon to find a unit with a great deal of equipment, but a small staff whose only function is to work with the designers and instructors to develop and provide learning experiences that make use of computers, video, teleconferencing, and so on.

*Involvement of Other Managers.* The HRD manager should involve other managers of the organization in staffing the HRD unit, primarily because those other managers are the clients of the HRD unit and the purpose of the HRD unit is to serve them. By involving those managers, the HRD manager reconfirms this stance and provides an opportunity for them to influence the selection process. Before recruiting additional staff, the HRD manager can approach selected line managers and ask for their guidance. This can be a matter of merely seeking information about their needs or of asking for specific recommendations of employees who would benefit themselves and the organization by transferring to the HRD unit. These employees would probably belong to Category II, but the HRD manager may also be looking for staff members who might want to become Category I's. The line managers are an important source for information about such potential employees.

If the additional staff are to come from outside the organization, specific line managers could be included on the selection panels. After all, the staff are being selected to serve the line manager, even though they are working under the HRD manager. This also means that line managers have to understand the roles and subroles. The line managers can be asked to identify those subroles for which they would like to have additional service or those subroles that they think are now adequately staffed.

## Conclusion

Staffing the HRD unit is a significant task for the HRD manager. To some degree the problems of staffing an HRD unit do not differ significantly from those of staffing other units in the organization. There are some differences, however, and the HRD manager must be aware of these in order to staff effectively. The HRD manager should be aware of other human resource units in the organization, what they consider their function to be, and how they staff.

Organizations have begun to recognize the importance of the HRD unit. There has been a significant growth in the number and types of people in the HRD field, as well as increased specialization. At one time, an individual in the personnel office was expected to be competent in all the aspects of human resources.

Since 1958, research has enabled us to identify three major roles of HRD staff: learning specialist, consultant, and manager. The role of manager is the focus of this book, whereas this chapter focusses on the roles of learning specialist and consultant. The learning specialist has three subroles (facilitator of learning, designer of learning programs, and developer of instructional strategies) and the consultant four (expert, advocate, stimulator, and change agent). Not every HRD unit will have an employee working in each of these seven subroles. The HRD manager, however, must be familiar with all the subroles and then try to fill those that are the most important to his or her organization.

Given the variety of roles and subroles, the HRD manager has alternatives about how to staff. All of these subroles can be handled by contracting for external services. Frequently, the HRD unit meets its goals through the use of both internal and external personnel. The internal personnel will generally belong to one of two categories. Category I employees are those who see HRD as their professional field. Category II employees are those whose major identification is with the organization. They are involved in HRD but do not intend to remain in that unit. They may be general managers who are cycling through the company, moving from one management position to another.

There are also Category III employees whose major job is not in the HRD unit, but who instruct on the job, thereby using learning to accomplish their own unit's goals. These may be managers and supervisors who conduct formal learning for employees of their units. Or they may be someone such as a safety director who conducts learning about safety for all the employees in the organization. The HRD unit also uses subject matter experts, employees who have a high degree of competence in some area and are assigned to the HRD unit to help design or conduct programs.

When selecting HRD staff, an HRD manager must first consider the regular staffing policies and practices of the organization. Then, the relation of HRD to other human resource units in the organization must be taken into account. Other managers in the organization should be involved in planning for the HRD staff, although the ultimate selection should still be in the hands of the HRD manager.

# Chapter 7

# Facilitating
# the Professional
# Growth of HRD Staff

The major purpose of the HRD unit is to provide for the growth, through learning, of all the employees in the organization and for some nonemployees as well. Such growth takes three forms: (1) improving performance on the present job, (2) preparing for a different job, and (3) furthering the general growth of individuals. Of course, this has been stated before as the basic taxonomy for HRD. But it bears repeating, for we will be discussing here the same taxonomy as applied to the HRD professional staff.

The reason for limiting this to professional staff is that the needs of the nonprofessional staff are usually provided for in the normal operations of the organization. But unless the HRD manager makes a specific effort directed toward the professional staff, very little will be done for them. As will be obvious, a good many of the points discussed in regard to staff will be applicable to the HRD manager as well.

### Relation to Categories

In the previous chapter we discussed the three categories of HRD staff (the professionally identified, the organizationally identified, and those who perform collateral duties). The last category will not be discussed here as its members do not form part of the professional staff. The HRD manager may have to provide some training for Category III persons, but there should be no intent to include them as staff. If a Category III is assigned to the HRD unit, however, that individual then becomes a Category II, and it may become necessary to provide professional growth experiences for him or her.

The major efforts of the HRD manager will be with those belonging to Category I. They consider themselves professionals and should be seeking to improve their present performance as well as looking for promotional opportunities. Here we do sometimes encounter a problem. Many organizations do not have the range of staff that can provide a clear career path for HRD people (Chalofsky and Lincoln, 1983). This is not unique to HRD. The same applies to many occupational groups within an organization such as lawyers, accountants, and even some engineers. In all these cases it is possible to be promoted, but only if the individual in question is willing to leave the professional field and move into general management or some other activity in the organization. This is a general problem with professional people that has yet to be adequately solved. How does an organization provide for "growth" when the opportunities within the particular professional field are limited? One approach has been to create higher-level jobs within that professional area that do not require moving into management. Thus, the U.S. Patent Office chose that route and created upper-level positions that recognized outstanding performance but did not require the incumbent to supervise or manage.

Not all organizations or fields have been that creative, however. For example, nurses join their profession because they want to care for patients. But if a given nurse is good at that, what happens? The reward is a promotion that takes the nurse a step away from the patient into supervision. From then on, more promotions are possible, but each one takes the nurse farther and farther away from the original motivation for joining the nursing profession. The same thing happens in our school system. To move ahead in the profession, a good teacher must sometimes become a poor supervisor or a poor principal! Once again, the prime motivation for the teacher was to work with students, but in order to receive promotions the teacher must move into supervision and administration—away from the students. There have been some efforts to reward good teachers through controversial merit pay systems. But as of the mid 1980s there was still no evidence that such an approach had provided an alternative for teachers. The challenge for the HRD manager is to devise some mechanism within the HRD unit to allow good staff members to advance and grow and still stay with the unit. We have not been able to find any evidence of such practices, though we feel they must exist. We hope that further research will uncover those practices for staff members in Category I.

### Performance Appraisal

A good growth program should start with performance appraisal. There are many reasons for evaluating performance, and one should be to discover if there is need for training and/or education. This is true for all employees throughout an organization, including the HRD staff. The form of that performance appraisal will vary, depending upon its purpose. Here the purpose is the improvement of performance or the identification of potential.

As with any other unit in the organization, the size of the HRD unit must be considered in making performance appraisal operational. If the unit is small, and all staff report directly to the HRD manager, then the manager is responsible for conducting the performance appraisal. If there is a unit composed only of designers, there will be a supervisor for that unit, and he or she will be responsible for initiating the performance appraisal and then passing it on to the HRD manager. In addition, the various supervisors will have their performance appraisals conducted by the HRD manager.

*Using Roles and Subroles.* One aspect of the appraisal should be carried out in terms of the roles and subroles discussed earlier. Various organizations have used this approach. When it was used by the Monsanto Company, the company was good enough to share its experience with us. Those in charge started the appraisal by having an in-depth discussion between the supervisor and each staff member using the role model in Chapter Six as a framework. They pointed out that they did not expect every member of the staff to fill all the roles and certainly not in the same fashion. Therefore, the first step was to identify, for the particular employee, exactly what subrole(s) that employee was filling. The discussion focused on the level of performance by that individual and the amount of time spent functioning in each subrole. After agreement on those two factors, it was possible to move into the performance appraisal stage.

An HRD manager can thus explore such alternatives as:

- Did the staff member want to stay with the HRD unit?
- Did the staff member want to continue in that subrole?
- Were there other subroles to which the staff member wanted to move?
- Would such a movement within the HRD unit be possible?

This appraisal process is essentially focused on staff members in Category I. For those in Category II, the process would start the same way in terms of the subroles, performance level, and time in the subrole(s). But the answers would be different and correctly so. There should be performance appraisals for persons in both categories, but the purpose and outcome of these appraisals will be different. Remember that Category II's are not interested in building a career in HRD but that they will nevertheless want to do the best job possible while assigned to the HRD unit.

*Data Sources.* In addition to the one-on-one appraisal meeting between supervisor and staff members, it is desirable to collect data from other sources that relate to the performance and potential of that staff member. One source would be those who have been served by the HRD staff member. If that staff member functioned mainly as a facilitator, then data should be collected from the learners with whom the facilitator worked. As a general rule, such data are accumulated while the learning is in progress or at the end of a particular course or program. It should not be gathered at the time of the appraisal. The HRD manager should not rely on data from only one program but collect data from a variety of programs.

If the staff member functioned as a designer, the data should come from those for whom the programs were designed. That would include the facilitator who had to use the program, and it might also include those line managers for whom programs were designed.

For the staff member functioning as a consultant, the HRD manager should confer with those whom the staff member serves. At one time, the Ford Motor Company used this approach. It had reorganized its corporate staffing of HRD, using the role model, into eight operating "departments," and the HRD manager assigned a lead consultant to each one of the eight departments. It was made clear that the initial performance appraisal data would come from the departments that the consultants were serving. The system worked very effectively.

Performance appraisals will differ considerably, depending on which subrole the staff member is filling. When a staff member is filling more than one subrole, the HRD manager will have to accumulate data from a variety of sources. These data should not be treated only statistically, as they are basically the perceptions of those involved. It may be possible to find a statistical base when appraising the unit as a whole, but quantified approaches have limitations when applied to individual performance.

But suppose that the HRD manager felt that quantification of performance was needed—where might it be used? For the facilitator, it can be in terms of learners enrolled in his or her classes, as in school systems. This assumes that the facilitator has some control over class sizes. To deal with the class size aspect, a formula could be developed, indicating the "load" for each facilitator. For a budget item center, this might work. For a cost center, however, it would be unworkable unless the facilitator was also involved in encouraging the enrollment of learners. In that case, however, the facilitator might become a salesperson, interested in obtaining large enrollments rather than in solving problems. The unit cost, as ascribed to the facilitator, might be low, and yet the whole process might contribute little or nothing to solving the problems of the organization.

This leads us to another data source—the line managers who have been served. The HRD manager should be in constant touch with the unit's clients, directly or by delegation, to see that they are being well served. That, however, is in program terms. The HRD manager must also seek data concerning the individuals in the HRD unit, although this is a difficult and delicate task. Few other units in an organization ask outsiders for data related to their own performance. But for HRD this is extremely important, as the competencies exhibited by the various HRD staff members to those they are serving outside the unit are an important part of the total image of the unit, as well as of individual performance.

After the HRD manager has accumulated the necessary data and arrived at agreement with the staff member, then a professional growth plan (or an individual development plan) can be mutually agreed upon. To implement those plans, the HRD manager and the staff member should explore possible resources.

### Resources

Some of the resources discussed here would be applicable to any professional in an organization, but there are others that are unique to HRD. The purpose of this section is to indicate some of the organizations that can serve as resources as the HRD manager helps the staff to grow professionally. It is also important for the HRD manager to recognize what must be done to identify and utilize those resources. It is more than a matter of just sending around memos or descriptions of programs. The HRD manager must be closely involved with the HRD staff members as they utilize these resources for professional growth.

*Professional Organizations.* One obvious resource is professional organizations. The largest one in the HRD field is ASTD. In addition, there are the National Society for Performance and Instruction (NSPI) and the American Association for Adult and Continuing Education (AAACE). Some HRD managers, particularly those in Category II, may not be familiar with these organizations so we will present a very brief picture of each.

When it was formed in 1942, ASTD was known as the American Society of Training Directors. The name was subse-

quently changed, but the original initials were retained. As of 1984
the organization had about 22,000 national members. There are
also over 100 local chapters, and they have about 25,000 members
who do not belong to the national association. ASTD conducts an
annual conference and exhibition.

The NSPI was originally formed about 1961 as the National
Society for Programmed Instruction. It drew heavily on the work
of B.F. Skinner and other behaviorists. Its first impetus came from
the military, and it produced a design model called the Instructional Systems Development model. The NSPI has chapters in the
United States, Canada, and other countries with a total membership of about 2,600. It conducts an annual conference.

The AAACE represents a combination of the Adult Education Association (AEA) and the National Association for Public
and Continuing Adult Education (NAPCAE). AEA essentially
focused on community adult education while NAPCAE focused on
public school adult education. The new AAACE has not only
combined those two areas but has also included HRD as a major
focus. In 1984 the membership was about 3,500, which was up
after a serious decline. The predecessor organizations had barely
survived grave financial and leadership difficulties. The new
organization appears to have solved its financial problems and is
now focusing on the professional side. It is taking a broader view
of adult learning than it did in the past, and is trying to attract all
who are involved in that field, no matter what their institution or
delivery system. It is actively seeking members in the HRD field,
that is, people who see adult learning as the basis for HRD. But it
remains to be seen if it can effectively compete for members with
the other two organizations.

These three major organizations depend essentially on their
membership, and the HRD manager should encourage his or her
staff to join as individual members. At this time the only criterion
for membership in those organizations is the willingness to pay
dues. All have explored some minimum qualifications, but none
have seen fit to pursue the question. AAACE and NSPI do have
different levels of membership, with a variety of benefits that are
available at some levels and not at others. It is also possible to join
any of these professional groups through an organizational

membership, but we question whether this is desirable, particularly for staff members in Category I. As professionals, they should have an individual identification with their professional organizations. For Category II's, the organizational membership might be preferable, so that as individual members of Category II move out there is still an existing active membership for their replacements. Whatever the category, it is preferable that the organization pay the dues for all those who are members. The HRD manager must therefore budget for that expenditure.

It is important for each HRD unit member (including the manager) to be a member of at least one of those organizations. The HRD manager should also encourage staff to become active participants in them. Staff should actively seek volunteer positions at the local and national levels. They should volunteer for committee assignments and should be willing to chair committees when called upon. This will help strengthen and build the professional organizations. In addition, such experiences within organizations can provide an excellent resource for staff growth. Those involved will be challenged by meeting with HRD people from other organizations as well as by the nature of the committee assignments that require research and study. It is unlikely that staff members belonging to Category II will become heavily involved, although ASTD seeks those Category II's who are HRD managers and has even appointed some to national committees and to the ASTD board of governors.

Being a volunteer takes time. Some of that time will come outside of regular working hours. But it is also possible that volunteer work in the form of meetings, writing reports, and speaking to others outside the organization will impinge on regular office hours. The HRD manager should make available a reasonable amount of time for any staff member who volunteers for activity in the professional organizations. It may also require some secretarial help, as well as some minimal resources in the form of copying charges and so on. But for the HRD manager, particularly a Category I, providing time and money is only the beginning. The HRD manager should model behavior for the staff by joining one or more of these organizations and being an active participant.

*Conferences.* All these organizations conduct conferences. While there is a tendency to criticize national conferences for being too large, particularly in the case of ASTD, conferences present two interesting opportunities for professional growth. The first is as a participant. HRD staff should plan very carefully what to do when attending a conference and how to make it a significant learning experience. The major focus should be on why an HRD staff member is going to attend that conference—what are his or her goals? The preconference program should be reviewed with the HRD manager and other staff. Plans should be made, beforehand, as to how what is learned at the conference will be shared, on returning, with those who did not attend.

Some learning will occur in the planned sessions, but there is also a great deal to be gained in just meeting and talking to other HRD people from different organizations and different parts of the world. The HRD manager should also provide for some kind of feedback when the participant (who could be the HRD manager him- or herself) returns from the conference. There should be a sharing of materials as well as of experiences. But this will usually not happen unless there is specific provision for it.

For multisite organizations, the annual conference presents another type of resource for professional growth. HRD people from the various sites rarely see each other. This is particularly true of multinational corporations. The annual conference of a particular organization can be a meeting place for these scattered HRD people although their encounters with one another should not be confined to cocktail parties or other social occasions. There is the possibility of significant professional growth, as well as of service to the employing organization, when these people arrange to meet several times during the conference. Such a staff group can form a temporary conference group (Nadler and Nadler, 1977) to increase the benefits derivable from the national conference.

Some professional organizations also have conferences at the regional level. Obviously they are not as large or as sophisticated as the national conferences, but they do provide a local or regional emphasis that is missing from a national conference.

An important feature of some national conferences is the exhibition, since it generally draws many vendors. ASTD, for example, usually has in excess of 500 exhibitors. The exhibition provides an opportunity for HRD staff to become acquainted with some of the latest technology and learning packages that are available, as well as other kinds of resources. The exhibit is too often seen as a filler or an extra. What is often overlooked is its benefit as a learning situation. Of course, you can spend a good deal of time wandering around a large exhibition area and learn very little for that investment of time, and you must control the tendency to pick up every brochure, advertisement, or piece of paper. That is the "locust" approach: Swoop down on each exhibit, get its handout, and move on. The intent, of course, is to carefully look at all that material when you return to your office. Actually, some of it never even gets that far. As you pack to return home, you find either that the material is too heavy or that you do not have space for it. As packing is generally done at the last minute, there is little opportunity to carefully screen all the material. The result—you leave it all behind!

A more organized approach to the exhibition can provide professional growth opportunities. At the outset, look at the total list of exhibitors. This is usually provided in the registration material, although at times it may be available only at the door to the exhibit hall. Given your reasons for being at the conference, what do you want to see at the exhibit? It may be very comfortable to visit exhibits and talk to exhibitors you know. It is nice to be recognized by them, particularly if you purchased their products. If you want ego satisfaction, it is readily available. But if you want professional growth, you must go beyond that.

One way to start, before going to the conference, is to identify the problems or needs of the HRD unit or the organization for which resources might be available at the exhibition. Then identify those resources on the list of exhibitors and visit them first. In the HRD field, the number of exhibitors at all conferences seem to keep growing. Therefore, select those that you feel you really need to see if the exhibit is to contribute to your professional growth. If time allows, you can visit the others.

The second opportunity for professional growth is as a presenter. The HRD manager should certainly look into the possibility of presenting at a conference and should encourage his or her staff members to do likewise. We have all heard the comment that one learns best by teaching. Something similar happens to a presenter at a professional conference. First of all, the presentation has to be designed with careful thought to the other professionals who will attend. Second, the feedback that one receives is another form of learning. Finally, although the presentation may be made by only one person from the HRD unit, it can become a growth experience for all. Each member of the unit can contribute to the development of the presentation even if only one of them is presenting.

*Institutes and Workshops.* In addition to conferences, most of the professional organizations conduct a variety of institutes and workshops. The AAACE conducts legislative workshops, as the bulk of their members are concerned with federal and state legislation related to adult learning programs.

*Publications.* The professional groups also engage in a variety of publication activities. Moreover, as the field continues to grow and change, the needs of HRD people will no doubt be reflected in the kinds of publications their professional organizations have to offer.

ASTD publishes a monthly publication called the *Training and Development Journal.* Some of its articles are refereed, that is, they must pass a panel of peers before being published. Many articles, however, are published without peer review. The types of articles vary greatly, but their focus is on the practitioner. There has been talk of an ASTD refereed journal that would contain research articles and more thought-provoking material, but that has not yet appeared. Therefore, at this time the HRD staff will have to look to other publications for the research in the field.

Other publishing is done in conjunction with various publishers. These journals or books are usually the products of the publishers' work, but they may be made available to a professional organization through a cooperative agreement.

The predecessor organizations of AAACE published journals as well as books. AAACE has continued this, putting out a monthly publication entitled *Lifelong Learning.* In 1984 there was considerable discussion about changing the name and focus of that publication. Its predecessor, *Adult Education,* had an excellent reputation for articles for practitioners, many of them volunteers. The new publication took a much broader approach and was criticized for lacking focus. It is possible that some new monthly publication may be published by AAACE, but it is not yet clear what that will be.

*Adult Education Quarterly* focuses on research and issues in the field. A refereed journal at a scholarly level, it focuses on various aspects of adult learning and the adult learner. (Note that in the early 1980s there was increased attention to the adult learner in the workplace, that is, on HRD.) In addition, AAACE works with publishers on joint book-publishing efforts as well as monographs and other relevant literature. Finally, NSPI issues a monthly *Performance and Instruction Journal.* It focuses on short, practical, informal, performance-oriented material—preferably one page in length.

As with other activities discussed earlier, the HRD manager must take positive steps if these publications are to be used for professional growth. The publications of these three organizations should be made readily available to all staff. Unfortunately, the process sometimes becomes self-defeating without the HRD manager realizing it. That happens when the routing process is used. First, the publication goes to the HRD manager. Given the pressure of other activities, it may take the HRD manager several weeks to finish reading the publication and to send it on its way. Then, at each stop on the routing slip, there will be an additional delay. By the time it reaches the third or fourth person, the publication may be many months old. The problem is not only that the material becomes dated but that there is little or no opportunity for interaction among the staff about critical articles.

One simple way to reduce the time lag is to have multiple subscriptions to some of the pertinent magazines and journals. Most of the professional organizations have provision for subscriptions that do not entail membership. The cost is less than that of a membership, and the HRD manager can subscribe to additional copies of those publications that will be most helpful for his or her particular HRD unit.

Another device is copying significant articles. The copyright laws keep changing, but most versions allow for copying printed material when the use is for instructional purposes and no money is exchanged. (However, it is not always easy to determine when this applies in view of the statement contained in most publications that warns against any kind of reproduction.) In any event, the HRD manager should view these publications as resources for professional growth. Provision should be made for sharing and discussing articles that are pertinent to the organization or that provide additional insights into various aspects of HRD.

The same process can be used with books. The volume of publishing in HRD has exploded and will continue to increase. It is not possible for any individual to read all the books that are available. One technique is to carefully review new books in the field and then purchase those that have some relevance for the HRD unit. When the book arrives, it should not disappear into the library or onto the shelves of the HRD manager's office. Rather, individual HRD staff members should be asked to volunteer to read a particular book. Then, the HRD manager should make provision for that reader to report on the particular book. After that, others may want to read the book, and the opportunity for this should be provided.

Reading is important, but it is not enough. HRD staff should also be encouraged to write for professional publications. The criticism is often heard that most of the articles in those publications come from professors and consultants. They appear to be the only ones who have the time and the need to put their ideas on paper. This is so, but it also means that material from practitioners is sorely lacking. HRD staff members usually lack the time for such activity, and there is nothing in the reward system to encourage them to write.

This places an obligation on the HRD manager. Able staff members should be encouraged to write for professional publications. But units should avoid the "publish or perish" syndrome, as not every staff member can be expected to find satisfaction in writing. But there are those who do, and they should be provided with the appropriate resources (time and secretarial help) so that they can contribute to the professional literature. As for the reward system, there is probably little that can be done within organizations to encourage publishing. There might be a psychic reward in distributing copies of published articles, but that may not mean much in organizations that place no value on publishing professionally.

*Other Publications and Groups.* As the field of HRD gained momentum, it was to be expected that others would see the desirability of moving into this market. That is good, but these other organizations and groups should not be confused with the professional organizations. A leading organization is Lakewood Publications, Inc. It publishes a monthly magazine, *Training: The Magazine of Human Resources Development*, and it also conducts conferences in various parts of the country at different times. Generally, while the presenters are not paid, there is no restriction about selling from the platform. This should not be interpreted to mean that the sessions are not valuable, as some well-known HRD leaders do appear as presenters. The HRD staff should be cautioned, however, that selling is not only permitted but encouraged, and therefore the presentations may differ from the ones found at the ASTD, NSPI, or AAACE conferences.

The HRD staff should also be encouraged to look outside the HRD field. There are other professional groups, such as the American Psychological Association and the American Academy of Management, that also offer conference opportunities and publication resources that relate to HRD.

We should also mention another group of organizations not specifically related to HRD. The question may well be, why, then, consider them? But keep in mind that one criticism sometimes leveled at HRD people (particularly Category I's) is that they don't know the business of the organization that they are serving. This is frequently true; and, if it is, the HRD manager should encourage some of the staff to attend meetings of organizations related to the business of the organization. These may be trade shows, as well as professional meetings and conferences. The purpose should not be to make the HRD staff competent in those areas but to enhance the ability of the HRD staff to understand what operating people are discussing and what they are concerned about.

*Academic Study.* A fairly new area of professional growth in HRD is academic study. It is not possible to be exact about when academic offerings in HRD first became available. In part, it would depend on one's definition of the field. Some academics in the field of adult education might contend that they have been offering HRD subject matter under the umbrella term of adult education for a long time, but this is a moot point.

Universities package their offerings in three forms. The first and most common form is study leading to a degree. The student is expected to take a certain number of credit courses and to meet other requirements, and thereby earn a degree in the selected field.

Here, of course, we are discussing graduate degrees. For the most part, undergraduate degrees in HRD have not fared well. One reason is that employers, when hiring for HRD positions, generally ask that the applicant have some kind of business experience. But such experience is usually not gained until after achieving an undergraduate degree.

The second form consists of taking courses for credit but not working toward a degree. This option is seldom chosen, as most students who want credit also want a degree. Some professions require a certain amount of credit work, taken periodically, in order to retain certification or licensure. HRD is not one of those, so the credit option may not be attractive unless the staff member is considering a degree at some future time.

The third form is the noncredit offering. In the past, this format was generally offered by a specialized part of the university, perhaps the continuing education or extension division or the university college. During the 1970s, however, the situation began to change, and one could find many regular faculties offering noncredit work both on and off campus. All three forms are resources for the HRD manager. The following discussion, however, will focus on the degree program as that is the one gaining the most attention.

We can note that George Washington University in Washington, D.C., offered a course titled "Employee Training" as early as 1948. We believe that this was the first academic offering in the emerging field of HRD. As the program grew, it began offering both the M.A. and the Ed.D. with a concentration in employee training. In 1965, one of the authors joined the George Washington faculty, and the following year the program name was changed to "Employee Development" to represent a broader view of the field. Three years later, the name was changed to "Human Resource Development."

For about ten years, George Washington was the only university offering graduate degrees specifically called HRD. By the end of the decade, however, others began to offer similarly labeled programs. Unfortunately, this proliferation created confusion in the field. As there was still no generally agreed-upon definition of HRD, some universities retitled previous offerings in order to use HRD somewhere in the title of courses or the program. Generally, this did not mean that they were offering new courses. A compilation by ASTD of some of the programs is evidence of that (see *ASTD Directory of Academic Programs in Training and Development: Human Resource Development 1983– 1984*, 1983). A review of those programs shows that the placement of some of them is in schools that have little or nothing to do with learning.

This introduction to academic resources is provided in the spirit of *caveat emptor*. The HRD manager should support the efforts of the staff to avail themselves of academic resources, but which ones? Titles tell too little. The HRD manager and concerned staff should request actual course outlines, should speak to alumni of those programs, and should determine the credentials and experience of the instructional staff. The program should be built on some model of the field that would indicate the competencies stressed in that program. As with most learning programs, we should start with the needs of the learner. One legitimate need can be to get an academic degree! There are those who scoff at such degrees (Berg, 1970), but it is interesting to note that the scoffers usually have already earned their degrees. In U.S. society, as in many places in the world, the earned degree carries some weight. Therefore, earning a graduate degree in HRD is a legitimate goal.

Some of the academic programs specialize in a particular area of HRD. Those that are labeled "Instructional Technology" tend to be media oriented. Some programs will specifically state that they center on communications and media, and some have an emphasis on computer-assisted instruction. Other programs focus on consulting, usually with an organization development emphasis.

The HRD manager and staff should identify the short-term, as well as the long-term, needs of those involved in academic programs. For the short term, the HRD manager may recommend a particular course or courses that do not lead to a degree. For those seeking a degree, the long range is more important. This distinction is significant, for we have found students (working staff members) coming to George Washington University in search of one or two courses that will cover the entire field. This is just not possible. The field is too big, and the required competencies cannot be acquired in one or two courses.

When using academia as a resource, the HRD manager must take some positive steps. For one, funds must be made available for tuition refunds. There are a variety of ways this can be done. Above all, the tuition refund practices should apply in the same way to the HRD staff as to others in the organization who are eligible for refunds. (Note that tuition refund programs bear significant tax implications that may not apply to other HRD programs.) For example, the "student" may be reimbursed for the entire academic program or for only part of it. One practice is to tie the level of reimbursement to the grade level of the employee within the organization.

It may also be necessary to provide time. HRD offerings vary at different universities. In some cases, all required courses are offered in the evenings, while in others the entire program is on weekends. Or the work may be concentrated into one-week blocks that are offered periodically. Note that most of these modes reflect the fact that the student body is made up of persons who are employed in the field and who therefore cannot attend the university on a regular full-time basis. Of course, the HRD manager could arrange for paid leave for a staff member to attend school full time. The staff member should have clear goals when entering an academic program, although that does not mean that he or she should have selected all the courses before enrolling. A good academic program should allow some flexibility to meet the new needs that can be expected to emerge as the learner goes through the program.

Must the staff member return to the organization? This is basically an ethical point, although it is also a legal one. Since the organization has been paying for the schooling, it is assumed that the staff member will return and use the newly acquired competencies for the benefit of the organization and its people. Some organizations require that the staff member sign a formal contract, although this usually contains some kind of buy-out clause. That is, if the staff member wants to leave, the costs of the schooling must be repaid to the company. Enforcing such a provision is frequently difficult. The staff member cannot be forced to remain with the company. The courts have ruled that this is in the category of "peonage," which is forbidden by our laws. Therefore, the HRD manager must plan carefully with each individual staff member when a degree-granting program is selected as a resource. The preceding is only a caution and should not discourage the HRD manager or the staff member from using the resources of universities.

*Self-Directed Learning.* We owe a great deal to Tough (1971) for his work in this area. In conducting his research—research that is still being expanded upon by others—he found that adult learners did not rely only on formal learning situations but often learned without a teacher or classroom. He labeled this self-directed learning. This has led to some confusion as it is also possible to be self-directed in a group learning situation. In our discussion here, however, we will use his definition of self-directed learning.

For the HRD staff, self-directed learning means learning that takes place outside formal situations. There are a variety of these possibilities, and some were discussed earlier. (For example, reading professional journals and books, attending conferences, and joining professional organizations.) The intent is usually to keep up-to-date in one's field (Nadler, 1982b).

There are many kinds of self-directed learning opportunities that are available to the HRD manager and staff. One common approach is reading books and magazines. In the self-directed approach, the learner may utilize another individual (the HRD manager perhaps) to help in identifying the material to be read. The learner may also seek out others (the HRD manager and HRD staff) as sounding boards—to discuss material with them and to focus on what the learner has learned from the reading. If the self-directed learner chooses a book to read, the HRD manager could purchase it, using unit funds. The book, of course, would be the property of the HRD unit rather than of the learner. This is an advantage for the unit, as it helps to build a professional library for the HRD unit.

Another approach is the field trip. We tend to think of this as a group activity, with a leader. But it can also be self-directed when the HRD staff member identifies something to see, a place to visit, or some person (outside the organization) to speak to. For the field trip the staff member needs time and perhaps some limited funds. The HRD manager can justify this expenditure of time and money quite readily by building in the requirement that the staff member share the outcomes of the field trip with other staff. Professional writing, discussed earlier, is another type of self-directed learning. We will not repeat what we said earlier on this point, but we do want to emphasize its use as a self-directed learning experience.

The range of approaches to self-directed learning is only limited by the imagination of the learner and the availability of resources. It is this aspect that the HRD manager must consider. It would be counterproductive to encourage the staff to be self-directed learners and then to fail to remove some of the organizational barriers that can hinder such learning.

*Mentoring.* One of the newer resources is mentoring (Zey, 1984). In mentoring, a person is selected who can serve as a role model, coach, and reinforcer for the learner. Preferably, the two should not be in a supervisor-subordinate relationship, though there are times when this cannot be avoided. We still have a great deal to learn about this resource, and the HRD unit should be at the forefront of this new learning experience. While there are some significant problems with this approach—it may become difficult to terminate the relationship and the mentee may develop excessive feelings of counterdependency as the relationship draws to an end—it has a very positive side. It provides the learner with a specific individual who will serve as a resource. The learner need not wait for the appropriate class or opportunity to try to solve a professional problem. Rather, the learner can contact the mentor at any time for help and guidance or just to talk to professionally.

After speaking to mentors, we have discovered that mentoring brings benefits to them far beyond the time they must give to it. The learner can raise issues that the mentor may have overlooked. The learner can ask questions that the mentor has stopped asking under the assumption that answers to them had already been obtained. Mentors have also commented very favorably on the stimulation they have received from learners.

For the HRD manager, there are some specific considerations when using the mentoring approach. For one, selection and preparation of the mentor are crucial. If the HRD unit is large, it may be possible to select mentors from within the HRD unit who can serve in that role for the younger and less experienced staff members. But if the HRD unit is small, the HRD manager will have to look elsewhere. If the mentor is chosen from within the organization, but outside the HRD unit, there can be the implication that the learner will eventually be transferred from the unit. Therefore, the HRD manager may have to look outside the organization. Experienced academics are one source, but the HRD manager must expect to pay for their services. Some people think that university professors should serve as mentors as part of their contribution to the community. At one time this may have been the practice, but it is certainly not in tune with today's marketplace. It is also possible to select a mentor from some other organization, though it must be stated explicitly that there will be no attempt to pirate away that individual. As even the explicit statement may not govern behavior, this approach must be used with extreme caution. The learner should enter the relationship willingly. Some staff members may not want a mentor. There is nothing wrong with that. Not everybody is comfortable learning in that mode.

On the negative side, mentoring has sometimes created the "crown prince" effect; that is, it is presumed that the learner is being geared to move into the mentor's job when the mentor moves on. This is one reason for being cautious about using a direct superior as a mentor.

There is, as yet, no research that enables us to list the criteria for a good mentor. It is a question of personality and "fit" between the mentor and the learner. We have observed, however, that both of them need some kind of preparation for their new roles. The learner must know how to use the mentor without becoming overly dependent or consuming an unreasonable amount of the mentor's time. The mentor must learn what the limits of mentoring are and how to help the learners without creating dependency.

## Conclusion

Professional growth of the HRD staff is an important responsibility for an HRD manager. There are few identifiable career paths in HRD, but the manager has the obligation to provide for staff growth and to offer staff members the opportunity to advance themselves within the organization. Performance appraisal is the appropriate starting place in planning for individual growth. The roles and subroles can be effectively utilized in performance appraisal as well as in planning for individual professional growth.

There are numerous resources for HRD staff members, and it is the responsibility of the manager to see that they are made available. Of course, it is still the responsibility of the individual staff member to take the initiative in utilizing those resources.

Academic programs are proliferating and should be actively considered when discussing individual development plans. This could include nondegree as well as degree opportunities. Consideration should also be given to self-directed learning as an important element of professional growth.

Provisions for professional growth must relate directly to the employee's category. The Category I staff member should be very interested in all forms of professional growth in the HRD field. The Category II employee can be expected to be much less interested in professional growth related to HRD. Staff in both categories will receive performance appraisals containing comments regarding appropriate professional growth opportunities.

The appraisals should relate to the categories or they will not have much meaning.

The employees' roles and subroles should also be considered when planning for professional growth. As conditions and people change, staff members may want to develop competencies in subroles other than those they are currently performing. The direction in which their growth will proceed must also be related to the needs of the line managers and the plans of the organization.

Many organizations can provide growth opportunities for HRD staff. The three major national professional organizations in the field are: American Society for Training and Development, National Society for Performance and Instruction, and the American Association for Adult and Continuing Education. All of these offer conferences, workshops and institutes, publications, and possibilities for leadership in the HRD field. There are also companies that have publications, institutes, and conferences that can contribute to the professional growth of HRD staff.

Academic opportunities for HRD staff are proliferating. At one time, only the George Washington University offered a graduate degree in human resource development with specific course work in that field. Now many more universities offer programs and courses, and the number continues to grow. Other possibilities for professional growth include self-directed learning and mentoring.

··⁂ *Chapter 8* ⁂··

# Managing Facilities and Equipment

Up to this point, we have discussed the philosophical foundations of HRD, the development of HRD policy, organizing, financing, budgeting, and staffing the HRD program, and HRD professional development—all the competencies that are needed for managing a successful HRD program. We now turn to another topic: HRD facilities and equipment. We believe that unless the HRD manager pays close personal attention to the planning and utilization of learning environments—the HRD facilities—even the most well-planned, carefully implemented, and professionally managed HRD program may experience serious administrative and logistical difficulties that will inhibit learning.

Of course, some HRD managers will say, "My job is managing learning programs for the human resources of the organization. I don't know anything about the facilities planning and management business, and I am not about to get into it now!" Others will ask, "What makes the design, purchase, maintenance, repair, and control of the HRD facilities and equipment different from similar activities in other units of the organization?" Indeed, it should not be difficult to plan and control HRD facilities and equipment when appropriate spaces have already been provided and office and classroom furnishings are already in the organization's equipment inventory. All that the HRD manager has to do is plan the facility layouts, schedule the moving date, and make sure that the furnishings and equipment are put where they belong.

This is especially true when the HRD manager knows that other staff units (for example, the architect's office in corporate planning or in the engineering department) do the planning and design of all facilities and equipment for *all* units of the enterprise, that other staff units have direct responsibilities for handling purchasing, renting, or leasing arrangements, and that still other units will handle maintenance. What planning or controlling does the HRD manager have to do?

In reality, however, an HRD manager's efforts toward managing and controlling HRD facilities and equipment are as important as they are complex. We consider particularly important the selection of the administrative and classroom furnishings and the choice of instructional media and equipment needed for the HRD offices, classrooms, laboratories, media production and storage areas.

## Design, Planning, and Control

The advantages of the HRD manager's having control over both HRD facilities and equipment are obvious to those of us who have had to share HRD facilities that were never originally designed or equipped to provide effective learning environments. As Finkel (1984) suggests, HRD learning environments must create specific kinds of surroundings in order to fulfill the needs of the HRD program participants and to satisfy the requirements for their learning. The design approaches used for planning most offices, schools, or plants will usually not result in effective learning environments for HRD. The responsive learning environment, in the context of an HRD learning activity or program, should be designed around the designer's understanding of the adult learning process. Unfortunately, most office or plant designers or planners have not studied adult learning processes and do not have experience in planning adult learning facilities.

It is all too often true that senior management approval of architectural and engineering plans for the design and equipping of new or refurbished existing HRD facilities is given without inputs from the HRD manager or staff. Throughout our consulting experiences, we have known of many senior managers who had not even considered giving the organization's HRD manager or staff an opportunity to make inputs to the proposal recommendations. When we ask why they hadn't, they reply along these lines: "The HRD manager and staff are responsible for the design and delivery of our learning activities here, *not* facilities engineering and construction. We have had the firm's architect and our engineering department design and build all our facilities. That's their business! The HRD manager is responsible for setting up the HRD unit offices and classrooms the way the HRD staff wants them, *after the construction is completed.* That's the HRD manager's business!"

Senior management decisions made without the HRD manager's inputs at the time of the approval of the architectural and engineering design specifications can produce poorly designed HRD facilities and equipment. Those decisions can result in the making of some very costly mistakes—mistakes that the HRD staff and learners will have to live with for years to come.

It is therefore highly important for the HRD manager to recognize that there are external resources that can provide assistance in designing effective adult learning environments. There are now many good facility planners, architects, human-factors engineers, media specialists, lighting consultants, interior designers, and purchasing consultants who specialize in the design and construction specifications of total HRD learning environments. The HRD manager should identify and seek out such experts and get the benefit of their professional advice in designing and planning HRD learning environments. These professionals can help by asking the "right kinds of dumb questions" that the HRD manager tends to ignore when trying to develop his or her facility alone. They can provide much assistance to the HRD manager in developing cost-efficient and effective HRD facilities.

## HRD Facilities: Policy Decisions

The HRD manager will have to review the organization's policy to determine if it requires or encourages its HRD activities to be delivered on a centralized or decentralized basis. Can the HRD unit's customers' different learning needs and required learning activities be accommodated in one centralized location, or will different types of learning facilities be required in various locations? Most often, it is not possible or desirable to locate *all* the organization's HRD learning activities in one place within the organization. The learning activities should be delivered in close proximity to where their varied target groups of employees, supervisors, managers, and nonemployees (clients, customers, and others) are employed or are to be served. This does not mean, however, that there is no value in conducting HRD learning programs in "off-the-ranch" facilities.

*Dedicated versus Nondedicated Facilities.* Before beginning the design and planning processes for the organization's HRD facilities and equipment, the HRD manager must also know whether the HRD program is to have its own *dedicated* classroom and/or classroom-laboratory facilities or whether it will have to share facilities with other organizational units. If the HRD activities are to be conducted in existing facilities that were designed as conference or meeting rooms and will be shared with various other types of managerial or employee groups not associated with the HRD program, the inputs of the other "users" of the spaces most certainly will have to be considered in the planning process. In the case of either dedicated or nondedicated classrooms, the HRD manager will have to know if the room size, physical layouts, and furnishings of the existing facilities will accommodate the learning activities planned for the subject matter to be taught in the HRD program.

*Internal versus External HRD Facilities.* Because organizations today are focusing more extensively on the development of their human resources, there has been a related expansion in the number of HRD learning activities conducted, many in *outside* facilities. Finkel (1984) suggests that the increase in the use of hotels, motels, and other rented conference centers is encouraging senior managers in some organizations to question all aspects of such off-site HRD activities—their cost, effectiveness, administration, and so on. And well they should be questioned, for unfortunately many of our present hotel or motel "conference" rooms were formerly guestrooms—designed for sleeping, not for effective instruction, learning, *or* conferences. The HRD programs of many of our largest companies are spending millions of dollars annually on the use of outside facilities, and this practice will probably continue. However, some organizations have now built or leased their own stand-alone, centralized, learning facilities or are at least exploring the idea.

Some of these centralized learning facilities include full hotel accommodations and "guest" recreation facilities, even though the facility is usually not open for use by the public. Examples of such corporate learning centers include the General Electric Company's Management Learning Center at Croton-on-the-Hudson, New York; the Federal Executives Institute at Charlottesville, Virginia; the Postal Service Management Institute in Bethesda, Maryland; and the International Typographical Union's Graphic Arts Crafts Training Center at Colorado Springs, Colorado.

*Identify Long-Range Organizational Learning Needs and Objectives.* Although there are different approaches to planning the design of HRD facilities, the acquisition of appropriate HRD facility furnishings, and the selection of required instructional equipment, expert planners agree that the HRD manager must first very clearly define his or her program's mission and goals. Most likely, the manager will also have to clarify some of the present HRD policies to see if any new policies will be needed before a new HRD facility becomes operative and any new equipment is put into use. Toward this effort, the HRD manager should, with senior management consensus, anticipate what the long-term employee and nonemployee learning needs will be and determine the requirements for the HRD program policy, mission, and objectives. This will require answers to such questions as:

1.  What clients will the HRD program serve and what will be their learning needs? Data should be gathered to determine:
    a.  the size and location of the target populations to be served;
    b.  the demographic characteristics of the identified target groups, such as age ranges, educational attainments, work experience, and cultural backgrounds;
    c.  identification of learning disabilities, learning motiva-

tions, and, most certainly, learning content (subject matter).

2. Will some of the learning programs require sophisticated classroom-laboratory facilities, unique equipment, or complex learning methodologies, or will traditional classroom facilities, instructional equipment, and adult education methodologies suffice?

3. Will transportation, housing, and food services for the learners be required?

4. What types of instructional technology will be employed in the HRD facilities? During recent years, rapid changes in educational technology have dramatically increased the availability of new instructional media and hardware. It leads one to think that the days when an instructor used the classroom "whiteboard" or overhead transparency and 35-mm slide projectors to illustrate a lecture may well be numbered.

5. Will the HRD facilities need computer-assisted instruction stations (requiring microcomputers with appropriate software), teleconferencing equipment (requiring use of optical fiber communication and satellite network linkups), high-powered color video or videodisc projection equipment, stop-frame 16-mm movie projectors, electronic teletraining blackboards, front- and rear-projection screens, among *some* of the instructional hardware gadgetry currently available.

6. Will extensive references be required for use by the learners while participating in learning programs so that space has to be set aside for a library and student study areas?

### HRD Administrative Facilities

Depending on the HRD manager's staffing decisions (the size and types of HRD staff), consideration must be given to planning the location, size, arrangement, and types of office furnishing and equipment required to house the HRD unit staff. In many organizations, HRD managers have decided to staff their HRD unit on a "mean and lean" basis. That is, they have decided to maintain a very small, but highly professional HRD staff team. They prefer to use the organization's own lead persons, supervisors, managers, and other subject matter experts as "adjunct" HRD faculty to deliver the majority of HRD programs instead of having a large number of permanent HRD staff. In such cases, the need for HRD office and administrative space is much less than would otherwise be the case.

*HRD Staff Work-Space Requirements.* Most HRD unit offices are very busy places. The HRD learning specialist staff members spend considerable time in their offices and work spaces, preparing for instruction and developing plans of instruction, lesson plans, participant handouts, audiovisual materials, and other instructional and job aids. Such work requires sufficient individual work space and storage space. The HRD learning specialist staff members have daily telephone or personal contacts, as well as meetings and conferences with a variety of subject matter experts, including graphic arts specialists, photographers, printers or instructional aid reproduction and duplication specialists, and other suppliers. Needless to say, each HRD staff member's desk should be supplied with a telephone, typewriter or word processor terminal, and the other "tools" and supplies needed to do a professional job.

The HRD staff members will often confer in their offices with individual learners from their classes to give additional out-of-class assistance, test makeups, and so on. The organization's employees and supervisors will come to the HRD unit's offices to meet with the HRD staff for guidance regarding external training, education, or development activities. The supervisors and managers will often come to consult with the HRD manager or an individual HRD staff member about a productivity problem believed to be due to a lack of skills or knowledge on the part of their employees or about other matters that may identify needed new HRD activities. To maintain any degree of confidentiality during meetings with "customers" or with other members of the staff, each staff member must have his or her own office space.

Many HRD managers today are providing sound-deadening, modular furniture offices for their HRD staff employees. These modular office systems allow for a typewriter or word processor terminal, a printer, conveniently built-in storage spaces, enough floor space for extra chairs for two visitors, and the creative work environment required for privacy. Separate small, closed meeting rooms equipped with a conference table, a telephone, and seating for fifteen to twenty people are provided in conveniently located areas near the individual's office module.

Before leaving this discussion of HRD unit administrative offices, we want to emphasize the need for adequate storage space. Ask just about any group of HRD learning specialists if they have sufficient office or classroom storage spaces, and their answer is almost always a resounding "No!" Of course, experienced HRD managers know that most HRD learning specialists have characteristics similar to those of packrats. Instructors tend to be collectors of all types of materials they plan to use in class— someday—and they will not part with anything unless forced to do so.

*Make, Buy, Rent, or Lease Decisions.* Because most HRD programs require a variety of instructional materials and different kinds of audiovisual equipment, some decisions have probably already been made about buying or leasing such materials and equipment if the organization's HRD program has been in existence for any length of time. Someone, whether senior management, the purchasing manager, or the HRD manager has probably decided what will be produced inside and what will be purchased, rented, or leased from outside vendors. For example, if the organization already has a well-established, fully equipped graphics department and a good printshop, it is likely that their services will continue to be used and not duplicated by the HRD unit. Moreover, an effective graphics shop can produce work that will compare most favorably with that available from outside commercial art firms. If there are no in-house graphics and printshop capabilities, however, the HRD manager must then estimate the requirements that will be needed to support the HRD activities. A small in-house graphics support staff can produce instructional materials with fast turnaround times. They can often give excellent service for a variety of instructional aids and materials, including visual transparencies, 35-mm slides, demonstration simulators and models, printed learner reference handouts, and job aids for a number of different types of audiovisual equipment. However, the luxury of having the in-house graphic and printing support may not justify the costs associated with salaries, shop spaces, and equipment. Given those costs, the HRD manager must ask if the services or materials can be purchased from commercial graphics arts houses or printshops or can be rented from vendors at much less overall cost to the organization.

*Instructional Technology Hardware Costs.* Have you purchased any new pieces of audiovisual hardware lately? If you have, you will know that their cost has climbed along with their technological advances. There are a great number of HRD managers in firms and organizations throughout the nation today who have decided that it is more cost effective to lease *all* their audiovisual equipment. The leasing arrangement with their vendor ensures that they are supplied with the latest models of needed equipment. The equipment is maintained on a scheduled preventative maintenance program, and any repairs required are made by the vendor-leasor.

*Required Learning Facilities and Equipment.* Obviously, there are different learning environment requirements for different types of HRD activities. For example, in job skills learning activities, there are often as many different learning environment requirements as there are jobs to be learned. It would be next to impossible to conduct a course in electronic equipment maintenance in a classroom in which no tools used in repairing or maintaining the equipment were available. Likewise, it would be foolish, and very dangerous, to teach a welding class in a classroom that had been designed to teach supervisory or management skills. The most important question an HRD manager must ask regarding HRD facilities and equipment is, How completely will the learning facility and equipment fulfill the requirements of the learning environments now and *in the future?*

## The HRD Manager's Fantasy Trip

Recognizing the fact that the majority of our readers will never be completely satisfied with their organization's HRD facilities and equipment, let us dream a little. Let us take an HRD manager's fantasy trip and see what would be needed to design and equip an "ideal" HRD learning center.

This morning at the weekly meeting of the senior management group, you were asked by the chief executive officer to develop a proposal to design and build a first-rate HRD facility. The new facility is to be equipped with the best of furnishings and the most up-to-date instructional technology. The chief executive officer wants the learning center to be a company showplace *and* to serve the learning needs of the employees, managers, and customers of your organization well into the next century. You have been given an almost unlimited budget for the project. Your proposal is to be completed in three months, giving the chief executive officer sufficient time to prepare his presentation to the members of the board at their year-end meeting four months from now. How, and with whom, would you begin developing the proposal?

Planning to accommodate the learning needs of the twenty-first century requires making a number of assumptions. As we suggested earlier, our HRD manager should first identify and seek out expert external consultants to help make the "right" assumptions. Designers of HRD facilities most often begin with space requirements. Just how big should your ideal classrooms and laboratories be? The answer, of course, is that it all depends on what learning functions each HRD facility is to serve. For example, if you decide that information systems and computer-assisted instruction are to be an integral part of your twenty-first century instructional methodology, then you had better ensure that adequate wiring is built into each classroom in the center. You must try to anticipate your target populations' learning needs and the instructional methodologies to be employed to serve those needs. Only then will you be prepared to give good answers regarding your HRD learning facility requirements.

Recognizing that your chief executive officer's proposed learning center is to meet the learning needs of some very diverse populations, you can assume that it should contain a variety of meeting rooms, classrooms, and classroom-laboratories. Each classroom should be uniquely designed to serve its different functions and to accommodate the number of learners most likely to use the room at one time. The proposed facility will probably require one or more of each of the four generic types of HRD learning environments: (1) multipurpose classrooms, (2) single-purpose classrooms, (3) single-purpose classroom-laboratories, and (4) an auditorium (a large meeting facility).

*The Multipurpose Classroom.* As its name implies, this can be used for a variety of HRD learning activities. Most classroom design experts will differ with HRD learning specialists as to the number of individuals who can effectively participate in an adult learning activity. The design consultants will suggest that thirty-two is the most workable number, with a maximum of forty. HRD learning specialists most often stress that fifteen to eighteen is an ideal number for *active* participation in the learning activities, with a maximum of twenty-five persons.

Whatever the maximum number of participants chosen for the room, design experts and knowledgeable HRD learning specialists will agree that a multipurpose classroom must be designed to allow room for participant movement, varied participant seating and worktable arrangements, and the application of a variety of instructional strategies and techniques. Facility design consultants, working closely with human-factors engineers, suggest that a multipurpose classroom should provide as much as seven to ten square feet per person for a theaterlike room, fifteen to seventeen square feet for a traditional classroom, and at least twenty-three square feet for a conference room.

Regardless of the total square footage of the multipurpose classroom, its inside wall room dimensions should permit a variety of participant seating layouts. Many HRD learning specialists suggest that two-participant study tables, (foldup style, trapezoid shape, six feet long by thirty inches wide) provide the greatest degree of flexibility for varied room seating layouts. In a thirty-eight-by-forty-foot classroom with trapezoid-shaped tables, for example, the room can quickly and conveniently be set up in a "hollow circle" or in "U," "V," "E," or "T" student table and chair layouts for active learner participation. Seating comfort is also important. Many of your HRD program learners will be used to active physical movement on their jobs, and the classroom learning environment will be foreign to them. It is important that the HRD facility be equipped with ergonomically designed fabric-upholstered swivel armchairs, with adjustable seat heights and firm backs. They should be designed for durability as well as for the comfort of the student.

However, it is important to note that a chair can just as easily be *too* comfortable as it can be too uncomfortable! For example:

> The authors recall the time they were conducting an advanced management learning program in a very plush learning facility located in an organization's executive development center. Each of us experienced difficulty in keeping the participants involved in their learning activities after the lunch break at noon. It seemed to be "naptime" for the majority of the participants. We tried every method we knew to keep the group awake and actively participating, to no avail. When we later mentioned our concerns to the program manager, he said, "Come with me. I want to show you something in the classroom." He had us sit down in the student chairs. They were softer than our easy chairs at home! No wonder the students had problems staying awake during the sessions after lunch. The program manager then told us that *every* instructor in the program had experienced the same problem. Unfortunately, when the center was designed, the decision makers did not check with the HRD manager or staff members to get their inputs regarding student chairs. Each chair had cost the organization more than $375, so it would be years before it could justify replacing them.

For lectures and visual presentations in multipurpose classrooms, the study tables can be arranged in regular or "chevron" classroom styles, with the instructor's table and chair, newsprint-pad easels, and visual aid screen at the front of the room. Some instructors prefer a small portable lectern placed on their "working" table, with a smaller table conveniently situated alongside to make it easier to use the overhead projector.

Facility designers and those who have conducted HRD activities in hotel and motel "conference" rooms agree that the most important dimension in a classroom is the height of the ceiling. Design experts tell us that, for a thirty-eight-by-forty-foot classroom, the projection screen should be eight feet high and should stand at least five feet off the classroom floor. With the screen at that height, the visual material being projected can be readily seen by everyone seated. Realistically however, that ideal would be most difficult to attain, for it translates into a classroom ceiling height of approximately thirteen and a half feet. Today, ten-foot ceilings are the rule in architecture, so you will have to adjust participant seating layouts and screen size accordingly.

HRD learning specialists often use adult learning facilitation techniques that require the participants to work together in small groups. Therefore, there is a need for small break-out rooms to be located in close proximity to the classroom or to have room dividers within the room itself.

As noted earlier, we have already entered an age of advanced instructional technology. Multiimage presentations, televideo communications transmitted by satellite that allow participants to enroll in concurrent learning activities at separate sites; and instant color video replay, along with videocassette-delivered learning programs, are commonplace today. Nevertheless, the instructor's writing surface in the front of the classroom (be the board black, green, or white in color, or require chalk, marking pen, or electronic pencil) still serves an important need. In addition, various classroom display boards, as well as 35-mm slides, 8- and 16-mm films, overhead transparency projectors, video cameras, and recorder/playback machines are certain to be used to supplement classroom instruction well into the next century. Consequently, classroom design experts support the view that new multipurpose classrooms should be equipped with both front- *and* rear-projection systems.

Many well-equipped classrooms today combine a large screen projector with two suspended nineteen-inch television monitors to help reduce participants' eyestrain. It is important for individuals to be able to shift their eyes and bodies around to look from one monitor to another during a visual presentation. A new high-powered video projector that projects images on a flat screen or even a painted wall, eliminating the need for monitors, has recently been introduced. This projector represents a significant breakthrough in helping to prevent eyestrain and stiff necks caused by watching video images on suspended television monitors.

The need for a flexible media system in the modern classroom is obvious to all of us who have had to work with limited facilities over the years. For example, front-projection visual presentations usually require a darkened room, which inhibits note taking by participants. With rear-projection screen systems in place, that problem can be avoided. Experts also tell us that a custom-built screen sixteen feet wide and eight feet high will ensure dual-image capabilities. Three vertical images or two super 35-mm slides can be projected together to fill the whole screen if needed.

Front-projection screens are being continually improved. The common problem we have all faced in using these screens has been glare spots on the screen surface. But the invention of special nonglare screen surfaces has virtually eliminated that problem. The new "whiteboard" front-of-classroom panels available today include magnetic surfaces and "dry-ink" write-on capabilities, and, at the same time, provide excellent nonglare visual projection screens. Their manufacturers claim that these "whiteboard" panels are so advanced in design that participants can sit at a ninety-degree angle from the screen and see as clearly as if they were in the front center row of a theaterlike classroom.

The back of the classroom should have a closed access corridor (with locked door) for a projection booth raised on a five-foot platform (to line up with the front of the room projection screen). The locked door and closed access corridor are recommended by everyone who has experienced the loss (by theft) of expensive audiovisual equipment or other types of instructional hardware. Many multipurpose classrooms today are designed so that behind the thirty-eight-foot-long wall, the projection booth area is approximately twenty feet wide, with ten feet left over for classroom storage (five feet on one side and five feet on the other side of the booth).

*Single-Purpose Learning Facilities.* For many years, organizations have established a variety of single-purpose learning facilities for specific employee and nonemployee learning needs. Most of the newly established, single-purpose learning facilities in recent years have been computer learning center facilities. The rapid advances in computer and computer software programming technology in recent years have made available a wide range of affordable microcomputers and relatively inexpensive courseware-authoring software systems. The color, animation, and even sound capabilities that are available in today's computer hardware and software make them appealing for a variety of HRD applications by the HRD learning specialists and their learners. But the unique architectural designs needed for the computer learning classrooms, the engineering and environmental requirements for wiring and air conditioning, the computer hardware and its software, plus the costs in both time and money associated with development of the actual courseware, make the initial investment in this single-purpose learning facility quite high.

One of the authors devoted almost a full year during his recent sabbatical leave to the design of a large computer-based job skills learning program for a client organization. He estimates that his four-person subject matter expert and instructional design team worked more than 300 hours to produce each hour of planned instruction! However, both he and his HRD client are most enthusiastic about the learning successes they see with those participants who use the computer-based training programs versus those who are still learning in a traditional classroom setting. HRD managers are also beginning to think about integrating computer-aided instruction or computer-based learning programs with the learning programs now available in new videodisc formats. Videodisc playback machines are today being set up and used in combination with single-purpose computer learning facilities by a number of HRD technical training programs in both Japan and the United States.

However, the computer and combined computer-videodisc learning center facility is but one type of single-purpose learning facility, and there are many other good examples of such learning facilities that are *not* based on technological advances in instructional technology. For example, by far the majority of pharmaceutical firms provide their "detailer" sales forces with training in learning facilities that include very comprehensive mock-ups of medical offices and drugstore pharmacy areas. These facilities are furnished so that the sales trainees can practice making "detailer calls" to physicians and pharmacists through role playing in real life environments. Most likely, the teller you do business with at your local financial institution first learned to handle your many different transactions in a simulated, fully equipped teller's cage at the institution's learning center. Many HRD units at our large retail department stores equip their employee learning centers with single-purpose classroom facilities that include cash registers, display racks, display windows, and other "tools" for learning effective retail merchandising and sales.

*Single-Purpose Classroom-Laboratories.* In our view, there is a difference between the single-purpose classroom and the single-purpose classroom-laboratory. We contend that the difference is one of magnitude relative to the dimensions and scope of the job skills to be learned, the necessary learning environments, and the tools and equipment that are prescribed by the nature of the job. However, the magnitude of that difference can be very substantial in initial capital outlays, as well as in year-to-year operating costs, for the classroom-laboratory facility, its tools, equipment, and staffing. Let us give an example.

For many years now, one of our nation's Big Three auto makers has operated a comprehensive automobile technician learning center for its dealers' mechanics in northern Virginia. The classroom wing of this single-purpose classroom-laboratory is equipped with the most modern instructional technology available. Also provided in the center's laboratory wings are numerous auto repair bays with lifts and work stations for mechanics (each bay complete with duplicate sets of mechanic's tools and diagnostic equipment), an electronic ignition shop, an auto body repair bay, a paint shop bay, and a fully supplied parts department. Before the auto maker's new models are introduced to the public, the learning facility receives at least one new model of each make of car and truck. The new vehicles must be stripped down into their component parts, analyzed, and rebuilt by the "mechanics in training" before they can be certified as qualified mechanics. This special-purpose classroom-laboratory is only one of several identical regional learning centers located throughout the country. Can you imagine what the annual costs are for such a learning center? Nevertheless, the company views it as a necessary cost of doing business.

*The Auditorium or Large Meeting Facility.* For meetings and conferences of large groups of up to 200 or more, a comprehensive learning center should have an auditorium with a raised platform (stage) and tiered seating and should be equipped with both front- and rear-projection screens, a sound-presentation and cordless voice-enhancement system with a tuner and a sufficient number of stereo speakers, and layered levels of lighting. There is always the need to have sufficient lighting, projectors with appropriate lenses, and sound capabilities in *all* learning facilities. That need becomes even more evident in larger size learning facilities.

All new classrooms today should have four levels of lighting: a subdued level of lighting for slides or films when the participants are expected to take notes; a second level, even darker, for presenting 16-mm movies; a third level, full lighting, for lecture-discussions and other group activities; and a fourth level, for illuminating only the front of the room (or the area behind the video monitors). Media specialists advise that the lighting circuits be split into three sections for independent control of the facility's illumination in the front, middle, and back of the room. The lighting should be controlled by a console from the front of the room, convenient to the instructor.

Audiovisual consultants suggest buying a good projector and then buying the lenses to match what you want to do with it. It was pointed out to one of the authors that the three-inch lens that came with his 35-mm slide projector gave only about 60 percent of the light on the screen that a five-inch lens would produce. Audiovisual consultants also recommend using xenon arc lamps in both slide and overhead projectors to light up either front- or rear-projection screens. In addition, they recommend investing in a five-inch lens for slide projectors, as well as long focal-length lens for overhead projectors so that they can be moved to the back of the room to reduce screen glare. Most of us know so little about lens sizes or types of lamps to use for the best illumination that we can certainly benefit from getting advice from the experts who do.

## Learning from Others' Mistakes

When we began our HRD manager's fantasy trip some pages back, you will recall that we started out suggesting that we look for external experts in a variety of disciplines and fields. We have also found that some of the best recommendations about learning facilities come from those who have recently built new HRD facilities or refurbished existing ones. They will be proud to show you their facilities, and some of them may even be willing to tell you *what not to do!* We encourage you to do the legwork necessary to visit such individuals and to discuss with them what you have in mind for your HRD facility—before you repeat their mistakes!

## Conclusion

Managers need to keep in mind that there is a return on the investment required to provide good learning environments for the HRD activities targeted for their employees in terms of increased productivity and customer satisfaction. The design and furnishing of an HRD facility today is far more complex and expensive than it was only a decade ago. The actual amount of annual financial support an organization's HRD activities need depends on the type and complexity of audiovisual equipment, computer hardware and software, and classroom furnishings chosen; the salaries of the HRD staff or the fees paid to contractors for instructional design and delivery; the learners' salaries; and any transportation and housing costs. These expenses can be significant and may be a major factor in an organization's decision regarding human resource development.

··· ⁊ *Chapter 9* ⊱···

# Building Supportive
# Internal and External Relations

$T$here is one element (subrole) of the job of the HRD manager that tends to be overlooked or at least to be given insufficient attention, and that is the necessity for maintaining effective relations, both within and outside the organization. This subrole is one that makes the job of the HRD manager different from that of other managers, particularly line managers. Maintaining relations must start with the HRD manager's understanding of what HRD is and what it contributes to the organization.

Let us think for a minute of the manager as the "person in the middle." In other words, let us picture the manager as a central figure who is affected by subordinates (from below), by other managers (at the same level), and by upper managers and executives (from above). This is just a limited picture, for there can obviously be other forces not so readily observable but equally important: stockholders, government officials, community leaders, and so on. It is a volatile situation and one that can exert tremendous pressure on a manager.

The HRD manager is even more emphatically the "person in the middle." Because few people in the organization are cognizant of the actual and potential contribution of HRD, the HRD manager must constantly relate to others, that is, constantly maintain relations. This can be done by the HRD manager, but it can also be delegated to others on the HRD staff. That delegation must be made very cautiously, however, as the persons performing this function are, in essence, "ambassadors of HRD" to those within and outside the organization.

Maintaining relations is an experience in two-way communication. One line of communication involves keeping others informed of what the HRD unit is doing, its goals, and its frustrations. By means of the other line, the HRD unit tries to identify what others in the organization are doing and experiencing. Most of what goes on in an organization has implications for the HRD function, but not all of it appears in formal reports or management meetings, although these are good sources of information. More important is the constant, daily interaction between the members of the HRD unit and people in the other parts of the organization. Through these interactions, information is shared and relations are maintained.

There is not full agreement that the need for maintaining relations is part of the job of the HRD manager. In a study conducted to determine the relevancy of the role model presented in this book, all the subroles were accepted above the 50 percent level by the respondents except this one (Theodore, 1977). It is possible that this particular subrole (or function) was not considered important because it does not produce any direct or observable results. In most of our organizations we tend to reward results, not efforts. Obviously, managers will tend to do those things that produce observable and/or measurable results. But the task of maintaining relations involves intangibles that are almost impossible to quantify.

## Marketing and Selling

We can clearly see the importance of maintaining relations if we relate the effort to the field of marketing and selling. Generally, marketing involves image building, providing product knowledge, and attempting to increase product recognition. Marketing is not intended to produce any direct results. Results are sought through selling, which requires activities or behaviors that can be evaluated in terms of orders written and final sales produced. Perhaps an example from the pharmaceutical field will enable us to see the distinction. As noted earlier in another connection, that field uses so-called detailers who visit physicians' offices, explain or "detail" the products, and generally provide advice and information, as well as samples. Obviously, the detailer is not selling, for the physician is not the ultimate consumer. Selling is done by other employees of the pharmaceutical company, those who are in direct contact with the pharmacists who fill the prescriptions written by physicians.

Similarly, in HRD, maintaining relations is the marketing element of providing and receiving information. Thus, if the HRD function is to help managers solve problems, then marketing becomes crucial for HRD, but little or no selling will be needed. Many articles have been written on "How to Sell HRD to Managers." The authors assume that HRD is a product that must be touted rather than a service that will help managers solve problems. If the HRD manager asks, "How can I sell my managers on HRD?" that manager probably does not fully understand the contribution that HRD makes to problem solving in the organization. This does not mean that there is never a need to sell, and we will discuss that aspect later. But first, let us look at maintaining relations in terms of internal and external activities.

The major purpose of maintaining relations within the organization is to make the product (HRD services and programs) highly recognizable to all the employees in the organization. Of course, the main effort should be directed at bringing HRD to the attention of the decision makers at the upper-management levels. It is important that the HRD manager not wait until a crisis arises before marketing. Then it is too late. At a crisis point, everybody in the organization is not only "marketing" but is engaged in a variety of activities designed to ensure survival for their own units.

Marketing HRD is a matter of advertising the availability of the HRD unit to those parts of the organization that have not yet used its services, although this does not mean that those who have used the HRD services should be ignored. Selling HRD, as discussed earlier, is usually inappropriate. If the HRD unit is organized as a cost center, however, it may be necessary to do some "selling," since the HRD unit will be in competition with vendors. The vendors are selling, as well as marketing, and the HRD unit is in a competitive situation. Again, if the HRD unit is organized as a profit center, it is mandatory that there be a strong selling impetus, but it should be focused more on external than internal customers. Here, too, as in the cost center situation, selling may be required to overcome competition from vendors.

In both situations (cost and profit centers), however, the HRD unit has a strong edge. Managers usually utilize vendors only when they do not see their own HRD units as meeting their needs. Through constant contact with those managers (maintaining relations), the HRD people are in the enviable position of being able to immediately identify needs and to respond appropriately. Vendors recognize the need to market and do it in many ways; but since vendors are external to the organization, their marketing activities must be conducted from a distance. The HRD manager has the internal edge and should use it diligently.

When HRD is marketed and sold externally, it is in the same position as any other product or service that is available on the open market. It must compete with others and generally has only limited data on what is happening internally in the customers' organizations. The major effort will then be on selling, for it is sales that will be counted when the profit and loss statement is drawn up. However, there must be some marketing effort to assess what can be sold. Market surveys are helpful and frequently necessary, particularly to identify potential customers. Mailings and exhibits at various conferences and meetings are essential to keep the HRD offerings at a high recognition level.

### Maintaining Internal Relations

This activity begins by identifying the various groups within the organization with whom relations should be maintained. Although these groups will vary from one organization to another, some will be found in almost every organization. It can also be expected that some members of the organization will belong to more than one of the groups identified in this discussion. We will first identify some of the groups that the HRD manager should focus on. Then we will discuss how the HRD manager can do this and how he or she can use the HRD staff to help accomplish the tasks in this subrole.

The most numerous group are the *supervisors,* whom we define as those people who accomplish the mission of their unit through the efforts of others. They are concerned with solving immediate, day-to-day problems, and they are usually the people who make the decisions about who will attend an HRD training program.

The most obvious and perhaps most important group is composed of the *other managers* in the organization. They are the people who usually make the decisions about whether or not to use HRD. The concern of these managers is generally with problem solving and short-range planning. They are usually not overly concerned with the day-to-day operations of the people they supervise—the supervisors.

Some managers will be at the same level as the HRD manager, while others will be above that level. This group can go up to the highest level of the organization, though it is customary to consider people at that level *executives.* In most organizations, there is no clear-cut point at which a manager becomes an executive, but executives are generally those who supervise managers and are concerned with long-range problem solving and planning.

In addition to supervisors, managers, and executives, the HRD manager should maintain relations with *various work units.* When there is an organizational chart or diagram that lists the various departments and units, the HRD manager should note these and arrange to be in touch with them. If the HRD manager chooses not to engage in such activity with a particular unit, it should be the result of a carefully arrived at decision and not merely an oversight.

If the organization has a *union* (and some organizations may have several), the HRD manager should maintain relations with the union personnel. This includes the shop steward, who is an employee of the organization, as well as the regular union officials, who are external to the organization. Since the HRD manager is outside the bargaining unit and a part of management, this relationship must be handled cautiously. The HRD manager must avoid being drawn into the position of being for or against the union. That is not the issue here. Rather, it is a question of how the union relates to the HRD effort and the impact of HRD programs on the union members.

For a multisite organization, the HRD manager must consider *locations*. The several sites may be in the same city or spread through various parts of the world. It is easy to overlook those that are off the beaten track. This is done by too many staff members of multisite organizations. The HRD manager should identify all the locations and plan to have some contact with each of them periodically.

Within organizations there are various kinds of *special groups*. These usually start as temporary groups but can become permanent. At this time, for example, there is a proliferation of quality circles. Some of these have been in existence for several years, under other names, while some are new and reflect an increasing trend toward participative management. The HRD manager should maintain relations with these groups in addition to providing any of the normal servicing that they require. For example, the HRD unit may have provided training for the leader and group members of the quality circle. That is service, not maintaining relations.

Another way to look at people in the organization is in terms of *professional identification*. If there are engineers in the organization, they will be an identifiable group even though they may work in many different parts of the organization. The HRD manager should see them as a group with whom relations should be maintained.

There are also numerous groups outside the organization with whom the HRD manager should maintain relations. One major purpose here is to keep posted on what is happening outside the organization that relates to HRD. It is too easy to be trapped into focusing only inwardly. There is also a responsibility, professional if you will, to keep others informed as to what is going on in HRD within one's own organization. Of course, there are the usual constraints of keeping company secrets. By having good external relations, the HRD manager can also keep informed about what is happening in other companies and in the field as a whole.

## Strategies for Maintaining Relations

Having discussed the groups with whom the HRD manager should maintain relations, we will now consider some of the many ways that this can be done. Obviously, maintaining relations is a time-consuming activity. Generally, it is not possible for the HRD manager to carry out this function alone, and others on the HRD staff should be involved in it.

*Attending Meetings.* The complaint is heard, too frequently, that "we have too many meetings around here!" This may be so, but it is important that there be an HRD presence at as many of those meetings as possible. Hence, the HRD manager must be prepared to attend numerous meetings outside his or her own unit. The most frequent and visible meetings are staff meetings. These are not always limited to the staff of a particular unit, and the HRD manager can probably arrange to attend as an observer. The purpose, for the HRD manager, is not to talk about the HRD unit's activities, unless he or she is specifically invited to do so. Rather, the HRD manager should listen to what is being said and, if and when appropriate, follow up on what he or she has heard.

The HRD manager may also be invited to a staff meeting to give an overview of the HRD function and operations. Under such circumstances, the manager must avoid taking up an inordinate amount of time. HRD may not be uppermost in the minds of the attendees at that time. They do not want, or need, an in-depth approach to adult learning or a detailed explanation of how training programs are designed. The HRD manager should ascertain, beforehand, how much time is being allotted for the presentation at that particular staff meeting. Frequently, the manager is given only ten or fifteen minutes. While this represents a significant challenge, the presentation must be kept within the time guideline and, hence, must be very carefully prepared. There may not be a second chance. It is also helpful if the HRD manager can determine how HRD arose as an agenda item.

It is preferable that the HRD manager be given an invitation to attend staff meetings on a continuing basis. To accomplish this, the HRD manager may have to seek out the initial invitation. Frequently, this is done through some personal contact. If the invitation is extended to the HRD manager, then that person should attend. At some later time, it may be possible to have an HRD staff member replace the manager. Alternatively, an HRD staff member may receive an invitation because of some particular qualification that he possesses. He may be invited in by the administrative group because he has a background in accounting. The administrative group may feel, rightly or wrongly, that only a person with such a background will be able to understand what is going on in the meeting. In that situation, the HRD manager would be well advised to step aside and designate the invited staff member to attend.

When attendance at staff meetings is for maintaining relations, not assisting in problem solving, the HRD person must resist the temptation to speak or comment in any way. Merely being an observer is not easy for many of us engaged in HRD, as so much of what we do involves the give-and-take of discussion. Caution must also be exercised in note taking, lest the HRD person be perceived as "spying." When attending meetings, the HRD manager (or other staff member) must be prepared to accept a relatively passive role.

There are other kinds of meetings, such as those of professional and trade groups. It is relatively easy to obtain invitations to those meetings; indeed, it may only require the payment of a fee. But attending such meetings can also foster a false impression, unless one is careful. For example, one of the authors was working with an organization in developing learning programs. It was an organization that was heavily involved in agriculture. The author was invited by one of the people in the organization to attend a meeting that focused on an agricultural topic. The invitation was accepted, and a long evening was spent listening to speeches and discussion related to agriculture. A month later, the author was invited to join the organization! He responded by expressing appreciation for the opportunity but noting that his professional area was HRD, not agriculture. For several years after that, he continued to receive letters and fliers inviting him to become a member.

On the positive side, however, two benefits came from attending that meeting. The first was an increased acceptance of the author by some agriculturists in the organization. They did not expect him to become an agriculture expert, but they did appreciate his interest in their specific area. Second, he obtained some insights into their language and perceptions that aided him in understanding the organization and its people.

*Making Presentations.* This is essentially what is called "making speeches." But, while making these presentations, the HRD manager must be able to demonstrate an understanding of adults. Usually, the presentations will be made in external situations. There are many groups, both community and professional, that look to the HRD manager as an expert on a variety of topics. Most of these topics are related to HRD, but it is not uncommon for external people to call upon the HRD manager for presentations on other topics. Such presentations should be seen as opportunities to help others understand HRD.

*Writing Articles and Papers.* Good writing skills are among the essential competencies of an HRD manager. In addition to the usual accounts of activities that are expected of somebody in that position, there are certain kinds of writing that fall within the category of maintaining relations. For example, many organizations have internal publications called "house organs." These are usually for internal distribution, although some organizations make them available to the general public. The HRD manager should seek opportunities to write articles for the house organ. The articles should be on various aspects of the HRD function, how HRD contributes to individual and organizational growth, and so on. At times, of course, the articles can focus on specific needs. For example, an organization may have embarked on a project for raising the ethical standards of managers, increasing employment of minority groups within the organization, or establishing new goals for strategic planning. The HRD manager may be invited, or may solicit an invitation, to write an article for the house organ on how HRD could contribute to meeting that particular organizational goal.

It is also possible for the HRD unit to have its own publication. Such a publication must be planned very carefully, however, for very few other units in the organization will be engaged in internal publishing. The HRD publication should provide a service to the organization, while at the same time helping the HRD unit to maintain relations. For example:

> One of the authors was the HRD manager of a large multisite organization. The HRD staff was small and could not possibly reach all the sites. Hence, the unit initiated a peer-mediated learning approach for supervisors at the various sites. After being selected by their managers, the supervisors attended a one-week program designed to enable them to return to their own units and conduct the supervisory training program.
>
> As the program grew, it became apparent that some device to facilitate communication among the various sites was needed. A small newsletter was begun. Initially, it was used only for linkage and networking for this program, and distribution at first was limited to those who had completed the one-week workshop and their managers. But as others in the organization began to express an interest in the newsletter (for example, department heads), their names were added to the distribution list. The newsletter published the names of the supervisors who completed the program. Then, as the supervisors actually began conducting programs, this information was also written up, and the names of their managers and organizational units were mentioned. As had been expected, other managers queried the HRD manager as to how they could also participate in the program.
>
> In time, other items were added to the newsletter to provide a broader picture of the HRD function and how it could help managers solve problems, take advantage of opportunities, and meet their goals. Over time, the newsletter not only became a significant element for maintaining relations in that multisite organization but it also brought additional

requests to the HRD manager for contact and work
with the HRD unit.

HRD managers should also write articles for the professional journals and related publications in the field of HRD.
While some of those articles will be written to share what the
managers are doing or thinking with their professional peers, the
articles can also be used to maintain internal relations. Particularly in our society, something that has been published has validity
and a life of its own. Depending on the focal point of the article
and the publication in which it appeared, there are several possible
ways for the HRD manager to use it in maintaining relations. For
upper-level management, it is more impressive to send the
publication with the HRD manager's article clearly marked rather
than just a reprint. For others, a reprint may have to suffice. It is
preferable, however, that the reprint be from the publisher rather
than a photocopy of the article.

*Availability.* A key element in maintaining relations is that
the HRD manager be readily available to everybody in the
organization at all times, although this is by no means easy to
accomplish. The need to talk about HRD can arise spontaneously
during any number of activities that may involve quite diverse
members of the organization. Being told, "You must make an
appointment," may signal a lack of interest on the part of the
HRD manager. One way for the manager to make him- or herself
available is to identify the groups we discussed earlier in this
chapter and then find ways to meet with them informally. Some of
those groups consistently eat lunch in the same place, either inside
or outside the organization. The membership of these eating
groups is usually not limited, and the HRD manager should have
lunch with the different groups on some planned rotational basis.

In many organizations, the HRD manager is entitled to eat
in the executive dining room. That is fine, but it can also be a
trap. Eating in the executive dining room each day may be good
for the ego, but can be disastrous for maintaining relations with
other levels of management. Wherever, or with whomever, lunch is
eaten, the HRD manager must exercise another critical competency—listening. A good deal of the conversation will have

nothing to do with work. From time to time, however, something will be said that gives the HRD manager a clue about a problem. Also, the HRD manager will from time to time be asked, "What do you people do in this organization?" What an opportunity (but not to lecture)! The HRD manager should keep the response brief and helpful. One is reminded of the story of the child who asked a parent, "Where did I come from?" The parent, after careful consideration, began the story of the birds and the bees. When the parent paused for breath, the child broke in and said, "My friend Johnny came from New York—where did I come from?" The HRD manager should keep that story in mind when responding to questions in informal settings and avoid the temptation to respond to a simple question by conducting a short training session on HRD.

To be available, the HRD manager must get out from behind the desk. But this produces a conflict. Many HRD managers have worked hard to earn the large desk, carpeted office, and other amenities that go with their position. We certainly do not recommend that the HRD manager be content with a plank and cardboard filing cases near the boiler room. To maintain relations, however, the HRD manager must be familiar with the concept of the "territorial imperative" (Nadler, 1984a). A person's office, or work space, is that person's turf. The "owner" of that turf is essentially in charge of whatever happens there. Anybody who comes in is a visitor, not an equal.

For purposes of maintaining relations, the HRD manager must move out and become a visitor on other people's turf. This can range from the chief executive officer to those engaged in activities at the lowest level of the organization. Obviously, the nature and extent of those contacts will vary, but what is important is the contact itself. In modern parlance—get out and walk around. That is not as simple as it sounds. It requires an understanding of how one should dress in different parts of the organization. It also requires a sensitivity to appropriate behavior and language. The HRD manager should not try to imitate the behavior found in different parts of the organization but should know enough about those factors to avoid the gaffes that can get in the way of maintaining relations.

*Advisory Committees.* Most well-functioning HRD units rely on advisory committees. There may be one major advisory committee, and the HRD manager's relationship to that group will be as a participating member with specific responsibilities. Essentially, participation on that committee is not part of maintaining relations. But there are other groups and committees that are organized on an ad hoc or temporary basis. They may be related to specific programs or activities within the organization. Sometimes the HRD manager will have stated duties on those committees, whereas at other times the role will be that of observer. The HRD manager should play a passive, but not inactive, role. It is too easy for the manager to slowly take over the advisory committee, and that is its death knell. The committees should be seen as a way of keeping open lines of communication, with everybody on the committee functioning as equals. We all complain about the large number of committees that we have to serve on. This is a valid complaint; but, at present, serving on a committee is still one of the best ways to maintain relations, not only for the HRD manager but for other staff managers as well.

### Using HRD Staff

By this time, you are probably wondering how the HRD manager can find the time needed to maintain relations and still get the other work done. One alternative, as suggested by the Theodore (1977) study, is to ignore this subrole and do nothing about maintaining relations. A more positive alternative is to recognize that the HRD manager is not the only HRD person responsible for maintaining relations. Every HRD staff member should see maintaining relations with others in the organization as part of his or her job. The responsibility for this role lies with the HRD manager; but, as with other activities, delegation can be very effective. In fact, the HRD manager should see this activity as one that is amenable to delegation. How a staff member handles this delegation could be a good indication of the ability of that staff member to handle similar managerial functions.

There are many other positive reasons for delegating these functions. One of these is that it may keep others from seeing the

HRD unit as the private empire of the HRD manager. Through effective use of delegation, the HRD manager can communicate to other managers that what the HRD unit teaches about delegation in training sessions, the HRD manager actually practices.

*Competencies.* As with all delegation, however, the HRD manager must take into consideration the individuals and the situation (Engel, 1983). Various times, in this chapter, reference has been made to competencies such as speaking, writing, and listening. Before making any assignment or delegation, the HRD manager should be sure that the HRD staff member has the requisite competencies for the job. If not, perhaps some training is required and should be provided. Of course, those competencies have implications for other activities, not only for maintaining relations. It is also possible, through delegation of this subrole, to uncover previously unknown competencies in HRD staff members. There have been situations where a staff member has done some writing of a nonprofessional nature, and where it was obvious that writing abilities did exist. It took very little to encourage that staff member to use his skills to write for professional publications.

*Personality.* As personalities vary, so will the use of delegation. It is not suggested that the HRD manager administer personality tests or become overly involved in psychological analysis of staff members. But, over a period of time, the HRD manager should develop some understanding of the differences among the individual staff members in the unit. There may be extroverts who enjoy speaking to groups, who can think on their feet, and who like the challenge of responding to surprise questions. But there may be others in the unit who prefer to write articles or perhaps to write speeches that others will deliver.

There are also those staff members who have the need for well-defined tasks and who want their efforts to be evaluated in a clear-cut way. Such staff members will have difficulty in most of the activities related to maintaining relationships since those tasks are usually situational and not well defined. Maintaining relations is a continuous activity, and there may never be any closure. Given the nature of the activity (that is, marketing rather than selling), it is impossible to evaluate performance quantifiably. The HRD manager can establish some criteria, such as the number of articles to be written or the number of staff meetings to attend. Such criteria will satisfy those who need quantifiable feedback on their performance. Nevertheless, maintaining relations is and will remain essentially a qualitative function.

This does not mean that the HRD manager types each staff member and then allows him or her only congruent kinds of opportunities. But a manager's insensitivity to differences among staff members may cause them to avoid anything that is related to maintaining relations. Personality factors are also reflected in the "interests" of different staff members. Some prefer to work within the organization, where relationships are known, rather than in the outside world, where relationships can be confusing and vague. Some prefer working with small groups and can develop excellent rapport with such groups. Others may crave the large audience and the opportunity to make it laugh or empathize. The permutations of personality, interest, and opportunities are innumerable. An HRD manager must avoid projecting his or her own personality into the picture when delegating to others—and be prepared for changes and surprises when delegating an activity in the area of maintaining relations.

*Availability.* Important as it is, maintaining relations is not one of those activities with a high priority. Staff members may be very interested in this activity but must give more attention to the programs and operations of the HRD unit. It takes time and energy to engage in the activities described in this chapter. Obviously, the staff of the HRD unit has only a limited supply of those resources. Attending meetings, writing articles, and implementing all the activities described in this chapter would obviously cut down on the time and energy available for other HRD missions. The HRD manager must search for a balance among all these activities.

Maintaining relations should not be perceived as additional work. If that is the perception of the staff, the HRD manager can expect less availability and less productivity when staff are called upon to make speeches, write articles, and so on. These activities should be considered part of the regular work of the HRD unit with high, though unquantifiable, payoffs for all concerned. It is also true that there are various forms of staff availability:

A new HRD manager was hired from outside the state for the Department of Welfare in the commonwealth of Pennsylvania. Among his job duties was providing HRD services to ten medical and surgical hospitals, twenty-two mental hospitals, and various units in the department itself. Although it was not a political appointment, the HRD manager was subjected to political pressures. There were others in the state government in a similar position. Every payday, the local press would list their names and salaries with the comment that "those salaries could be going to good Pennsylvanians rather than to the carpetbaggers."

HRD headquarters were in Harrisburg, but some of the staff members were located in other parts of the state. Although the HRD manager visited with them individually in his travels around the state, he decided at one point to bring them together in Harrisburg for a staff meeting. A meeting was arranged for a Monday morning.

On that morning the Harrisburg staff arrived at 9:00 A.M. to get ready for the 10:00 A.M. meeting. At 10:00 A.M. the HRD manager entered the conference room, but nobody else was there. By 11:00 A.M. there were only two people there—the HRD manager and the one staff member stationed in Harrisburg. The HRD manager left the room and wandered through the building looking for the rest of the staff. They were found in the snack bar! The snack bar had small tables, holding no more than three people. The four field staff members were each sitting at different tables talking to one or two members from the headquarters staff.

As agreed, the HRD manager and all the staff met for lunch. During that time the HRD manager said that he would like to share a case study with them. Changing a few of the facts, he described what had happened that morning. He conjectured that he had gotten that reaction, in part, because he was a "carpetbagger." The staff readily saw the point being made and then explained the situation to the HRD manager. They were not resentful, quite the contrary. He was the first professional HRD manager they had ever worked for. Previously, they had all worked in Harrisburg and had rarely gotten out to the various sites around the state. When he was hired, the HRD manager had negotiated for a travel budget and for the provision that the HRD staff members could live in their home communities but travel in designated territories. Other units did not have similar travel budgets. The other managers in the Department of Welfare, at various levels, were sitting in Harrisburg and only communicating with the field by phone calls and letters.

Various managers had heard, through the informal communication network (the grapevine), that the HRD staff was coming into Harrisburg from the field. On Monday morning, they started calling the staff members and arranging to meet them on neutral ground—the snack bar. From 9:30 A.M. to 12:00 noon, the staff had been meeting with managers from different units. They were responding to questions as to what was going on out in the field as well as relaying questions and messages that the managers preferred to send informally.

In essence, the staff members were being asked to serve a necessary communication function. This provides an excellent example of how HRD staff members can maintain relations. A significant result of this activity was increased attention to the HRD unit. It began to receive more requests for assistance than it was able to handle with its limited staff. (The HRD manager was later asked to increase the staff and its functions.) The HRD unit continued the process for some time with alternate Monday mornings being kept open so that staff could be available at the snack bar. In the afternoons, the HRD unit held its staff meeting.

Another spin-off was that the HRD manager began using the snack bar for the same purpose. It meant drinking more coffee and eating more donuts than he wanted or needed, but his presence there on an irregular schedule successfully removed the "carpet-bagger" label.

## Conclusion

Maintaining relations is an important part of the work of an HRD manager. It sometimes receives too little attention for it is not quantifiable and there is no direct relationship between it and the productivity of the HRD unit. When maintaining relations, the HRD manager must avoid selling. It is easy to slip into that mode, but if that happens, the audience will react with the resistance one can expect from a sales pitch. Instead, the HRD manager must be involved in marketing the HRD unit and function. This requires a well-planned and well-implemented series of activities designed to keep all concerned constantly informed of what HRD is and how it contributes to meeting the goals and mission of the organization.

Maintaining relations involves both internal and external contacts. Internally, there are supervisors, other managers, executives, various work units, the union, different site personnel, special groups, and those with a professional identification. Employees can be expected to be members of more than one group. External groups will be dictated by the local situation.

The HRD manager can use several techniques to maintain relations, including attending meetings within the organization, making presentations, writing articles and professional papers, and serving on various committees. The HRD manager must be constantly available to all the individuals and groups within the organization. And the manager should be prepared to delegate some activities to others on the HRD staff. An effective program for maintaining relations will help many people recognize the contribution of HRD to the organization.

···{ *Chapter 10* }···

# Strategic, Long-Range, and Short-Range HRD Planning

$T$his chapter deals with the HRD manager's role in planning for HRD in the organization. This planning function might be called the cornerstone of HRD management. If planning does not precede implementation, there will be little chance of having effective or efficient HRD units, HRD learning programs, or other HRD services.

*Planning* became an important topic during the early 1980s, and numerous individual managers and management teams are now learning how to do sound planning. In public seminars and in learning sessions at professional and trade group conventions and regional conferences, managers are offered such planning topics as time management, strategic planning, functional planning, planning for technological change, employee career development planning, marketing planning, and the like. In addition, consulting firms now provide specialized consultation services on the planning process to assist individual managers and management groups.

The word *planning* conjures up a variety of activities. HRD managers do all kinds of planning for all kinds of different responsibility areas. They plan their own and their subordinates' work for the day, the week, the month, the year, or even years into the future. They plan for HRD staff allocations and utilization. They do the HRD budget planning. They plan for the acquisition, maintenance, and utilization of HRD facilities and equipment.

They plan learning activities, the HRD program, and schedules of delivery. And, most certainly, the effective HRD manager must plan for the future. All such management actions require a systematic approach to planning. In operationally defining the term *planning*, one is referring to a *process*. What results, in implementation, is the "plan."

As consultants to numerous HRD managers over the years, the authors have frequently heard, "I really don't do HRD planning as such, for it's our business to respond to the needs of our operating groups by providing the learning programs they want. Meeting their needs, not ours, is our plan!" "How can I plan for HRD when I'm not privy to the organization's strategic plans? The real strategic planning done here is what goes on in the chief executive officer's head!" "HRD planning? You've got to be kidding! The nature of our business is such that crisis management is the rule, not the exception, around here!" Unfortunately, such excuses for neglecting to plan for HRD have not only resulted in ineffective HRD programs but have also contributed to the ultimate demise of HRD units (or the departure of HRD managers) in such organizations.

Scheduling of HRD learning programs that do not meet the needs of the organization's mission, goals, or objectives is symptomatic of little or no HRD planning. Keeping up with what is on the "market" in the HRD field and budgeting for what is "new" seem to be the focus of such shortsighted HRD planning efforts. Many learning programs today are offered because they are currently popular, *not* because they are needed. Some of our readers will recall when many organizations' management development programs consisted of at least one segment (if not more) devoted to sensitivity training, to transactional analysis, or, more recently, to stress training. It seems that many individuals today believe they must have stress training. For some, as in the past with T-groups, such learning experiences have taken on a mystique all their own, with some graduates coming to wear a mantle of religious fervor: "You *must* enroll in stress training in order to be saved . . . from yourself, your job, your spouse, your boss!"

HRD practitioners have often been accused of being faddists. Unfortunately, it seems that some HRD managers' and HRD learning specialists' major planning interest focuses on what new learning schemes or packages can be purchased and conducted for the employees and managers of the organization. They tend to view their major management responsibility as that of being a broker of learning activities. They should be serving in the far more important roles of in-house HRD consultant and solver of production or personnel problems directly related to the actual needs of the organization. Such HRD managers seem not to recognize that the major focus of the HRD unit's mission should be its learning programs, that is, HRD activities designed to bring about changes in performance, to solve organizational performance problems, or to anticipate such problems and contribute to their solution in advance.

## Management Planning Mechanisms

A variety of new planning mechanisms and processes have had to be developed to cope with the turbulent technological, economic, and social changes that first surfaced during the 1960s. Halal (1983) points to the development of new "coping" mechanisms, including organizational development programs, consumer affairs departments, quality of work life efforts, public policy committees, future research studies, and issue management systems. However important these new developments have been in helping organizations adapt, the most comprehensive new management function designed to ensure corporate survival is a body of theory and practice known as *strategic planning*.

The unusual degree of complexity associated with organizational planning probably explains why the art of strategic planning is so poorly understood. It is almost incomprehensible to some managers. No wonder most executives still engage in the more traditional forms of planning and decision making rather than relying on strategic planning, which requires them to use a formal, systematic process and way of thinking. As Tracey (1981, p. 46) suggests, "Successful management of HRD . . . hinges on the development, articulation, and communication of several

different but closely related types of plans." There are three types
of management planning efforts common in organizations today.
They are *strategic planning, long-range planning,* and *functional*
(operational or short-term), *planning.*

Since there is little agreement on specific definitions for the
terms associated with organizational planning, let us make the
following operational definitions:

1.  Simply stated, *strategic planning* is the organization's road
    map to tomorrow. It is the process by which organizational
    planners make projections of where the enterprise wants to be
    at a given point *sometime in the future.*
2.  *Long-range planning* defines management's authority and
    responsibility for carrying out the tasks required to achieve the
    organization's objectives for at least one business cycle
    (usually a fiscal or calendar year). It describes the courses of
    action through which the organization will produce its
    products or services (accomplish its mission). And lastly, long-
    range planning determines how the organization's resources
    will be allocated to achieve its goals.
3.  *Functional planning* is used to direct the day-to-day opera-
    tions needed to implement and manage the activities required
    to accomplish the organization's goals and objectives as
    described in its strategic and long-range plans.

## Strategic Planning

Many HRD managers think that they are doing strategic
planning when, in fact, they are involved in long-range planning.
Unfortunately, the term *strategic planning* is used in many
different ways. Ben Tregoe and John Zimmerman suggest that
organizational management use strategic planning to determine
what "business" the organization should be in and what resources
are needed to be in that business—sometime in the future. A
strategic plan not only sets the organization on a firm and steady
course but also helps to maximize the use of its available resources
and to identify needed additional resources: financial resources

(capital), physical resources (plant and equipment), and human resources (people).

Strategic planning is today the key ingredient for *all* organizational planning. It forms the catalyst for long-range planning and is the basis for functional planning. Management experience has clearly shown that functional planning cannot be successful over any extended period of time without a strategic plan in place. Likewise, long-range planning efforts made without seriously considering functional plans become another management exercise in futility.

Strategic planning, although not actually recognized as such until recently, has always been a necessity. An organization's performance has always been the result of someone's good planning and execution. Very few organizations have become successful by relying on the management team's pure, dumb luck! But strategic planning is not only a necessity for growth. When an organization is faced with an unstable economy, restructured production and management environments that have created new products and new industries, or intense competition in world markets, that organization must do strategic planning to survive. Although strategic, long-range, and functional planning are separate management responsibilities, each is dependent on the other, and they must be carefully interwoven by management planners.

Strategic planning should be a way of doing business—all organizations that survive do it. It is the broadest type of planning conducted by an organization, whether small, midsize, or large. Strategic planning carves out the turf or scope of the enterprise. Strategic planning may result in a formal written plan or, in the case of smaller organizations, in an idea that exists only in the mind of the owner or manager. As an organization gets larger, a formal written strategic plan becomes a necessity, as more people need to be made aware of the organizational objectives so that they can do their jobs more effectively.

Unfortunately, there are a number of roadblocks to effective strategic planning. The following represent some of the more common and serious blocks to strategic planning found in organizations today (adapted from Hennecke, 1983a):

1.  *Too little involvement by top management.* Although strategic planning requires use of a participative method that involves all levels of management, the chief executive officer must provide the overall direction, parameters, scope, and statement of purpose for the strategic plan.

2.  *Too much emphasis on planning process.* Some management teams tend to be far more concerned with the techniques of planning than with efforts to inject real substance into their strategic plans.

3.  *Product and/or market myopia.* Because many managers are blinded by their successes with existing products, services, and markets, they avoid taking advantage of organizational growth opportunities. Strategic planners should always be forward looking and should not be restricted in their thinking by current organizational operations.

4.  *Too much numbers crunching.* Strategic planning sometimes gets blocked by financial managers and accountants who make it a static budgeting tool. Effective strategic planning requires creative risk takers who can bring forth new ideas and alternative courses of action.

5.  *Unfounded optimism.* Unfortunately, some management teams occasionally get carried away with their own creativity and optimism or fall prey to the phenomenon known as "group think." They tend to forget that "Murphy's Law" may prevail (that is, whatever can go wrong with a strategic plan, probably will!). A certain amount of guarded optimism, along with some carefully thought-out contingency plans, is always in order.

6.  *Too much emphasis on immediate payoffs.* Strategic planners must remember that the organization's functional, short-term planning should always be congruent with long-range goals and objectives.

7.  *Top management disunity.* Unfortunately, the same senior managers who can work in close harmony when making day-to-day operational decisions do not always agree when setting corporate strategy. Their unified statement of mission and purpose is mandatory if strategic planning is to work.

8. *Lack of management support.* Even when the senior management group is in agreement on strategic goals and objectives, their plans cannot be implemented without the cooperation and support of middle managers.

9. *Confusion between planning efforts.* Strategic planning is concerned with organizational direction, not how long it takes to accomplish a specific task. Some managers become confused about the focus of their functional and long-range planning efforts.

10. *Lack of faith in planning.* Some managers, very often even some HRD managers, believe that planning is a gross waste of their time. They feel that most organizational plans become obsolete as soon as they are published. In addition, some HRD managers can recall personal experiences in which their carefully thought-out strategic plans were "bought into" by senior management only to be ignored and/or go awry at the first sign of a downturn in the economy.

## Long-Range Planning

Long-range planning provides the organization with a blueprint for accomplishing its future goals, showing how it will get to where the strategic plan indicated that the organization should be. Unfortunately, few managers have psychic powers or clear enough crystal balls to be able to accurately foretell the future and make long-term predictions for their organizations. Long-range planning projections should be made for no further than three to five years ahead. Planning ahead for longer periods of time is dangerous because of all the unforeseen economic, social, market, political, and technological changes that can occur.

The organization's long-range plans are usually in the form of an overall statement of its mission, goals, and objectives, complete with resource (financial, physical, and human) requirements and other pertinent factors that may affect the organization's desired future growth and the nature of its "business." Such long-range planning projections are based on past performance, as well as on the management team's assumptions regarding future growth and business opportunities.

One should recognize that since the consequences of decisions based on long-range plans may not be felt for several years, it is difficult to determine if a long-range plan is progressing on target or if the results will be relevant to the actual conditions that will be found to exist five or more years later. Despite these shortcomings, however, a management team should not neglect to make long-range plans. In fact, it has little choice but to try to anticipate future changes, based on the best of available data. Members of the team must plan for the organization's future operations, taking all possible assumptions into account, and then be able to synchronize their short-term (functional) objectives and long-term goals into a cohesive, comprehensive organizational plan.

It is important to point out here that traditional long-range planning is often based on short-term plans—that is, the organization's planners plan to do more of what they are already doing successfully. Thus, in doing long-range planning, many HRD managers fall into the trap of unjustifiably projecting *present* realities and trends into the future. An organization cannot simply assume that its current products, services, or technologies will be the same tomorrow. As one senior corporate planner suggests, "Our long-range plan cannot commit tomorrow's resources and energies to securing yesterday's markets." At the same time, of course, long-range planning that does not consider the organization's current functional plans is an exercise in futility.

Effective long-range planning helps the organization to adapt to change. The future stability and growth of an organization, however, depend on its ability to accurately predict future changes in its customer base, technology, competition, the need for its products and services, government regulations, and many other critical variables. To be truly effective, long-range planning should be ongoing, not a one-shot effort. The plan must be continually updated as more reliable data become available. Such an effort gives managers an up-to-date early-warning system that will allow them to spot potential problems when they can still be resolved.

There are five basic characteristics of an effective long-range plan:

First, the plan identifies long-term goals (that is, exactly where the organization wants to go and what it wants to do or become at a future point in time as determined by the organization's strategic plan.

Second, the plan alerts managers to both opportunities and challenges that the organization will encounter long before they become realities. This encourages responses that will take advantage of those opportunities and minimize the risks associated with the identified challenges.

Third, the plan projects the organization's needs for financial, physical, and human resources in order to reduce the likelihood of overcommitting such resources to unprofitable actions.

Fourth, the plan develops alternative courses of action to achieve the organization's mission, goals, and objectives. The planning decision process encourages managers to seek the alternatives most feasible in light of the organization's limited resources, its strengths, and its weaknesses.

Fifth, the long-range planning effort provides the framework for periodic reviews so managers can measure progress and, when necessary, make the changes required to get the organization back on track.

To illustrate the use of long-range planning in HRD, let us cite some common examples:

1.  The HRD unit's instructional design staff will, by the first quarter of next year, redesign the current learning programs for entry-level job skills for manufacturing technicians using Computer-Assisted Instruction (CAI) as the primary instructional delivery medium in order to accommodate anticipated changes during the next two years in hiring patterns for new technicians and in manufacturing processes. The program will use individualized instruction strategies with computer-assisted instruction as a primary instructional delivery medium.

2.   During the coming year, the HRD unit will design and conduct an organizationwide employee learning needs survey to identify required training, education, and development activities, at a cost of not more than $ _____ , to be completed on or before _____ .

3.   Due to the planned expansion of the company during the next three years, the HRD unit will create at a cost of not more than $ _____ a new supervisors' and lead persons' on-the-job training skills program by the end of the current fiscal year. This program will be designed to improve their interpersonal skills in coaching and counseling newly hired employees.

### Functional Planning

Managers need to plan for the direction of their day-to-day operations. Effective functional planning is a line and staff manager's daily operational tool. The tasks required to accomplish organizational objectives are often stated in terms of quantifiable results and specific time frames. If the short-term goals and objectives can be set in quantitative terms—numbers of programs produced, participants served, earnings, costs, or sales figures—senior managers can determine on an ongoing basis how well the unit is progressing toward achieving established objectives and can evaluate the functional plan itself.

Functional planning also informs management what the unit's objectives are, what tasks and organizational resources are involved, who will carry them out, how they can best be accomplished, and the time frame required for completion. However, to implement functional plans, the HRD manager must have reliable, accurate, and timely data. Such data are usually based on forecasts, which in turn are based on past organizational or unit performance or past assessments of future requirements. In the case of HRD planning, for example, an in-depth analysis of the current year's HRD program activities and the data gathered and prioritized from a recent needs assessment will both be important ingredients of the HRD unit's data base when it develops functional plans for the coming year.

Some examples to illustrate HRD functional plans follow:

1. During the second quarter of the year, the assigned HRD unit learning specialist team, working with the appropriate subject matter experts from the manufacturing department and the new equipment vendor-supplier, will design, field test, and implement by the first quarter of the coming year a redesigned job-related, manufacturing technicians' entry-level and updating job skills learning program using individualized instruction strategies, with computer-assisted instruction as a primary instructional delivery medium.

2. The assigned HRD unit staff will on or before June 1 of the coming year consult with the management and union representatives of each of the organization's divisions and departments to identify the most efficient approach for the design of an organizationwide employee learning needs survey to be conducted during the last quarter of FY-____ .

3. The assigned learning specialist staff members of the HRD unit will by the end of the year have completed the instructional design work on the new supervisors' and lead persons' on-the-job training skills program, focusing on their needs for improved interpersonal skills in coaching and counseling newly hired employees. The new program will be designed, field tested, and ready for scheduling classes with members of the target population by January 1, 19____ .

### Preparing for the HRD Planning Process

There is no question that all HRD managers and their units can benefit from strategic planning. There are, however, many questions regarding what form HRD planning should take and how it should be done. In the 1960s when strategic planning was used almost exclusively by corporate giants, it was most often based on technical data generated by planning specialists using computer mathematical models and other complicated forecasting techniques. Strategic planning today has become far more practical and less complicated. The planning process is now usually carried out not by planning specialists but by an organization's managers, who are familiar with operational realities and procedures. Plans developed by managers generally represent more realistic reflections of the organization's strengths, weaknesses, and potentials than did the plans generated in the rapid-growth period of the 1960s.

HRD units that help their organizations to survive the 1980s will not be able to rely only on short-term plans that are implemented and performed on an annual fiscal or calendar year budget cycle. This type of HRD management planning typically begins with one- or two-year budget forecasts, followed by reviews, evaluations, changes, senior management briefings, and finally the chief executive officer's approval of the HRD unit's annual budget and functional plan. This type of planning gives little attention to, or direction for, long-range unit objectives. In organizations where this kind of planning process is employed, the HRD manager often feels that by the time the plan has been completed and approved, he must start the process all over again.

The concept of a rigid HRD management plan is outdated because HRD planning today must reflect the constantly evolving and fluid nature of the organization's business as it strives to cope with competition, as well as changes in technology, markets, and its product or service mix. An HRD unit's accomplishments and its strategic plans for the future cannot be summarized or synthesized in a static annual report. HRD strategic planning must be flexible and tailored to the organization's strategic plans and to its senior managers' leadership styles. It cannot be oriented toward the counting of HRD programs, numbers of participants served, and the like. Most certainly HRD managers should not be inhibited in their planning outlook by past performances or by presumably hard-and-fast rules that cannot be broken.

HRD strategic planning should always be a participative effort. While organizational leadership is provided by the senior management team and the organization's mission, goals, and objectives are provided by strategic, long-range, and functional plans, the HRD manager should retain the primary responsibility for HRD planning. However, the organization's line and staff managers who are the customers or clients of HRD programs should share responsibility for developing and implementing the HRD strategic plan, since the HRD program's business is to serve their needs, their work schedules, their priorities. This participative process of HRD strategic planning provides a realistic framework for future HRD programming and services. It also helps to ensure that there will be fewer surprises in the future. Some examples will illustrate the need for participation in HRD planning:

> The HRD director of a large department store in the Washington, D.C., area was responsible for human resource development of the employees of the downtown store and its eight suburban stores. Early in the first week of October, she was called into the office of her manager, the store operations vice-president, and asked to do a "little" training project before the first of the coming year. Beginning on January 2, 1976, in addition to the store's own customer charge cards, the stores would begin accepting Visa, MasterCard, and American Express charge cards. All sales employees would have to learn how to process each of the new charge cards. "Oh, by the way, each charge card system is handled differently," said the vice-president as the HRD manager left his office.

> This unplanned-for request for new HRD learning activities came at the most inopportune time of the year—the beginning of the biggest selling season of the year, the Christmas holiday season. The HRD manager was already scheduled to provide sales training for new part-time employees at all the stores. She now had just three months in which to design, schedule, and deliver a new learning program for a total of more than 1,500 full- and part-time employees. Needless to say, her short-term HRD plans had to be revised somewhat drastically.

> But what was most upsetting to her about this late request for an HRD activity was this: The management decision to accept the three additional charge cards had been reached in February of the previous year at a senior management planning

retreat. The credit policy to accept only store credit cards—a policy that had been in effect more than twenty-five years—was to be changed. Unfortunately, the HRD director was not invited to senior managers' planning retreats, and her manager, the vice-president of store operations, had not considered the effects of delaying to inform her about the decision.

The second example has a far different ending. In this case, the corporation's planning efforts involved all levels of the line and staff management team.

There were three HRD managers in a very large, major corporation operating in the mid-Atlantic region. Each of them had primary responsibility for HRD in a different operating division within the organization. The organizational planning process adopted by their corporation's senior management required a systematic step-by-step approach that began at the lowest level of management—the first-line supervisory team—continued on to the next level of management, and finally reached the senior management team. Then the planning process went back down through the levels of managers to the first-line supervisor again.

Each of the HRD managers conducted a one and one-half day off-site planning meeting with his program manager (first-line supervisor) to determine what the program managers believed would be realistic performance objectives for the HRD unit in question. The objectives were stated in terms of one year, three years, and five years—identifying not only what presently was, but also what was believed should be, the business direction of the respective units. The objectives were clearly defined, and the HRD manager and the program manager agreed that vague goals such as "growth" or "doing more of the same" were useless. Next, they identified what they believed to be the key factors that would determine the unit's success or failure. Most often, only a few major factors determined the unit's overall results, so the first-line supervisors planned strategies to implement or control their performance outcomes. Each unit listed one-, three-, and five-year plans with identified key determining factors (including estimated resource requirements, new business ventures, and the like). The units recommended planned implementation and control strategies that were then carried up by the HRD unit manager to the next level of management planning. In turn, the manager's peers and the immediate manager repeated the process in a two-day planning meeting for the division, taking into full account the recommended plans and strategies produced for the unit levels of the corporation.

The HRD managers' immediate supervisor, the divisional vice-president, then repeated the planning process in a week-long strategic planning meeting with the chief executive officer and other members of the senior management group. At the conclusion of this senior-level planning conference, each senior manager held meetings with subordinate managers, and they, in turn, held meetings with their subordinates to finalize each division's and unit's long-range and functional plans. In this company, every member of the management team was involved in the planning process and its unique bottom-up approach to strategic planning. The organization's senior management group saw value in eliciting its lower-level managers' planning ideas and implementation strategies.

The motivational aspects of the approach are obvious, as exemplified by the old Pennsylvania Dutch saying, "He who helps build a glass house is the last to throw stones at it!" If lower levels of management make direct inputs into the organization's strategic plan, quite naturally they will support it when the time comes to take action on behalf of the plan. The organization's senior managers recognized the fact that although the majority of lower-level managers tend to be somewhat conservative in their functional planning efforts, they can also be highly innovative when given opportunities to make inputs into the planning of the enterprise's future destination.

## Management by Objectives

Earlier attempts at improving the quality of organizational planning efforts have also found adherents. For example, during the 1960s and well into the 1970s, many executives and HRD managers became enthralled with the concepts and processes of management by objectives (MBO), which was first described by Drucker (1959). MBO provided a systematic means of obtaining the commitment of individual managers and their subordinates to accomplish specific performance results that would contribute to the organization's goals. The basic tenets of MBO included (Beck and Hillmar, 1972; Gregold, 1978; Drucker, 1971):

1.  Specific qualitative and quantitative performance objectives must be developed for each organizational unit and, ultimately, for each individual employed in the unit.
2.  Target plans for each unit and each employee must be developed jointly by the individual and his or her superior.
3.  The target plans of each employee and individual unit must be keyed to the organization's objectives.
4.  Each performance objective must have clearly defined performance indicators (measures of accomplishment), and commitment to accomplishment of the objective must be obtained.
5.  The objectives and indicators provide the basis for self-appraisal by the employee (or unit) and for reviews by the superior.
6.  The MBO concept recognizes that individual performance is best when the individual sets the objectives.

The process of developing "objectives" began by establishing a clearly defined mission statement for the organization or the HRD unit. The mission statement provided an operational definition of the business in which the organization was involved. The mission statement was proactive, in that it established direction and business parameters and offered opportunities for future growth and creativity. In other words, it was the forerunner of a strategic action plan. Not only did the mission statement describe what the organization was presently doing, it also projected what the organization would try to do in the future. The statement attempted to respond to such questions as, "Why does this unit exist?" "Whose needs should we be meeting?" "What resources must we manage in order to be effective?" The mission statement also described the unique and distinctive contribution that the unit or the individual employee should make to the accomplishment of the mission. The HRD manager first identified, with his or her manager, what the overall role of the HRD unit would be in helping the organization to achieve its long-range and short-term goals and objectives. The HRD manager's mission statement reflected the broad parameters of the unit's efforts, carving out both present and future business aims. Once refined and approved by senior management, the mission statement was disseminated to all members of the HRD staff to ensure that everyone understood it.

In addition, it was left to the HRD manager to specify the actual functions or major activities the HRD unit would carry out to support the unit's mission and goals. The HRD manager also described the major accountabilities of the HRD unit in broad functional statements. These statements most often included references to such HRD responsibilities as making HRD policy recommendations; assessing employee career training and development needs; designing and delivering learning programs; purchasing, scheduling, and maintaining dedicated HRD facilities and equipment; and assisting line managers with their responsibilities for human resource development.

These functional statements were couched in broad terms to identify the "what" of the operational activity areas of the HRD unit. From these functional statements, very specific key results statements were written describing what the unit or the individual was actually expected to produce or accomplish. The extent of success or failure to achieve the results (outputs) was determined by the performance measures (indicators) that identified the degree of accomplishment desired for each identified key result area. The term *key result area* denoted the importance of the specific activities. The key results of an HRD unit or of an HRD staff position were the critical reasons for the existence of the unit or the position.

***MBO Objectives Statements.*** The next step in the MBO process was to establish statements of objectives that would identify the specific efforts to be taken to maintain, improve, meet, or change the performance results of the individual key results areas of the HRD unit or the HRD staff position. The objectives statement described the what, when, how much, and estimated cost (in terms of effort and/or expense) of the action to be taken. The objectives statement also established a target date for completion. However, it did not indicate the how of the proposed action or who was to be involved in its accomplishment.

Two, and sometimes three, different types of MBO objectives were established in HRD units: long-term objectives, short-term objectives, and, in the case of the individual staff member, individual career development objectives.

***Long-Term Objectives.*** These objectives, which were stated in very broad and general terms, focused on a period of time stretching two to three years into the future. The long-term objectives stated the specific conditions that must be accomplished if the objective was to be considered successful. For example:

1.  Within the next two years, to have two qualified candidates from within the current HRD staff from whom to choose in making appointments to HRD program manager positions.
2.  To improve the capability to accomplish primary HRD functional responsibilities within the present staffing and budget allocations, to conduct a cost-benefit analysis on all HRD activities within the next two years, and to determine which HRD programs can be eliminated.

*Short-Term Objectives.* These objectives provided the measurable end results to be achieved within a given period of time, usually up to one year. The short-term objectives were stated in very specific terms; each statement began with an action verb and identified a single, specific end result, a due date, and a cost estimate:

1. To increase the HRD unit's internal consultation services to the operating units by 15 percent in the next fiscal year, within established budget and current staffing allocations.
2. To develop a new computer-based basic mathematics skills learning module for entry-level engineering technicians, meeting the HRD department's established instructional design criteria, within the next nine months, not to exceed 500 work hours and $3,500 support expense.

*Individual Career Development Objectives.* Recognizing the importance of human resource development for the HRD staff, some HRD managers encouraged staff members to identify their continuing professional education needs as an integral part of the MBO process. For example:

1. To increase my skills and knowledge as an HRD learning specialist, I will enroll as a master's degree candidate in HRD on a part-time basis at the local university and will complete the degree requirement by _____ by using the company-approved tuition reimbursement plan.
2. To participate in the National Society for Performance and Instruction (NSPI) annual conference in San Francisco from April ____ to ____ , 19____ , at a total cost of no more than $ ____ for registration, hotel, and transportation.

*Indicators.* The indicators were the significant measures that an HRD manager monitored to determine whether progress was being made (or if problems were being encountered) within a particular key result (an HRD unit's or a staff member's individual major accountability). For example, an indicator of success in an HRD learning specialist area might be the completion of a specific phase of an instructional design project within a given time period. Indicators, when identified, help to determine if an objective needs to be established to improve or to accomplish the key result. Using the example of the instructional design project again, an indicator might be the accomplishment of 60 percent of the project during the first quarter of the coming calendar year. Other examples might include computer-based training instructional frames produced per work hour, staff turnover, employee absenteeism, customer complaints, or failures to meet deadlines.

*Action Plans.* The action plan consisted of the activities undertaken to accomplish specific objectives. Plans set forth milestones (a time schedule) for achieving the objective and for assigning individual responsibility. Action plans were to be directly related to the key result area concerned and described the how of the specific objective by detailing the specific activities undertaken for its accomplishment.

*MBO Review Sessions.* The single most important part of the MBO process in terms of encouraging the concept of participative management was the review sessions. The primary purpose of these frequent meetings between the HRD manager and his or her immediate superior or between the manager and a subordinate was to discuss their performance with regard to the key result areas of their jobs, to identify any problems they had encountered, and to focus on the accomplishment of results.

During their MBO review session meetings, the superior and subordinate would strive to agree on what the subordinate had yet to do to accomplish the previously planned key result actions. These review sessions also reflected both the superior's and the subordinate's degree of enthusiasm, commitment, and involvement in the participative management process.

The review sessions were important in encouraging two-way communication. If the subordinate required the superior's assistance, needed additional resources to accomplish his or her key result activity, or had encountered difficulties in accomplishing a particular key result objective, the review session could be most helpful in communicating these needs to the superior. The session also provided an effective mechanism for communicating

the need to change or amend a previously agreed on key result
action or performance indicator.

In many ways, the processes used in implementing MBO in
the 1960s and 1970s are applicable today to the implementation of
strategic planning efforts in organizations. Without good communication and a commitment to achieve that is shared by all the
players, the organization's strategic plans become difficult, if not
impossible, to either implement or accomplish.

### HRD Goals and Objectives Setting

The HRD manager must have access to an extensive
internal and external data base related to the many different forces
that can impact either positively or negatively on the HRD
program operations. Good analysis of the following kind of data
by the HRD manager is mandatory:

1. The organization's strategic plans, goals, and objectives. As
   Tracey (1984) suggests, HRD programs must be based on the
   enterprise's goals, objectives, and plans if they are to be
   effective.
2. Projected changes in the organization's future operations, new
   products, new services, market penetration, demographics of
   its client-customer base, and new organizational output
   procedures and techniques, many brought about by advances
   in technology. All such changes will have impact on managing the HRD function and upon HRD activities and their
   delivery.
3. Federal, state, and local laws and regulations that affect
   human resources management and HRD.

### Conclusion

Planning is the cornerstone of an HRD unit. Without
effective proactive planning by the HRD manager, the HRD
activities, programs, and services will be managed by others.
Fortunately, many HRD managers have become skillful in using
effective strategic planning techniques and processes. They are no

longer managing their HRD units using the "no-win" reactive modes of the past. Their HRD plans are directed toward fulfilling the goals and mission of the organization they serve.

The key result activities of the well-managed HRD unit focus on helping to resolve problems of productivity through well-designed and implemented learning programs. In addition, the HRD units assist the organization in exploiting its growth opportunities by providing both direct and consultative support services to the line and other staff managers in the development of their human resources.

··˧ *Chapter 11* ꜱ···

# Supervising Programs and Staff

$S$upervision is necessary to bring the whole HRD program effort together and make it work. The items discussed in this chapter often consume a significant amount of the time of the HRD manager. But if the HRD unit is well staffed, some or all of these functions can be assigned or delegated to others. This will leave the HRD manager less encumbered and therefore able to take a broader view of his or her responsibilities. It will allow him or her more time to be involved formulating policy, maintaining relations, and working with organization leaders in other areas of human resources. Generally, however, the HRD manager will be performing at least some of the tasks discussed in this chapter.

## Scheduling

Formal learning, which makes up the bulk of HRD activities, requires the utilization of various resources, including such resources as space, staff, and equipment. Great care must be taken so that all needed resources converge in the learning situation at the appropriate time and in appropriate amounts. Some HRD managers have said that they come to feel like air traffic controllers. There are airplanes getting ready to take off (HRD courses ready to start); there are airplanes in the air (courses in progress); and airplanes getting ready to land (courses nearing conclusion). There are airplanes being worked on for maintenance (courses being designed or redesigned); there are people waiting for passengers (supervisors waiting for learners to return to the work site)—and the analogy could continue. The result, for HRD managers, much as with air controllers, is an inordinate amount of tension and pressure to meet the expectations and needs of others. Fortunately, the analogy does not continue into the life and death area, although HRD can be a factor in the survival of an organization.

*Notification.* The selection of learners should be the responsibility of the line supervisor. In some organizations, however, employees can self-select (or at least self-nominate) themselves to attend HRD courses. This form of voluntary learning is highly desirable; and, presumably, instructors need not be concerned about the motivation of such learners. Unfortunately, however, it is not always possible to determine the reasons for self-selection. They may be entirely appropriate ones, or individuals may simply want to get away from their work situations or their supervisors. In the majority of cases, however, the employee will be directed by the supervisor to attend a particular course. This directive should not come as a surprise to the employee. There should have been prior discussion between the supervisor and the trainee about the existing problem and the need for the course, if it is a question of training. If the course is for education, then they should have discussed it in terms of the career development of the employee. It could be for the individual's personal development, but that will more commonly be the case when it is a matter of self-selection.

Since the employee was selected by the supervisor, that supervisor must be in the loop for notification. The notification should be sent in sufficient time so that both the supervisor and the employee can plan ahead. When there is no formal notification process, it is not uncommon for the employee to be informed on the day preceding the opening of the course. This does not allow for the physical and psychological preparation required for effective learning. Climate setting is important in learning, and a short lead time in notification contributes to setting a negative climate.

The content of the notification will vary in each situation, but there are some general elements that are essential.

First, the title of the course should be given. Recognize, however, that titles alone do not always communicate much. Therefore, information should be provided about the objectives and content of the course.

Second, the employee should know why the course is being offered to him or her—and why it is being offered at that time. This focuses on whether it is training, education, or development for the particular employee.

Third, some courses require that work be done by the learner before the courses begin. The most frequent type of such work is reading a text or completing a review of other written material. The readings might include the organization's policy manual, position papers from leaders in the field, or reports of recent research. Not all prework involves reading. There could be a self-administered questionnaire or some other instrument that would enable the employee to look at his or her own behavior, performance, values, and so on. There are a wide variety of prework possibilities that can enhance and facilitate learning. But the learner needs sufficient lead time to build the prework into his or her regular work schedule.

Fourth, the learner and supervisor should be provided with exact details about when the course will start and when it will end. The course may involve a block of time—say, three consecutive days—or it may be spaced over a period of several weeks. The place where the course will be offered may be internal or external and should be specifically designated.

Fifth, if the venue is internal, there will be logistical concerns such as a place to have lunch, a specific contact person, and so on. When the venue is external, the situation becomes even more complicated. Provisions may have to be made for travel. If the learner is driving, parking can be a significant problem. The company regulations on travel and reimbursement should be made explicit. It is also helpful to include information on appropriate dress, social activities, emergency contacts, and similar items.

Sixth, while what the individual learns is crucial, we should never forget that the organization is paying for what that learning will produce. The notification should be as specific as possible about learning and performance expectations and about follow-up after the course. What form of evaluation can be expected? When will it be done? Who has the responsibility for it?

Notification, then, is more than just a matter of sending out a brief memo. Good notification communicates the interest of the HRD unit in the learner as well as in the course.

The form of the notification is also important. In a large HRD program, it may seem impossible to send out individual notices to each learner for each course. But it only requires a simple computer program to produce letters that are personally addressed to each learner. That should be the minimum. Beyond that, it is also possible to provide each learner with information, such as the items just discussed, that relates specifically to him or her.

The way the notification is delivered will almost certainly vary. But upper-level managers tend to expect some informal contact through a visit or phone call before the selection of employees is made. In fact, if there has not been any prior contact, they may not give much importance to the notification. Attention must also be paid to the sensitivity of supervisors. Some supervisors resent any notifications to their employees that have not gone through them. This may seem unreasonable when the supervisor has selected the employee who will attend, but logic is not the point. Rather, the HRD manager must understand the style and desires of the supervisor and conform to them, unless there are some overriding reasons not to do so. If there are such reasons, they should be discussed with the supervisor prior to notification.

In some organizations, lists are posted on unit bulletin boards giving the names and courses for selected employees. This of course, requires much less work than the notification process that we have been discussing, but it is also much less effective in establishing a good learning climate. If possible, HRD managers should avoid notification in that impersonal fashion regardless of how much time and energy it would save them.

Let us turn to the self-selected learner—the employee who volunteers to attend an HRD course. This is not unusual in an organization whose HRD unit publishes course lists and catalogues or posts courses that are available internally or externally. The approval of the supervisor might be required, but that is by no means always the case. If the HRD operation and policy in the organization support self-selection, then notification must follow the same process as in the case of those who are selected by supervisors. If possible, however, there should have been some prior discussion between the supervisor and the employee.

*Timing of Courses.* Generally, in HRD units there are several courses in operation at any given time. Thus, special efforts to plan and coordinate their timing and sequence are required. The number of courses that can be offered will be a reflection of the resources available to the HRD unit and the philosophy of the HRD manager. Organization policy will also play a part. The policy may be that the major portion of the HRD offerings should be staffed by in-house people. The HRD manager may be limited to using only the people on the HRD staff, or there may be a provision for utilizing line personnel. If the budget and policy allow for the use of external resources, the timing and sequence of courses will have to be coordinated with procurement.

Whenever possible, courses should be offered as needed. Realistically, this cannot always be done when group instruction is involved. For budgetary reasons, a minimum number of participants may be required to make the course cost effective. The challenge to the HRD manager is to offer the course as close to the time of need as possible. The timing factor has contributed to increasing emphasis on individualized learning. The goal here is to offer the course at the time the employee needs it, in an individual learning mode. This generally means using the computer or some similar delivery method that allows a person to learn on his or her own. There are those who contend that even interpersonal behavior can be learned alone, while others take the position that to learn interpersonal behavior the learner must interact with other people. The position of the HRD manager on this point will govern what topics are offered for individuals.

There are still many organizations that offer HRD in the same way that colleges and universities do. For example, McDonald's has its Hamburger University for its franchises, as well as its employees. It is run like a college, and the company has found that method to work well, given the learners and the subject matter. Regular courses are offered, since that has proven to be an extremely efficient way to handle the large groups that are involved. When an organization has a small number of employees, or less turnover than in a fast-food operation, the appropriate timing of courses may not be so readily ascertainable.

The days or months during which courses should be offered must reflect the living cycle of the organization. A retail establishment should probably not offer a large number of courses before holidays such as Easter and Christmas. But almost every organization has times that are better or worse than others for offering courses. A mark of the efficient HRD manager is to know those times. In a large organization, there may be a variety of appropriate times for courses, depending on the work of each unit or department. In a small organization, such opportunities will tend to be fewer in number. A small organization has to make more compromises and cannot allow for too many differences among units.

*Sequence of Courses.* A program is made up of a group of courses. The sequencing and relationship of the various courses should be evident to all who are interested in taking the program. The optimum situation is to be able to follow the stipulated sequence, but it may be necessary to vary it, depending on the individuals who are enrolled. A new employee, at any level, can be expected to have had prior learning experiences. These may put the employee out of phase with the sequence being offered. It is easy to have a policy that says that everybody must go through the same sequence, but that can prove unnecessarily costly and engender negative feelings in the learners and their supervisors. The sequence should be determined by the appropriate person or group in the HRD unit, after appropriate consultation. Provision should be made, however, for individual differences.

*Consulting Services.* In addition to scheduling courses, the HRD manager must also schedule the consulting activities of the HRD unit. We are assuming, of course, that the HRD unit includes staff who have the necessary consulting competencies. Scheduling consulting activity is much more difficult than scheduling courses. It is possible to anticipate the learning needs of individuals based on factors such as career development plans, introduction of new equipment, changes in technology, and similar identifiable needs. But much of consulting in HRD is centered on problems that require fairly rapid solutions. Consulting also involves much more personal relationships than does offering a course. When a course is offered, the learner is usually prepared to accept whichever facilitator shows up. It would be a very rare case where a learner would refuse to attend a course because of the facilitator. By contrast, in consulting, the personal rapport between the consultant and client is a crucial element. When scheduling internal consultants, the HRD manager must weigh a variety of factors, but the most critical one is the anticipated relationship between the manager-client and the consultant.

If these two have had a prior relationship, it is fairly easy for the HRD manager to build on that or to decide that they are not compatible. When there has not been a prior relationship, the HRD manager has to closely examine the competencies, personalities, and styles of the consultants on the HRD staff to determine which one can be most effective with the particular manager who is seeking assistance. The HRD manager's choice is complicated when HRD staff members function as both facilitators and consultants, which is not unusual. The HRD manager can easily be tempted to reassign a consultant, who is functioning as a facilitator, out of a course in progress in order to respond to the need of a manager. But this is hardly fair to the learners in the class. Assigning a new facilitator, after a course has started, can be detrimental to the learning situation and should be done only when absolutely necessary. To complicate the situation further, the HRD manager must consider how necessary it is to respond to a manager's request at a particular time. How will a delay affect the problem and the relationship with that manager-client? The responses to these questions are what sometimes causes the HRD manager to seek external consulting resources.

### Preparing to Offer Courses

Learners come to the classroom and find that everything is in place. The seats are arranged in an orderly fashion, the air conditioning is set just right, and all the lights are working. The needed materials and equipment are in place. Indeed, it looks as though someone has been very busy establishing the appropriate physical climate for learning. Obviously, the work was done by the staff of the HRD unit. They were assigned, by the HRD manager, to make sure that all the logistics were planned and delivered. Some of the work was accomplished by clerical or paraprofessional workers. But the final check must be done by a professional staff member, usually by the supervisor of that program or by the facilitator who will conduct the course.

## Review of Courses

An essential element of preparation is the constant review of courses being offered by the HRD unit. Some courses will be the direct responsibility of a supervisor within the HRD unit, while others may be provided by external sources, through contracting. In both situations, someone must be designated as the "supervisor." In a small organization, with few in-house courses, the review process is relatively easy. It would be helpful to have a monthly review, but it may not be necessary to go through the process that frequently. If a large number of courses are being offered, however, it is desirable and even necessary to have at least monthly reviews. The scheduling of courses will have to be reviewed carefully and often, particularly if there is limited classroom space. The review may reveal the immediate need to obtain some temporary space or to begin to plan for more permanent space.

The equipment required for HRD has become a major concern, and many allow themselves to get swept up into current fads. New instructional technology is of course important for learning, but there must be a balance. There are the old standbys such as overhead projectors and 16-mm movie projectors. Video, in some form, has also become standard, although the kinds of video systems in use have been changing. The computer is fast reaching the point of becoming a standard piece of equipment, but we will have to await further developments before its actual position can be assessed. During a review session, the HRD manager should have the staff analyze newly marketed equipment in light of present and anticipated needs. This can also lead to an in-depth exploration of the utilization of instructional equipment and examination of other equipment that might be desirable.

The review should cover more than just logistics. Courses will be in various stages of development or implementation. Everybody on the staff, including the nonprofessionals, should be kept up-to-date on the progress of those activities. The mistake is often made of thinking that in cases where the staff is small, there is no need for formal review. But situations can arise where there is overlap and even conflict among the duties of staff members. Another reason for review is to make sure that each course has at least one identified person who is responsible for it. It is not expected that the person so designated will actually arrange the room or provide the ice water and markers; rather, that person is responsible for seeing that such things get done. Many organizations develop logistic checklists on the basis of checklists that can be found in the literature (Margolis and Bell, 1985).

The HRD manager should use these review sessions to look at the operations of the unit. Are there activities that can be improved upon? How do the activities that are conducted relate to the competencies of the various staff members? Are there new challenges that can be used to help staff members grow? A very busy HRD unit can readily become so involved in meeting deadlines and delivering courses that it loses the broad view. It is up to the HRD manager to provide the bigger picture that goes beyond everyday problems and concerns.

### Procurement of Resources

Whether an HRD program is internal or external, at some point there will be a need for procurement activities, which consist of identifying the need for a resource and the possible ways of obtaining it, contracting for the resource, overseeing (supervising) its use, and, finally, evaluating how it was used. The resource will generally be a product or service. It may be used for a single course, a part of a program, or an entire program. There are some resources that can be used for several programs. These will generally be in the area of equipment and materials and were discussed elsewhere as part of the facilities required for HRD. The focus here is on personnel or off-the-shelf programs.

*Identifying the Need.* The process starts with the identification of a need, particularly one that cannot be met directly by the resources of the HRD unit. A common need is for facilitators-instructors, particularly if the HRD manager has adopted the policy of limiting the number of HRD staff in the subrole of facilitator. In other words, the manager has decided to have the HRD staff do as little direct instruction as possible but instead to provide other HRD services. The increasing emphasis on utilizing various kinds of technology in learning situations has also created needs that cannot all be met directly by HRD staff. Again, the need for consultants varies, and the HRD manager may not be able to satisfy all those requests at any given time.

Some needs for particular kinds of HRD people can be readily identified and planned for. Other needs arise with little or no notice. An unanticipated problem may produce the immediate need for a consultant, and one may not be available from the HRD staff at that time. Or a problem may require a facilitator with competency in a subject matter outside the ken of the HRD staff. Specialized types of instructional strategies (devices, aids) may be needed that are not currently available within the HRD unit. The need must be established carefully. The HRD manager must determine if it is a "one-shot" or an ongoing need. That determination will influence the steps that follow.

*Identifying the Resource.* From here on, there will be a separate discussion of internal and external procurement. An internal resource is one that can be obtained from within the organization, while an external resource is obtained from an outside vendor who sells a product or service. We made the following point earlier but feel the need to emphasize it here. It is unfortunate that it is so common to use the word *consultant* when referring to an external resource. This is fallacious for two reasons. First, there are internal people who are also consultants. Second, the external people may merely be providing a facilitator or a packaged program, not doing consulting. Therefore, we will use the word *vendor* for those external people.

The identification of internal resources can be difficult, as few organizations have a catalogue that lists persons with the competencies that might be required on the HRD staff. The process of identifying internal resources requires the HRD manager to discuss this with the HRD staff who meet and work with people from many parts of the organization. The most commonly used internal resources are the subject matter experts. They are people who know what has to be learned in order for an employee to perform. (Note that subject matter experts are not expected to know how to organize material so that it can be taught and learned. That is the function of the designer.) The HRD manager cannot possibly find all the needed subject matter expertise within the HRD unit. Hence, unless subject matter experts are used, there will be severe limits to the kinds of programs that can be offered by the HRD unit. But the utilization of experts should not be confused with the increasing trend for line units to provide their own facilitators. Facilitators and subject matter experts represent two different kinds of resources.

The use of external resources may be governed by policy and culture in an organization. There are still organizations in which the feeling exists that external people cannot function as effectively as those who have grown up within the organization. This may still be true for certain subject matter areas, but it is becoming less so. Even the Type Z organization (Ouchi, 1981) must sometimes procure external HRD resources.

A major difficulty faced by the HRD manager is to identify those vendors who can meet his needs. One approach is to develop a network of other professional HRD people to whom he can turn. The HRD manager, faced with a need, can contact another HRD manager and seek advice and assistance in identifying a resource. This has the added advantage of enabling the manager to obtain information about vendors that is not available in the brochures that come in the mail every day. (Brochures, by the way, present their own problems. Some HRD managers keep these brochures and consult them when a resource is needed. That sounds like a good idea, but few managers have found a way to file that information so that it is readily retrievable. This has led to another external resource, a publication titled *The Trainer's Resource,*

1985, which is a listing of packaged programs organized in a retrievable form.)

Universities and colleges have long been an external resource. They do not advertise as frequently or as consistently as other vendors, though this has begun to change as these institutions have come to recognize the vast market available to them. The HRD manager is no longer surprised to receive brochures from these institutions, as vendors, or to see them mount exhibitions at various conferences and meetings.

There are many printed guides, but two deserve some special mention. ASTD and *Training* magazine publish annual guides to the marketplace. To be listed, a vendor must submit information in the prescribed form and sometimes is required to pay for the listing. The policy of these publications is always subject to change, so it is not possible to say how a vendor gets listed, except to note that neither publisher screens the listing. There is no known method at this time to generally evaluate the performance of a vendor prior to listing.

Not all external resources are brought in-house. There are innumerable public seminars available, and there are times when it is more cost effective to send an employee to one of those. In some organizations, the HRD unit is called upon to approve requests for attendance at public seminars or conferences. This is generally the case when the budget is in the hands of the HRD unit, as in a budget item center. When the budget is under the control of the line manager, the HRD unit may be bypassed. This is unfortunate, for in many cases the HRD manager could give valuable advice about those seminars.

*Contracting.* When the resources used are internal, there is usually no need to sign a formal contract. Despite this, steps should be taken to ensure that all parties concerned recognize the obligations and expectations implied. A manager may assign a lead employee to be a facilitator for a specific course. There should be agreement on preparation time, actual class hours, and any follow-up time that is needed. Also, how is this to be billed? In some organizations, there is no financial implication when an HRD manager obtains the services of a line person. In other organizations, this requires either a requisition or some kind of paper formalizing the relationship. It can also mean that the HRD unit is to be billed for the time the line person is away from his or her regular job doing HRD work.

In government organizations, resources cannot be obtained without stipulated paperwork. This is also the practice in some private sector organizations, while others rely on a more informal method. Most written contracts contain a section that describes the scope of the work to be done in terms of tasks or outcomes, though some contracts for services cannot be made that specific. It is important that both sides, the HRD manager and the vendor, reach as complete an agreement as possible, although this may require considerable perseverance and they may end up simply agreeing not to agree.

An HRD manager related the following:

> I received a phone call from one of our operating units seeking my help in obtaining an external resource person who could handle a session for them using the nominal group technique (NGT). Naturally, I asked for more details. That particular part of our organization was concerned with cost containment and peer review in hospitals. Its members were planning a two-day workshop during which a group of selected physicians would review the data. They would then call upon an external resource to assist them in prioritizing the medical list, using the NGT.
>
> I accepted their decision to go outside the organization, though I think we could have handled it through our unit. As we discussed their need, it became clear that their objective was, on the third day, to have the physicians assign priorities to the items they had been discussing the previous two days. When I asked why they had selected the NGT, I was told that one of the physicians on the planning committee had been in a workshop several years earlier where the NGT was used. He thought it was great. He wanted to use it in this situation.

I questioned whether that was the best technique to use, and when he insisted on it I contacted a professional I knew (let's call him Smith) to see if he was interested. He was willing to explore it. The planning committee notified me that it wanted to talk directly to Smith, so the balance of this story is his.

Smith told them that he did not want to be locked into that technique until there had been further mutual exploration. If they insisted on using NGT, he was prepared to provide the names of others who would do that. They finished the conversation with him with the usual statement, "We will be in touch with you."

Several weeks went by, and Smith did not hear anything. Then he received a call from another member of the planning committee, who said that the committee liked his approach and would be interested in exploring it further. Smith then got back to me, and we were able to set up a meeting where he and I described other ways of helping the group prioritize the material. Agreement was reached on using a different technique (a modified Delphi), and the planning committee was now satisfied. It then asked me to handle the contracting for Smith's services.

If a contract concerns a product, it is fairly easy to stipulate exactly what that product will be. If it is a packaged program, there will be a title or code number that specifically identifies it, but the HRD manager must still exercise caution. It is not uncommon for vendors to change the contents of a package. There is nothing wrong or immoral about that practice. Rather, new materials are constantly being developed and old ones modified and improved. But while the new product may be better in the eyes of the vendor, it may not be seen the same way by the HRD manager, who had contracted for the product previously reviewed.

HRD managers can also contract for a combination package that includes both a product and a service. There are programs that offer a product but require that the facilitator be certified by the vendor. This is the case with the managerial grid, the KTA problem-solving program, and others. In developing the contract, the HRD manager must be sure that there are internal resources that can be linked to the external resource. Although this would probably have been explored earlier, it must be made specific at the time of contracting. The contract might even include the names of the internal people who are to be trained by the vendor.

When an employee will be attending a public seminar or conference, the title and dates make the scope of work explicit. As part of the procurement, the HRD manager may also have to obtain details about travel, accommodations, and any extra charges that might arise. Organizations that utilize public seminars and conferences generally have guidelines for handling the costs. In each case, however, the guidelines should be reviewed to see if they are still pertinent to the particular situation.

*Supervision of the Contract.* The responsibility of the HRD manager does not end with awarding the contract or making an oral agreement. When dealing with a product, the HRD manager must determine if the product contracted for has actually been received. Usually this task will be delegated to others in the HRD unit. For example, if it is merely a question of counting books, that would be a poor use of the HRD manager's time. But it may be necessary to review the content of the books, particularly if they have been written or modified for this particular organization. This professional task should either be done by the HRD manager or assigned to an HRD staff member with the competency to render a professional judgment.

A contract for services requires professional supervision. It is not sufficient to contract for the service and then go on to something else. The HRD manager has the responsibility of verifying that the appropriate professional service has actually been performed. In large organizations, where contracting for services is the general practice, there will probably be HRD staff members who devote a good deal of their time and energy to supervising the performance of contracts. Supervising a contract for services requires time and tact. The vendor may be a "big name" in the field. The HRD manager may feel inadequate to supervise that vendor, but must do so nevertheless, since he or she is responsible for performance under the contract. If the vendor, no matter how well known, does not perform well, it is the HRD manager who will get the negative feedback and who must be prepared to cope with it. (However, when the performance is above the level expected, it is very rarely the HRD manager who gets the accolades.)

There is a significant problem that arises when utilizing external resources for services, namely substitution. Let us say that an HRD manager contracts with an organization to provide a facilitator or consultant. At the time of negotiation both sides are in agreement as to the specific person, from the vendor's side, who will staff that contract. At the time of actual performance, however, the vendor may send in somebody else! The reasons for this substitution can vary; the originally designated person may be unavailable for personal reasons or because of illness, and so on. But no matter what the reason, a substitution has taken place. At the point of delivery, usually little can be done. The learners are in place in the classroom, and the course must proceed. The managers are waiting to meet with the external consultant, and it would be detrimental to the whole effort if those meetings had to be canceled.

If the contract was in writing, the HRD manager could consider taking legal action. This has been done, but only in rare cases. More often, the HRD manager has simply been put on notice as to that vendor's practices, and this should guide their future relationship, if any. It may mean that the HRD manager will never use that vendor again. However, if it is necessary to do so, the manager should insist on some right of refusal, at a given date prior to the start of the course or the meetings.

*Evaluation.* Anytime there has been procurement of a product or service, there should be an evaluation. Where products are concerned, the evaluation is relatively easy to accomplish. The contract is usually fairly explicit about the product, and it may be possible to perform the evaluation in quantifiable terms. For services, or a mixture of products and services, evaluation becomes more difficult, although some of the general rules of evaluation would apply here (Deming, 1982; Denova, 1979; Kirkpatrick, 1976; Morris, Fitz-Gibbon, and Henderson, 1978; Phillips, 1983). In addition, the HRD manager should make provision for some kind of report or record. When many resources (both internal and external) are used, there may be several supervisors involved. Each will produce an evaluation of a particular resource. If those evaluations are not shared, resources that have already proved inadequate may be used again.

When the resource is internal, the evaluation may be part of the performance appraisal, but this is generally not the case. If the resource is a Category III person (collateral duties), it would be unusual for the HRD manager to do a performance appraisal. It is necessary, therefore, for the HRD manager to develop some internal system to provide an evaluation of the performance of non-HRD employees when they do HRD-related work.

For external resources it is relatively easy to develop and record an evaluation. The evaluation should be more than a "happiness ratio" or some other instrument that simply rates the performance of the facilitator or consultant. The expectations of the HRD unit will be different from those of the learners, though there may be some overlap between them. The external resource should be involved in developing the evaluation criteria and should later receive feedback as appropriate. Many external resource people seek such opportunities, but fear that they might represent impositions on the HRD manager who contracted for their services. Actually, the time needed would not be a burden on the manager and would probably be welcomed.

Public seminars and conferences should also be evaluated, particularly the former. Conferences may be "one-shot" affairs that will never be repeated in the same way. Public seminars, however, are generally offered the same way each time. Once the HRD manager has approved or contracted for attendance of an employee (at any level) at a public seminar, it is important to get an evaluation. Here, too, the "happiness ratio" should be avoided, and the evaluation should focus on the relation of the seminar experience to the previously agreed-upon objectives.

## Announcements and Catalogues

An output, in HRD, can be a printed catalogue or list of courses. There are times when such publications are extremely helpful, although there is a contrary point of view that holds that those catalogues communicate to others that HRD is essentially a school within the organization. This always raises the question of whether maintaining a school is an appropriate use of the limited resources available in any organization. Earlier we noted that we see HRD as a problem-solving tool. Some problems can be solved by regular classrooms within organizations. The point is, What image does the HRD manager wish to convey to the rest of the organization? If it is that of an internal problem solver, then the indiscriminate use of catalogues is self-defeating.

By no means are we suggesting that the HRD manager avoid all printed announcements of available learning opportunities. It is necessary to dispense information about such opportunities, and it is the task of the HRD unit to do that. Once an HRD manager gets into the catalogue business, however, it becomes an instrument that feeds on itself. Rarely will a new catalogue be thinner than its predecessor. The tendency is for it to get bigger, and it may eventually become a shopping list rather than a resource. Moreover, catalogues are of doubtful value when it comes to line managers. The line manager with a problem usually wants to talk to somebody. The first point of contact between the line manager and the HRD unit, when a problem arises, should not be a catalogue. If the catalogue is seen as the HRD unit's response to a problem, the line manager may call in an external HRD resource.

Announcements of HRD activities should be distributed when there is a general need in various parts of the organization for a specific course, such as a clerical, supervisory, or technical course. In a small organization, personal contact will be more helpful than an announcement. In a large or multisite organization, the personal approach is less feasible and usually not cost effective. Announcements will be needed, but they should be used cautiously, and great care should be given to their wording.

Frequently, a great deal more than just content is conveyed by an announcement.

A significant issue is the distribution of announcements. There are implications in the method of distribution that must be carefully considered. If announcements are sent only to supervisors and managers, they may not get down to potential learners. But if a course is going to be conducted for the purpose of training, then the announcement should definitely be routed through the supervisor, for that is the person who can most readily determine whether his or her employees need the course. For development, direct distribution to all employees is certainly in order.

In the case of education, matters are more complicated. If there are individual development plans, then the announcement of a course should be sent to those who will need it according to those plans. In the absence of such career development plans, the notices could be sent to supervisors who wish to prepare employees for promotion or transfer. If the announcements are sent directly to all employees, it signifies that promotion and transfer are items negotiable by each individual. Before issuing an announcement, HRD managers should carefully consider how the process of using announcements relates to the policies and practices of the organization.

### Reports and Records

Some HRD managers abhor paperwork, but for HRD it is essential. The actual entry work should be assigned to clerks, but the development of the record system must be under the direction of the HRD manager. In a large organization, with a big enough staff, this might be a delegated function. If so, delegation should be done cautiously and its results reviewed periodically. The data available from the system are crucial to the effective functioning of the HRD manager.

A discussion of reports and records must include a discussion of the role of the computer. Software packages designed specifically for HRD record keeping emerged in 1984. The vendors claimed many virtues for their various systems, all of which would supposedly be very useful to the HRD manager. But the few we tried at that time did not live up to expectations. They were the first generation, however, and we fully anticipate that by the end of the decade there will be extremely useful software packages for HRD.

If the organization has a mainframe computer, the HRD manager should possess a terminal capable of accessing its data. There will be production and sales figures that can provide clues about possible HRD needs. There will be reports from other parts of the organization that will enable the HRD manager to keep abreast of activities and plans. In many organizations, personnel files, as well as data from other human resource functions, are in the mainframe. It is up to the HRD manager to be sure that relevant HRD data are available through the organization's computer.

Each organization has its own criteria as to the number and types of reports required. Those that are mandated by other parts of the organization should be provided by the HRD manager. We cannot possibly indicate what those might be, as they vary greatly from one organization to another. Generally, however, reports related to budget and fiscal performance are required, as discussed in Chapters Four and Five. The HRD manager can initiate some reports if that is permitted in the organization. He or she should take care, however, to avoid those that rely on "body counts," that is, on reporting how many people attended programs. This, once again, emphasizes the school aspect of HRD rather than the contribution it can make to the regular goals and missions of the organization. When possible, the HRD manager should report on achievements. These data will come from evaluations of the results of courses and programs. In every case, the HRD manager should double-check the reports before distribution with the units or individuals covered by the report. There may be other factors to which the HRD manager was not privy that could influence how the report should be written and distributed.

Reports and records also allow for recognition. Many HRD managers have academic degrees and therefore do not think very highly of certificates, especially when the certificates only signify attendance at a given course. But for those who have received few certificates or diplomas in their lives, they can be important. If the

HRD unit services employees outside the United States, these kinds of awards can be even more important. In some countries, diplomas and certificates are looked upon very favorably. The fact that an employee has received one is frequently entered into the personnel file of that individual. Framed certificates can be observed on the walls of offices and homes. They signify an accomplishment by the individual—and can also serve as publicity for the HRD function. The HRD manager must keep records showing the certificates awarded to employees.

### Working with Line Managers

The supervisory subrole of the HRD manager includes working with line managers. In a small organization, the HRD manager can do this directly. In a large organization, direct contact may not be possible, and delegation of some of the contacting may be necessary. The kind of contact required here is different from that described earlier in Chapter Nine. The purpose of the contact here has a direct bearing on anticipated, in operation, and completed programs.

After a course, there should be feedback and follow-up (Broad, 1980; Nadler, 1982a). The HRD manager should work closely with line managers, before the HRD activity is offered, to ensure that adequate provision will be made for evaluation and follow-up. After the program, the HRD manager should take the initiative to implement the follow-up. Without fail, the line manager should receive feedback on the course. This raises a possible ethical issue, however. Should the HRD manager divulge a grade or other feedback concerning an individual employee? There is certainly no agreement on this question, and it should be explored before the course is even announced. The HRD manager may find that the line manager wants data on individual classroom performance of selected employees. Some would argue that this can defeat the process of learning. When a person is about to learn something new, that person should be in the position to try out new behaviors without worrying too much about failure. If performance is reported back to the supervisor, might this not encourage low-risk behavior, which is an obstacle to learning?

There are as yet no solid research findings on this question. Accordingly, all we can do is alert the HRD manager to this problem and urge that each HRD manager take a position in regard to it.

The real evaluation is in terms of improved performance in the work situation (unless the objective was development). If training was the purpose, the supervisor who sent the employee to the course should be directly involved in evaluation. Indeed, the HRD manager cannot possibly do any evaluation on the job without the support and assistance of the supervisor. When the purpose was education, the situation becomes more complicated. At the time of the course, the future supervisor of the employee may not be known. It is counterproductive to follow up on the present job, since it was not the target of the course. The HRD manager should track those who have been educated so that evaluation and follow-up can take place when the employee has been transferred to a new position and new supervisor.

Aside from the specific areas mentioned, the HRD manager should constantly strive to relate to all managers, at all levels, to keep HRD relevant to the changing goals and the mission of the organization. Again, this is not a question of simply maintaining relations, but of something much more specific. The HRD manager should meet with other managers to explore concrete needs to which HRD could be a response. In addition, the HRD manager should work closely with managers in other human resource areas. Conflict frequently occurs when the areas of operation are not discrete, as in human resources, and a legitimate approach can be interpreted as incipient piracy. The HRD manager should encourage open and continual communication with other human resource managers, as well as foster joint planning.

## Conclusion

Supervising is an essential task of the HRD manager. The activities of the HRD unit should be under constant review, not only the end results, but the entire operation. All the planning, organizing, staffing, and budgeting coalesce in the actual delivery of services.

Given the limited amount of resources available in any organization, careful scheduling is required so that the HRD unit can respond to the most important needs of the organization and of individual employees. If courses are offered, care should be given to ensure that they relate to the need that prompts the learning. Where several related courses are offered, there should be a logical sequencing. The learner must be able to become totally involved in the learning situation without having to interrupt it to return to the work unit. Learners must be carefully selected so that the HRD program is relevant to them and beneficial to the organization.

In addition to providing courses, the HRD unit should also be able to provide consulting services. Scheduling is an important consideration here, too, because the HRD unit needs to respond to requests for consulting as rapidly as possible.

The HRD manager is also responsible for procuring resources. This should start with identifying the need for a resource and then exploring ways to fulfill that need, either internally or externally. When using external resources, the manager must know how to contract and how to monitor performance of the contract.

The HRD unit will produce announcements and catalogues listing their offerings and activities. These must be carefully prepared because they reflect the image of the unit. Attention must also be paid to the appropriate method of distribution.

As with other units in an organization, the HRD unit must keep appropriate records and make reports. The reports and records should be tied into the organization's regular reporting systems. Particular attention should be paid to ensure that records and reports already maintained by other units of the organization are not regenerated by the HRD unit.

··⁌ *Chapter 12* ⁌··

# Current Issues and Trends

$T$he previous chapters have covered the basic elements of the job of the HRD manager. Additional factors that affect the manager will be considered in this chapter. Some of these topical areas are changing so rapidly that including them in the body of the book would have made certain portions time bound. We decided, therefore, to put these at the end of the book. This is intended not to diminish their importance but rather to highlight the controversies and issues in HRD, a field that is changing rapidly—a characteristic of any dynamic professional field.

The dynamism of the field suggests that managers who are looking for traditional and predictable positions should avoid entering the field of HRD. As recognition of the importance of HRD to organizations and individuals increases, it is possible to see more areas where HRD must be considered. It is not a function that can be isolated in an organization.

### Employee Assistance Programs (EAP)

There has been an increasing concern about people, as individuals, in the workplace. At one time, not too many years ago, when organizational emphasis was on the person as an employee rather than as an individual, it was considered inappropriate for an employer to delve into anything that was not directly related to the work situation. The general position within most organizations was that, above all, the individual's privacy should be respected. Now, however, it has been recognized that many

247

aspects of a person's life affect how he or she performs in the workplace. It would be very rewarding to be able to say that this happened as a result of the movement toward quality of work life. In fact, however, the movement occurred because organizations discovered that they were suffering significant losses in productivity because of such matters as alcohol and drug abuse.

For a time, organizational employee counseling was restricted to career counseling. Slowly the recognition has evolved that people need help with more than just their careers. However, there are some significant legal and ethical issues that must still be clarified in this area. Take, for example, an employee who goes to a company counselor, also an employee, and admits to the possibility of having a drinking problem. The following exchange might take place:

*Employee:* I wanted to talk to you because some people seem to think that I have a problem with alcohol. I drink but I am not an alcoholic! I know when to stop. I also know that I need a drink when the tension and stress get too high on the job.

*Counselor:* Have you ever done any drinking on the job?

*Employee:* Sure—and so have many other people around here. They don't talk about it, but one of these days we are going to have a catastrophe here.

*Counselor:* Has your drinking increased recently?

*Employee:* It sure has, with all this emphasis on productivity and quality circles. Sometimes those quality circles sound like Alcoholics Anonymous. But I've got it under control. I just wanted to talk to somebody about it. I feel better now. Thanks.

A simple situation? Not likely. What is the responsibility of the counselor? If the counselor was not an employee but was working in a community setting, the answer would be clear. The conversation would come under the counselor-client relationship, and professional ethics would prevent the counselor from sharing that information with anybody else without the explicit consent of the client. But when the counselor is an employee of the same organization, do similar ethical principles apply? By no means has this been settled in the counseling profession. The company is paying that counselor to help employees, but what if the counselor receives information that, if passed along, could prevent future accidents? Does the counselor have the right to withhold that information from the organization? This question has yet to be clarified.

EAP is a natural development in a changing workplace that has seen increased interest in individuals. The trend is a good one, but it is not without its problems. We see too many people, including HRD people, pushing into this area without fully understanding the implications of what they are doing and without being technically qualified to deliver the required personal services. So we might well ask, What is the place of HRD in all this? It is fairly evident that career counseling (Gutteridge and Hutcheson, 1984) can indicate the need for HRD. The same might apply to other aspects of EAP, such as stress management. And, as with many other needs of employees, when learning is required there is a place for HRD. If EAP continues to expand, it will no doubt generate additional HRD needs. The HRD manager should be aware of this and explore areas of cooperation.

At the same time, however, the HRD manager should avoid moving into the management of EAP programs. They generally require other competencies than an organization can expect from its HRD manager. For example, in the federal government, the HRD person is given the title of Employee Development Specialist (EDS). In *The Employee Development Specialist Curriculum Plan* (1976, p. 7), "career counseling" was included as one of the roles of the EDS: "One does not necessarily have to be an EDS in order to do career counseling; but, *as the need exists for the service, EDS's with their knowledge of developmental opportunities* are logical people to provide the service" (emphasis added).

In other words, since a need exists, the EDS person should fill it. If that were the case, HRD people would be extremely busy—doing other people's jobs. It is unclear what is meant by "developmental opportunities." If it means HRD opportunities, that is fine—except that knowing what those opportunities are is an answer to questions that have not yet been asked. Who should ask those questions? We believe that career counseling is the responsibility of the supervisor or of the human resource utilization or personnel people. If they are not doing a good job, then HRD should help improve their competencies rather than try to usurp their duties. There are also the problems of organizations that do not have career development *systems*. There are highly competent professionals in the area of career development who can help organizations develop such systems and clarify the roles of the employee, supervisor, and HRD unit in them.

## Legislation Affecting HRD

For the most part, most practitioners in HRD tend to ignore the question of legislation, particularly at the federal level. The usual position has been that the less one gets involved with the government, the better it is. However, after saying that they did not want to get involved in the war on poverty, many companies then rushed out and got government contracts to run urban Job Corps camps, adult basic education (literacy) programs, and other activities under the Economic Opportunity Act of 1964 and its subsequent iterations.

We also remember the time when many HRD people said they did not want to get involved in government programs. But when one of the authors mentioned a few of the relevant programs at a meeting of HRD managers from the private sector, he sparked a good deal of enthusiasm among the group. The result was an article (Nadler, 1969a) that received wide attention. Indeed, it was reprinted in the *Congressional Record*.

Since then, there has been an increasing amount of legislation related to HRD, although HRD may not be specifically mentioned in the titles of the bills or acts in question. The legislation covers such items as allowable deductions for HRD programs, reporting of HRD programs by employers and employees, and tax breaks for hiring, training, and employing people from identified disadvantaged groups.

To date, most legislation at the state level has not had too much of an impact on HRD, but that could change. Some state laws will mirror those of the federal government, but legislation can also be expected that will relate to local issues.

The question has been raised as to the appropriate role of an organization such as ASTD vis-à-vis legislation (Davidson, 1977). One answer is that there is nothing wrong with lobbying, and the law allows a professional organization to do that without losing its preferred tax status. Moreover, it should be noted that our legislative bodies are increasingly passing laws that have both a direct and an indirect impact on HRD. It is easy to sit back and do nothing—and then complain about government interference. It is better to become involved in the political arena and endeavor to influence the lawmakers. We are not advocating, in this book, the positions that should be taken on legislative issues. Rather, we are stating that it is the responsibility of an HRD manager to keep upper management informed of political issues and to be prepared to advise them on the implications of those issues for the organization and HRD.

### Shadow System

As HRD has grown in importance, more and more people and groups have become aware of its contribution. Previously, it was ignored. Indeed, we can recall having to justify to a dean why our graduate HRD program was in the School of Education and Human Development rather than in the School of Business! That has changed radically, and many education faculties have discovered that they missed a great deal by ignoring the kind of learning that occurs in the workplace. One study (Eurich, 1985) notes that HRD activities provided by corporations enroll 8 million people— the same number of students as are enrolled in colleges and universities. Eurich also notes that the figure for "corporate classrooms" is probably understated, as it does not include on-the-job training.

Given the increased attention to HRD, it is interesting to note that it has been described as a shadow system or the third leg of our schooling system. All these are somewhat pejorative terms implying that somebody has been trying to get away with an illegal system (Zemke, 1985). Another approach, taken by some, is to argue that private companies are concerned only with making money and that therefore their offerings in HRD programs do not provide the broad base for learning that is offered by colleges and universities. There is the implication that HRD programs should include that base, but do not.

Previously, the offering of degrees had been considered the private preserve of institutions of higher education. As of this writing, however, a number of private companies had begun to grant accredited postsecondary degrees (Eurich, 1985). All of these have been accredited by the usual nongovernmental bodies:

> Arthur D. Little Management Education Institute (M.S.)
> DeVry Institute of Technology (Bell and Howell; B.A. and A.A.S.)
> MGH Institute of Health Professions (Massachusetts General Hospital Corporation; M.S.)
> Hamburger University (McDonald's Corporation; A.A.S.)
> Northrup University (B.S. and M.S.)
> Rand Graduate Institute (Ph.D.)
> Wang Institute of Graduate Studies (M.S.)
> Watterson College (Jostens, Inc.; associate degrees)

There are also a number of postsecondary institutions sponsored by professional organizations and societies:

> American College (National Association of Life Underwriters)
> American Institute of Banking at Boston
> Industrial Management Institute (Midwest Industrial Management Association)

Institute of Management Competency (American Management Associations)

The College of Insurance (Insurance Society of New York)

There are probably many more accredited higher education institutions that are not part of the traditional higher education system. Some of these institutions start by providing courses only for their own employees or members. But it does not take long, apparently, before those institutions become open to the general public and therefore in competition with the more traditional institutions.

As one could expect, higher education institutions want to reserve that field for themselves. Some of these institutions have argued that they can do a better job of providing HRD than can a private company's internal unit. They argue that they have more extensive resources, have been in that business for a long time, and are prepared to make the necessary changes in their delivery systems (eliminate a semester basis, as one example) to accommodate them to the world of work. The challenge to those universities is to become competitive. If they do, it is possible that some HRD activities will move out of private companies and into institutions of higher education.

## Placement of HRD

We are often called upon to recommend where HRD should be placed in an organization, but this question is misleading. It implies that there is one best place for HRD and that, if that place can be found, HRD will function at its optimum. The placement of HRD should be the result of factors already discussed in this book, such as an organization's philosophy, its policy, its staffing, and so on, and we do not wish to repeat those points here. Rather, let us consider the trend we see evolving regarding the placement of the HRD unit in organizations.

One school argues that HRD should be placed as close to the point of delivery as possible. This would put the HRD unit within the various operating units. The major work of such HRD units would be directly related to the daily work of the particular unit where it was placed.

Another possibility is to have the HRD unit, as a staff unit, located where one would expect to find similar staff units in the organization. In this case, it would usually be part of the total human resource function. Given such a placement, coordination and cooperation with other human resource functions would be more readily accomplished. The HRD unit in this configuration would deliver some generic learning programs, such as supervisory training, while the technical programs would probably be delivered by an HRD unit at an operating level.

A third possibility is to have an HRD unit that reports to the top level of the organization, making it equal to such senior management support areas as corporate planning. Such a unit would report directly to the chief executive officer or to someone at some similar top level. It would be a small unit and might consist of only one or two HRD professionals. They would not deliver any programs but would serve strictly in a consulting relationship to the highest levels of the organization. If there were a strategic planning function at that level, the HRD unit would provide direct input and be part of the strategic planning team.

Some readers might think that we are here describing the progression of the HRD manager from the operating level of the organization to its highest level. That is not the case—at least not at present. This is not a description of the career ladder for the HRD manager. Indeed, there will be HRD managers at all three levels, but they will be quite different kinds of managers. The HRD manager who is concerned about delivering HRD programs may not be the type of HRD manager who can work effectively with strategic planning for human resources. The HRD manager at the top corporate level might not even be a manager in the traditional sense. Rather, he or she would have taken on various executive duties.

The first two HRD placements described, the operational and the staff, are the most common. The last, at the highest level of the organization, is just emerging. Its future depends, to a great degree, on the type of HRD managers put in those positions. The opportunity has arisen for HRD people to be heard at the top levels of the organization. Whether any will remain at that level depends on the value of the service they can render to the organization. The paradox is that organizations tend to appoint general managers at that level, and this would exclude the Category I HRD person who could bring sound HRD input to the situation.

## International Ramifications of HRD

At one time, by an international company, one meant a U.S. company that manufactured its products in the United States and then exported them. But this has slowly changed. There are now U.S. companies, for example, that set up manufacturing, assembly, and/or distribution facilities in various parts of the world. Of perhaps even greater significance is the fact that there are many non-U.S. companies now operating within the United States. Among the most prominent are the foreign auto companies such as Honda, Toyota, Volkswagen, and Renault. Less well known are the various companies that function in the United States under U.S. names but that are partly or fully owned by organizations outside the United States.

As related to HRD, the international function usually involves sending HRD products and services from an American company to its counterpart in another country. This is sometimes referred to as technology transfer. This is not just a matter of giving away technology but rather of focusing on how to get the foreign branch to operate as effectively as the company does in the United States. There has long been the belief that it is important to send somebody "over there" who has the technical know-how. This myth has remained, despite the experience of the 1960s that showed that it was extremely important to know how to transfer that technology. A study has shown that in the communications industry, when working internationally, a very high value is placed on knowing how to help others to learn.

The political situation has also caught up with us. During the period from 1950 to 1970, foreign countries welcomed all the help they could get. Getting an overseas assignment in HRD was easy, either directly through a company or as a "consultant." By the 1980s, however, this situation had changed considerably and can be expected to change even more. Host countries are now insisting that American companies (and other multinational companies) train and educate people from the host countries, so that they can enlarge their own capabilities. In the HRD field, this becomes evident when one looks at the proliferation of HRD professional organizations in many places outside the United States.

Conflicts do arise, in the HRD operation, when an American HRD manager perceives the local people in the host country as being barely able to read and write, much less handle HRD. In fact, there are some very sophisticated people in HRD operations in foreign countries. In 1985, George Washington University completed setting up an M.A. program in HRD in Singapore. Among the student body were HRD people from Honeywell, Mobil, Daimaru, Rockwell, Fujitec, Hewlett-Packard, and General Motors. All these were Singaporeans! Some of the students noted that their biggest problem was with HRD managers from the States who looked upon the Singaporeans as if they had just emerged from the jungle. In most cases, the American manager did not have a degree in HRD and had never even studied the subjects related to HRD. He or she may have known in a general way what the company had done in HRD, but had no idea of why it was done or how a given program might contribute to good adult learning practices. Even less did that state side HRD manager know about the cross-cultural implications of learning. We do not want to overgeneralize. There are some U.S. companies in the international arena that have excellent HRD managers, and the results of their efforts can be found in some of the publications of the international division of ASTD.

During the rest of the 1980s, the concept of international HRD will have to be redefined. The role of the United States as a leader in HRD has changed and will change even further as time goes on. This does not mean that the American HRD manager will not have something to offer. But the HRD manager who was effective internationally before 1980 will find that there will be different demands and challenges in the balance of this century.

### HRD and Productivity

The concern of management with productivity in organizations is certainly understandable. But a difficulty here is that too many people use the word *productivity* without bothering to define it. Unfortunately, this tendency has increased and has left us with a great deal of confusion. If the HRD manager is to make any contribution in this area, it is important for him or her to have a clear understanding of what is meant by productivity. The major confusion, in discussing *productivity*, is that it is too often used interchangeably with *production*. These are two very different concepts, as can be illustrated by a simple example. Figure 1 shows the typical production situation.

**Figure 1. Production.**

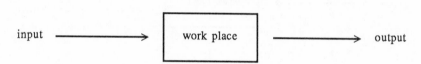

The basic concept of production is that there are inputs, shown by the arrows on the left-hand side of the figure, that produce outputs, shown by the arrows on the right-hand side. Let us assume that you want to increase production. This can be done by introducing the necessary additional inputs, as shown in Figure 2.

**Figure 2. Increased Production.**

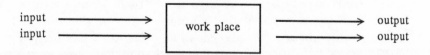

Of course, there is no guarantee that an additional input will produce an equivalent output. For example, the additional input may be a matter of additional worker hours. When employees work overtime, however, their rate of production may be lower because of fatigue and similar elements. Another common way to increase production is to purchase new or additional machinery or other means of production. In each case, the input requires some additional expenditure.

We have seen what needs to be done to increase *production*. To increase *productivity*, we do not make additional inputs, as shown in Figure 3. But how, then, can an increase in productivity be accomplished? The clue lies in the box situated between the arrows. Called the *workplace*, it encompasses a broad range of factors.

**Figure 3. Increased Productivity.**

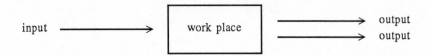

In some situations, productivity is increased by a practice called the *speedup;* that is, the worker is required to produce more units per hour. This was depicted by Charlie Chaplin in the classic film *Modern Times*. Even if you did not see that film, you may still have seen or experienced the phenomenon in your own work life. The order is given for each worker to produce more of whatever it is that is produced, and the machinery is geared to go faster—to increase output—without any adjustment in inputs. If the speedup works, it can reduce unit cost and raise productivity, but its long-range cost to the organization can be extremely negative.

Similar practices have also been tried. Many of these practices have benefitted the company but not the worker. Consequently, the work force tends to view increased productivity as just another name for increased exploitation. This need not be the case, however.

Another way to increase productivity is through capital investment. Taking a negative example, we might note that the American steel industry has been criticized for its low productivity.

That factor has prevented the industry from competing effectively in price with steel factories in Japan and Germany. There may be several reasons for that low productivity, but a major one is that there has been very little capital investment in the American steel industry over the past fifty years. In fact, many American plants are using equipment that is even older than that. With such outmoded equipment, it is impossible to increase productivity.

Ironically, the Japanese and German steel industry had an unusual advantage. During the Second World War, their steel mills were virtually destroyed by Allied bombing and had to be almost totally rebuilt. This was done not by merely replacing previously existing plants but by introducing modern postwar technology. It is not being suggested that we need a war in order to replace equipment, though sometimes employees who must use outmoded equipment may feel that it will take a "bomb" to wake management up to reality. The bomb can be a loss of market or a profit and loss statement dripping red ink.

Productivity is related not only to the physical aspects of operations but also to the company's collective state of mind, which is reflected in the philosophy of the organization. To increase productivity, HRD managers have been urged to explore such interventions as quality circles and MBO. Such activities in the area of participative management can be helpful in increasing productivity, but only if there is a state of mind (philosophy) at management levels that supports the interventions. Yoji Arai of the U.S. office of the Japan Productivity Center has continually emphasized to U.S. managers that support for quality circles must start at the top of the organization. The quality circle must become a way of thinking among upper levels of management that can then permeate the organization.

Rather than being the product of Japanese ingenuity, quality circles were something the Japanese observed when they came to the United States between 1955 and 1964 as part of our foreign aid program. An important question that has yet to be addressed is: If we were doing so well then that the Japanese chose to adapt our ideas, how did we lose that edge? (Nadler, 1984b).

In an earlier section of the book we defined HRD and the three activity areas of training, education, and development. Here again we have a situation where, if the HRD manager does not differentiate among the three, the value of HRD to the organization can be lost.

Development, as defined earlier, has little or no effect on productivity, although it can have an impact on morale and make employees feel better about their jobs. That is, when development activities are offered as part of the HRD program, employees will probably get the message that management views them as more than just extensions of machines and that management is using company resources for them even though this will produce no direct bottom-line results. Education is important, but it is learning for the future. It may result in increased productivity when the employee moves on to his or her next job, but it should not be expected to have any immediate effect on productivity. Training, however, is highly focused on productivity. The learning received in a training program is intended to produce a different performance level on the job. When related directly to quantity output, training can be expected to show an increase in productivity.

One of the major problems faced by an HRD manager, in this area, is how to measure the impact of HRD activities on productivity. It has been said that what cannot be measured has no bearing on productivity. If the organization does not have a recognized way of measuring productivity, the HRD manager should encourage it to focus on that problem. Until there is agreement in the organization on how input/output is to be measured, it will not be possible to get a current productivity index. And without that baseline number, it is impossible to evaluate how HRD can improve productivity. A major contribution of the HRD manager is to make general managers aware of this problem—one that must be faced when an organization is concerned with productivity.

### Committees

It is expected, in many situations, that the HRD manager will utilize a series of committees in implementing the HRD program. There are various types of committees including advisory, technical, subject matter, and evaluation committees. Let us look at some general guidelines for committees and then at those that relate directly to HRD.

*Committee Structure and Operation.* In a work organization, participation in committees is seldom voluntary. Employees at all levels are assigned to committees for various reasons related to the work situation. There may be some few cases where an individual volunteers to serve on a committee, but that is certainly not the norm. Being an active member of a committee usually means being away from one's regular work situation. This is certainly the case at the lower levels of the organization. As we move up the organization, committee work becomes more the norm and is considered part of one's regular work load.

In the United States, there is a good deal of negative feeling about committees, as evidenced by such folk sayings as "a committee works best when there are three members, one of whom is on sick leave and another out of town." Nevertheless, we do have numerous committees functioning in the workplace. Generally, they seem to serve a purpose, so let us briefly look at some of the factors that make for effective committees.

A committee should have a *focus* and *purpose*. Everybody should know what the committee is expected to do—recommend, decide, react, or advise. A committee can do one or more of these, but the functional aspect of the committee should be stated at the outset.

A committee should have a *defined life*. A committee's life begins when its members are identified and a meeting is called. The end of the committee should be just as clearly marked. Sometimes the end comes naturally, as the committee members complete an assigned task. It is all too common, however, to find that the life of a committee drags on while attendance at meetings begins to fall, agendas and minutes are no longer disseminated, regular meetings are skipped, and slowly it becomes obvious that the committee is no longer serving any useful purpose. Rather than that kind of ending, a committee should have a built-in sunset clause, which states that the committee will end on a given date unless some positive action is taken to keep it going.

There should be some form of *record keeping* for a committee. This can range from informal memos to minutes that are read and approved at subsequent meetings. Each committee must decide for itself the kind of paperwork required to enable that committee to achieve its goals. For some committees, no records are needed either during their functioning or at their termination. For other committees, a written record for the files is mandatory.

*Types of Committees.* The HRD manager can use a variety of committees, but they should be based on specific needs. The most common form of committee is the *advisory committee*. Unfortunately, this title does not tell what the committee is supposed to advise about. Also, sometimes HRD managers use advisory committees to do more than advise. If your organization requires you to use that kind of title for a committee, be sure that the members of the committee know whether they are expected to advise or to do something else.

Advisory committees commonly function in the area of tuition refunds or reimbursements, according to a recent study of HRD policy in organizations (Spector, 1985). (The words *refund* and *reimbursement* indicate only the manner of payment. In both cases, the organization pays all or part of the employee's tuition.) Frequently, a committee is established to ensure that the available funds are distributed appropriately. Such committees rarely concern themselves with training, education, development, or any other of the real objectives of the HRD program. The focus tends to be on equitable distribution of the available funds, whatever "equitable" happens to mean in that situation.

Another type of HRD committee, also frequently termed advisory, is called upon to respond to the overall HRD plan for the organization, as presented by the HRD manager. This type of committee can be used when the bulk of the HRD contribution to the organization will be in the form of course offerings for the next year. Such a plan should have been preceded by an intensive needs survey and should be related to performance appraisals and the career development system in place in the organization. Too often, however, it is the result of a questionnaire that reflects what employees want, not what they need. Seldom will such a needs survey address the real problems of an organization or how HRD can be used to solve those problems. That aspect of HRD is least well served by a committee.

More positively, a committee can perform an *oversight* function; that is, it can look at the total HRD function and advise on how it could more effectively respond to the needs of the organization. This serves a variety of purposes. For example, it keeps the HRD unit looking at some of the broad issues of concern to the organization rather than just running classes. It also helps the HRD manager to remain in touch with the concerns of other managers, as they relate to the goals and mission of the HRD unit. Finally, such a committee can help the HRD manager avoid the trap of being efficient (doing the job well) but not being effective (doing the wrong job).

There can also be committees to deal with specific operational areas. For example, if there is a new plant start-up, the HRD manager might form a committee to look at the HRD needs connected with that change. The same holds true when new equipment or technology is being introduced. If the organization uses committees to deal with such changes, the HRD manager should try to be named to those committees but should also suggest the need for special subcommittees to examine the implications for the HRD programs in the organization.

In a large organization with several sites, a committee involving representative people from the different sites can be used to make sure that all sites are being served appropriately by the HRD unit. Also, the exchange of information about HRD made possible by such a committee can be helpful to all concerned. In a small organization, the HRD manager is often faced with the problem of too many committees and too few people to serve on them.

There is an interesting dilemma facing some committees, particularly in cases where the members are located at some distance from each other. It then becomes costly, in terms of travel and time away from the job, to bring the committee members together. This is where technology can play a part. It is possible, for example, to have a meeting by means of a telephone conference call. Or moving up the technological scale, an organization can use closed-circuit television. This is available through several sources, including AT&T and Holiday Inns, both of which have special sites for such meetings. At George Washington University we have an instructional television facility that can also handle a closed-circuit meeting, and there are other universities with similar facilities.

It is also possible to use the computer, particularly when the meeting requires the sharing of information. A computer conference is much different from a regular conference. In computer conferencing, all the committee members need not be on-line at the same time. They can communicate with one another at the times that are most appropriate for each member, within a given number of hours or days. Each member of the committee can read, from the computer, what is being communicated to the other members. As needed, it is simple to produce the hard copy that most people still prefer. The use of computers for conferencing is still evolving, and newer techniques and technology can be expected to emerge.

But while additional technology is continually being made available to us, many people nevertheless still prefer the face-to-face meeting. You hear complaints that meetings are time consuming, but the same people who make these complaints will elect to spend time in a committee meeting rather than use some of the technology that is available. Hence, although the HRD manager should recognize the possibilities of the various kinds of meetings and technology, he or she should also consider the desires of the committee members.

## Culture

At various places in this book we have made reference to the concept of *culture* as it related to the themes of particular chapters. Given the increasing interest in organizational culture, it seems appropriate to devote some additional space to that topic.

One of the problems here is the difficulty in finding an acceptable definition of the term *culture*, although there are some areas of general agreement that can serve as a basis for discussing the topic. Nadler (1969b) defines culture as the habits and customs that people develop to cope with change. Schein defines culture as "a pattern of basic assumptions—invented, discovered, or developed by a given group as it learns to cope with its problems" (1985, p. 9). Both definitions have an important commonality. Culture is not something mandated from on high within an organization or a country. Rather, culture is something developed in the ranks, and it is developed as a coping mechanism. If there is no problem or change, cultural mechanisms do not develop. They are a result—a reaction to something that a group has had to deal with. But that question brings us into several other areas where there is less agreement at this time.

One difficulty in discussing culture lies in establishing what culture is in its experiential mode. Nadler speaks of "habits and customs." That is, culture is manifested in observable *behavior.* Culture is not found in people's minds but in what they do, how they behave. Schein focuses, rather, on the "assumptions" that people make. We believe, however, that it is possible to identify those assumptions from the way people act them out, so we are back to viewing culture as behavior. And in terms of the focus of this book, that is, people working in organizations, behavior is the major concern.

Not all behavior in an organization is cultural. There are times when the cultural behavior becomes so formalized that we must refer to it as *institutionalized* behavior. This behavior usually starts as a response to some sort of change. As an example, let us take a unit in an organization in which cultural behavior evolved with regard to smoking. The impact of the surgeon general's report, lobbying by groups such as Americans for Smoking and Health, and general awareness of the problems caused by smoking on the job began to produce some cultural changes. A consensus was reached by a group of employees that there would be no smoking on the job in their unit. There was no ruling or vote on the matter. Rather, over a relatively brief period of time, it became evident that smoking on the job was not considered desirable behavior in the unit. Ashtrays were removed, as well as boxes that had previously contained cigarettes. Thus, a new cultural imperative had emerged as a result of external stimuli; and over a period of time, it became so well accepted that it was institutionalized— it became the norm.

Those who did not conform to this new cultural norm found themselves left out of some activities; for instance, they were no longer welcome in the lunch group. Moreover, smokers became the butt of pointed remarks, and antismoking cartoons were placed on the unit bulletin board. As with any emerging cultural behavior, the smokers had several options. One was to ignore the new cultural norm, which is a form of testing it. If it was not truly an emerging culture, it would disappear. In fact, however, those who tested the norm were treated in ways that were meant to communicate the new culture to them.

Not all employees, however, stopped smoking, and some of those who found it necessary to smoke on the job requested transfers to other units where the cultural norm allowed smoking on the job. Such transfers might have meant some loss in promotional possibilities and even less desirable jobs. For others, who preferred to remain in the unit, another cultural behavior developed. On their own initiative they found a seldom-used stock room, close to the work site, that they used as a smoking room. The nonsmokers knew about the smoking room, but it was ignored since it did not function counter to the new no-smoking culture. The nonsmokers did not want to stamp out smoking, only to make it unacceptable behavior on the job.

Put yourself in the place of a new employee coming into that work unit. It is unlikely, at the outset, that you would be told about the no-smoking norm. It would simply be a question of "everybody knows," which is another way of saying that it is cultural behavior, not a rule that has been written down. This is part of the problem that must be recognized when we discuss culture and behavior. Cultural norms are taken for granted by those who follow them. They often do not see the need to tell others about these norms. Those who need to know will be acculturated—they will learn the appropriate cultural behaviors as they become part of that group.

Legal norms are officially mandated by policy, regulations, and other written documents. They appear in the manuals, memos, and other paper generated by those in positions of authority. Legal norms are fairly easy to understand and deal with, since they establish what is expected of employees. When one deviates from legal behavior, the system has various forms of punishment. There are also specific rewards for performing in accordance with expected legal behavior. That does not mean that everybody complies but simply that there is a yardstick against which to measure behavior. In the smoking case we have been discussing, it would become a legal question if there were a ruling that prohibited smoking on the job. As with any such legal injunction, however, other cultural behavior will develop if employees wish to continue their smoking practices.

We have selected the smoking situation to make the distinction among the three forms of organizational behavior because smoking is a readily observable activity. There are other forms of organizational behavior that are much more difficult to observe, but the pattern and relationship of the three norms (cultural, institutionalized, and legal) will be there. We have also selected the smoking example because there is no one correct response to it. If there were, then it would not be an instance in which cultural behavior is crucial.

It is possible that various units within an organization will have very different cultures. This applies to small organizations as well as to medium-size and large ones. Some refer to the cultures in these units as *subcultures,* but we prefer to call them *microcultures.* This is not merely a semantic difference. Using "sub" implies that a particular culture is subordinate to and less important than some larger unit, and that may not be the case. The culture of the total organization is not found by adding up all its microcultures. Rather, each unit has its own culture that is different in some aspects from what can be identified as the macroculture of the organization as a whole. It is a case where the whole is not the sum of its parts.

While it is satisfying to see the increasing awareness of this aspect of the work situation, what does this mean for the HRD manager? Obviously, it highlights the need for an understanding of the organization's culture. The HRD manager occupies a unique position in an organization. The very nature of the position requires that the HRD manager work with all the units of the organization. Therefore, the HRD manager must recognize their microcultural differences. The legal and institutionalized practices must also be recognized, but they are easier to discern. Since the HRD manager must deal with many different kinds of units, it is very easy to make cultural blunders. Those in the unit assume that "everybody knows" the culture. The challenge to the HRD manager is to isolate the cultural behaviors endemic to the individual units of the organization.

It is not possible to list all the cultural behaviors to which the HRD manager must be sensitive. That list has not yet been developed in any literature we could find, but here are some of the more obvious kinds of behavior:

- *Dress:* What is the appropriate clothing to wear in different parts of the organization? This does not mean that the HRD manager must be a chameleon or have an extensive wardrobe on hand in the HRD closet. Rather, when preparing to attend a staff meeting, the HRD manager should consider what the cultural dress code is for that group. When visiting in other parts of the organization, the HRD manager should be aware of what clothing indicates about status and work assignments.

- *Food and eating:* To what places do people in that unit go for lunch or other meals? What do they generally order? Ethnic foods? Health foods? There are times when this aspect of cultural behavior is used as a "rite of passage" to see if the HRD manager will be accepted by the group.

- *Language:* This is probably the most difficult kind of cultural behavior to deal with. Each microcultural group has its own language even though they may all use English. There are words that will have special meanings for those who are part of a given microculture. Using the "wrong" (culturally inappropriate) language with a group can produce a barrier to communication with that group. It is not expected that the HRD manager will come to know all the language behaviors in a group, but he or she should recognize that they do exist.

- *Space:* This refers to how space is used and the appropriate place for certain functions. For example, does coaching take place at the employee's work station or in the supervisor's office? Is it appropriate to talk business at lunch, given the place (cafeteria, executive dining room) where lunch is eaten?

This has been an exceedingly brief discussion of microcultural behaviors. But the intent was simply to make you aware of the possibilities of organizational culture, as they relate to the managerial functions of the HRD manager. Once you have developed some familiarity with the organizational culture as well as the various microcultures, you must then make sure that your HRD staff acquires the same sensitivity. Indeed, the attempt to understand different cultures should be a generally agreed-upon norm (culture) within the HRD unit.

We cannot leave this discussion, however, without some brief reference to learning, which is the focus of HRD. A culture can be learned, but it is difficult to teach. The HRD unit should not try to initiate employees into the microculture of an operating unit. That can only be accomplished by those within the unit who are part of that culture. But it is important that the designer of a learning program be sensitive to, if not knowledgeable about, the content and learning experiences within a learning design that might be counter-cultural. For example, if change is the objective, whether through direct learning or indirect consultation, the designer must recognize that if it is counter-cultural, the change may not bring about the desired result. In addition, attempts are sometimes made to bring about change by altering the structure of an organization. This change, however, may bring about cultural behaviors different from the anticipated ones.

As more studies are done on organizational climate, it should become possible, to provide an HRD manager with how-to-do-it information in this area. For now, he or she can turn to some of the already existing literature on cross culture (Harris and Moran, 1985; Lippitt and Hoopes, 1978; Harris, 1984; Reynolds, 1984b), although the emphasis in these works is on different countries or organizations rather than on intraorganizational culture.

## Career Ladders

As with any position, HRD managers want to know what the career opportunities are in their field. We have discussed some aspects of this question in earlier chapters on staffing and organization. Our intent here is to look at some broader issues related to the careers of HRD managers.

If you belong to Category II, you know that your career ladder is outside the HRD field. Your assignment in HRD may be for several years, but it is anticipated that you will move on. We hope that this book will be helpful to you while you are part of the HRD unit. It should also help you to understand some aspects of HRD that you may not have experienced during your assignment in this unit. If you belong to Category I, the question to explore is, How did you get to be an HRD manager? In a large organization, the movement is generally from learning specialist, usually a facilitator, to supervisor in the area of HRD management, to HRD manager. In a small organization, with a limited number of people in HRD, you may have joined the organization as the HRD manager. Where do you go from there?

As with any concern about career development, one of the most important questions is, What are *your* aspirations? Do you want to continue in HRD, recognizing that this may not bring you to the highest levels of the organization? The cultural norm in the United States still appears to be that each of us should continue seeking promotion. But perhaps this will change as more of the products of the postwar baby boom move into the age brackets where they expect to become managers. There may not be sufficient jobs at those higher levels, and the cultural norm may develop that moving up is not the only way to achieve in our society.

In some organizations, position is determined by the number of people who report to you. This does not appear to be a good criterion for the HRD manager, since the emerging trend is to return a good deal of the operational side of HRD to the line managers, which reduces the number of people on staff in the HRD unit.

Another way that the importance of a position is judged is by the size of the budget. How a unit is organized is very important, and an increase in the HRD budget may not be the best way of determining whether a manager is moving up the career ladder or not.

What we also see happening is a broadening of the job of the HRD manager, and one possibility for the HRD manager is to move into other human resource areas. This involves more than just taking on additional functions, because different areas require special competencies that are often distinct from those required for a human resource developer. A manager who wishes to take on the responsibilities of a human resource planner or human resource career developer, for example, should plan to obtain the necessary competencies before promising to deliver services.

Prior to 1970 one rarely, if ever, encountered the title vice-president for human resources. This position slowly emerged during the latter part of the 1970s, as people came to recognize that human resources was a broad area with a wide variety of specialties. In organizations where there were industrial or labor relations units, which usually meant the existence of strong unions, the position was in most cases held by the lawyer who previously led those industrial or labor relations programs. In organizations, the personnel director was moved into the higher-level position. Depending on the individual, the human resources unit either became a bigger personnel unit or grew into the broader concept of human resources, with all its specialty areas. It is still unclear, from a career ladder perspective, how organizations will generally fill the new position of vice-president of human resources.

But it is certain that there will be new and increasing challenges for the HRD manager who wants to remain in the HRD field. The impact of newer technologies will constantly be changing the dimensions of the HRD function. Small high-tech organizations, for example, are beginning to recognize the need for HRD professionals in their organizations to keep their scientists and engineers at the cutting edge. Moreover, it appears that demographics will begin to make for a different kind of learner— one more highly schooled than in the past. We have been told that those who have more schooling want to be involved in continuous learning. This will present some new and interesting challenges for the HRD manager. It can also mean increased recognition and prestige in the organization.

## Conclusion

The job of the HRD manager is wide ranging, exciting, and challenging. This applies whether he or she belongs to Category I or Category II, or whether he or she is in a large organization or a small one. The job of the HRD manager is to do much more than merely run a school in the company. A good HRD manager can make significant contributions to the success of the organization. It is a complicated job that requires competency in more than just management and in more than just learning. The HRD manager's job is a synergistic combination of both those major fields.

# Addresses of Relevant Associations

American Association for Adult
and Continuing Education
1601 Sixteenth Street, NW
Washington, DC 20036

American Society for
Healthcare Education and
Training
840 N. Lake Shore Drive
Chicago, IL 60611

American Society for Training
and Development
Box 1443
1630 Duke Street
Alexandria, VA 22313

Association for Educational
Communications and
Technology
1126 16th Street, NW
Washington, DC 20036

Council on the Continuing
Education Unit
13000 Old Columbia Pike
Silver Spring, MD 20904

International Federation of
Training and Development
Organizations
c/o Derek Wake
7 Westbourne Road, Southport
Merseyside PR8 2HZ
United Kingdom

National Association for
Industry-Education
Cooperation
235 Hendricks Boulevard
Buffalo, NY 14226

National Society for
Performance and Instruction
1126 Sixteenth Street, NW
Suite 315
Washington, DC 20036

National Society of Sales
Training Executives
1040 Woodcock Road
Orlando, FL 32803

# References

*Academic Programs and the World of Work.* Alexandria, Va.: American Society for Training and Development, 1983.

Alden, J. (ed.). *Critical HRD Research Issues.* Alexandria, Va.: American Society for Training and Development, 1982.

Allio, R. J., and Pennington, M. W. (eds.). *Corporate Planning: Techniques and Applications.* New York: AMACOM, 1979.

Anderson, R. E., and Kasl, E. S. *The Costs and Financing of Adult Education and Training.* Lexington, Mass.: Lexington Books, 1982.

Armstrong, J. S. *Long-Range Forecasting, from Crystal Ball to Computer.* New York: Wiley, 1978.

*ASTD Directory of Academic Programs in Training and Development: Human Resource Development 1983–1984.* Alexandria, Va.: American Society for Training and Development, 1983.

Bain, D. *The Productivity Prescription.* New York: McGraw-Hill, 1982.

Barney, D. J. "Technical Programs." In L. Nadler (ed.), *The Handbook of Human Resource Development.* New York: Wiley, 1984.

Baum, A., and Valins, S. *Architecture and Social Behavior.* New York: Wiley, 1977.

Beck, A. C., Jr., and Hillmar, E. D. *A Practical Approach to Organizational Development Through MBO: Selected Readings.* Reading, Mass.: Addison-Wesley, 1972.

Beckhard, R., and Harris, R. *Organizational Transitions: Managing Complex Change*. Reading, Mass.: Addison-Wesley, 1977.

Behringer, H. R. "Training Facilities—XEROX International Center for Training and Management Development." *Training and Development Journal*, 1977, *31*, 48–51.

Berg, I. *Education and Jobs: The Great Training Robbery*. New York: Praeger, 1970.

Birnberg, J. G., and Craft, J. A. "Human Resource Accounting: Perspective and Prospects." *Industrial Relations: A Journal of Economy and Society*, Feb. 1981, pp. 2–12.

Blake, R. R., and Mouton, J. S. *Consultation*. Reading, Mass.: Addison-Wesley, 1976.

Blake, R. R., and Mouton, J. S. *Managerial Grid III*. Houston, Tex.: Gulf, 1984.

Blank, W. E. *Handbook for Developing Competency-Based Training Programs*. Englewood Cliffs, N.J.: Prentice-Hall, 1982.

Brewster, J. H. "A Study of an Emerging Occupational Group—State Directors of Law Enforcement Training: Their Backgrounds and Perceptions of Their Role." Unpublished doctoral dissertation, School of Education and Human Development, George Washington University, 1972.

Broad, M. "Identification of Management Actions to Support Utilization of Training on the Job." Unpublished doctoral dissertation, School of Education and Human Development, George Washington University, 1980.

Broderick, R. "How Honeywell Teaches Its Managers to Manage." *Training: The Magazine of Human Resource Development*, 1983, *20* (1), 18.

Caplan, E. H., and Landekich, S. *Human Resource Accounting: Past, Present, and Future*. New York: National Association of Accountants, 1974.

Carnes, W. *Effective Meetings for Busy People*. New York: McGraw-Hill, 1980.

Cavallaro, S. J. "Identifying Human Resource Development Competencies at U.S. Coast Guard Resident Training Centers As Applied to the School Chief Role." Unpublished doctoral dissertation, School of Education and Human Development, George Washington University, 1984.

Chalofsky, N., and Lincoln, C. I. *Up the HRD Ladder: A Guide for Professional Growth.* Reading, Mass.: Addison-Wesley, 1983.

Commission on Planning Adult Learning Systems, Facilities, and Environments. *Directory of Consultants for Planning Adult Learning Systems, Facilities, and Environments.* Washington, D.C.: American Association for Adult and Continuing Education, 1974.

Connell, H. S., III. "Sales Programs." In L. Nadler (ed.), *The Handbook of Human Resource Development.* New York: Wiley, 1984.

David, T. G., and Wright, B. D. (eds.). *Learning Environments.* Chicago: University of Chicago Press, 1975.

Davidson, R. J. "Perceptions of the Activities Necessary to Gain a Voice in Federal Legislative Policy Matters for the Human Resource Development Professional." Unpublished doctoral dissertation, School of Education and Human Development, George Washington University, 1977.

Davies I. K. *Instructional Technique.* New York: McGraw-Hill 1981.

Davis, R. W. "Financial Aspects of HRD." In L. Nadler (ed.), *The Handbook of Human Resource Development.* New York: Wiley, 1984.

Deming, B. S. *Evaluating Training Programs: A Guide for Training the Trainer.* Arlington, Va.: American Society for Training and Development, 1982.

Denova, C. *Test Construction for Training Evaluation.* New York: Van Nostrand Reinhold, 1979.

Dibner, D. R. *Joint Ventures for Architects and Engineers.* New York: McGraw-Hill, 1977.

Drucker, P. F. *Managing for Results.* New York: McGraw-Hill, 1959.

Drucker, P. F. *Management: Tasks, Responsibilities, Practices.* New York: Harper & Row, 1971.

Drucker, P. F. *Management: Tasks, Responsibilities, Practices.* New York: Harper & Row, 1974.

Ebersberger, S. "Human Resource Accounting: Can We Afford It?" *Training and Development Journal*, 1981, *35* (8), 37–41.

Eitington, J. W. *The Winning Trainer*. Houston, Tex.: Gulf, 1984.

*The Employee Development Specialist Curriculum Plan: An Outline of Learning Experiences for the Employee Development Specialist*. Washington, D.C.: U.S. Civil Service Commission, 1976.

Engel, H. M. *Handbook of Creative Learning Experiences*. Houston, Tex.: Gulf, 1973.

Engel, H. M. *How to Delegate: A Guide to Getting Things Done*. Houston, Tex.: Gulf, 1983.

Epstein, J. "Line Managers' Perceptions and Expectations of the Operational Function of an Employee Development Specialist in a Federal Government Research and Development Organization." Unpublished doctoral dissertation, School of Education, George Washington University, 1971.

Epstein, J., and Nadler, L. "Managers' Views of Employee Development Specialists' Roles in an R & D Organization." *European Training*, 1972, *1*, 239–252.

Eurich, N. P. *Corporate Classrooms: The Learning Business*. Princeton, N.J.: The Carnegie Foundation for the Advancement of Teaching, 1985.

Fildes, R., and Wood, D. (eds.). *Forecasting and Planning*. New York: Praeger, 1978.

Finkel, C. "The Learning Environment: Its Critical Importance to Successful Meetings." In L. Nadler (ed.), *The Handbook of Human Resource Development*. New York: Wiley, 1984.

Finkel, C., and Nadler, L. (eds.). *Succeed in Facilities Planning*. Info-line: Practical Guidelines for Human Resource Development Professionals. Alexandria, Va.: American Society for Training and Development, Apr. 1985.

Finney, H. A. *Principles of Accounting—Advanced*. Englewood Cliffs, N.J.: Prentice-Hall, 1946.

French, W. *The Personnel Management Process*. Boston: Houghton Mifflin, 1964.

Gallessich, J. *The Profession and Practice of Consultation: A Handbook for Consultants, Trainers of Consultants, and*

*Consumers of Consultation Services.* San Francisco: Jossey-Bass, 1982.

Gelbach, D. L. "Designing the Training Room of Your Dreams." *Training: The Magazine of Human Resource Development,* 1982, *19,* 16–21.

Gill, W. B., and Luke, A. W. *Facilities Handbook for Career Education.* Washington, D.C.: National Institute of Education, 1976.

Glazer, R. R. "The Role of the Staff Developer in School Systems As Perceived by Incumbents and Their Supervisors." Unpublished doctoral dissertation, School of Education and Human Development, George Washington University, 1983.

Goad, T. W. *Delivering Effective Training.* San Diego, Calif.: University Associates, 1982.

Goldstein, I. L. *Training: Program Development and Evaluation.* Monterey, Calif.: Brooks/Cole, 1974.

Gouldner, A. W. "Cosmopolitans and Locals: Toward an Analysis of Latent Social Roles." *Administrative Science Quarterly,* 1957, *57* (2), 281–306.

Gregold, W. C. *Management by Objectives: A Self-Instructional Approach.* Vol. 1: *Strategic Planning and the MBO Process.* Vol. 2: *Objective Setting and the MBO Process.* Vol. 3: *Performance Appraisal and the MBO Process.* New York: McGraw-Hill, 1978.

Gutteridge, T. G., and Hutcheson, P. G. "Career Development." In L. Nadler (ed.), *The Handbook of Human Resource Development.* New York: Wiley, 1984.

Halal, W. E. "Strategic Management: The State of the Art & Beyond." Washington, D.C.: George Washington University, 1983. (An article adapted from *The New Capitalism.* New York: Wiley, 1985.)

Harris, P. R. (ed.). *Global Strategies for Human Resource Development.* Alexandria, Va.: American Society for Training and Development, 1984.

Harris, P. R., and Moran, R. *Managing Cultural Differences* (2nd ed.) Houston, Tex.: Gulf, 1985.

Head, G. E. *Training Cost Analysis: A Practical Guide.* Washington, D.C.: Marlin Press, 1985.

Heimsath, C. *Behavioral Architecture.* New York: McGraw-Hill, 1977.

Henke, E. O., Holmes, R. L., and Conway, L. G., Jr. *Managerial Use of Accounting Data.* Houston, Tex.: Gulf, 1978.

Hennecke, M. "Strategic Planning, Part 1." *Small Business Report,* Feb. 1983a, pp. 28–32.

Hennecke, M. "Strategic Planning, Part 2." *Small Business Report,* Mar. 1983b, pp. 28–32.

Hennecke, M. "Strategic Planning, Part 3." *Small Business Report,* Apr. 1983c, pp. 21–24.

Hennecke, M. "Strategic Planning for Human Resources." *Training: The Magazine of Human Resource Development,* 1984, *21,* 25–34.

Herold, A. K. "A Study of the Job Behaviors of Persons Responsible for Directing Continuing Education Projects/Programs for the Mental Health Field." Unpublished doctoral dissertation, School of Education and Human Development, George Washington University, 1973.

Herous, G.A.M. *Continuing Professional Education—How.* Homewood, Ill.: Institute for Continuing Legal Education, 1975.

"Honeywell: Management Development at This Corporate Giant Is Considered an Investment in the Future." *Training: The Magazine of Human Resource Development,* 1983, *20* (1), 20.

*How to Read a Balance Sheet.* (2nd ed.) Switzerland: International Labor Office, 1985.

"The Human Factor." *Productivity Measurement and Analysis,* no. 24. Tokyo: Asian Productivity Organization, 1984.

Januszewski, C. S. "The Simple Secret of Design Criteria." *Training: The Magazine of Human Resource Development,* 1975, *12,* 40–45.

Jewell, D. *Public Assembly Facilities.* New York: Wiley, 1978.

Kaiser, H. H. (ed.). *Managing Facilities More Effectively.* San Francisco: Jossey-Bass, 1980.

Kirkpatrick, D. L. (ed.). *Evaluating Training Programs.* New York: McGraw-Hill, 1976.

Koontz, H., and O'Donnell, C. *Principles of Management: An*

*Analysis of Managerial Function.* (5th ed.) New York: McGraw-Hill, 1972.

Kubr, M. (ed.). *Management Consulting: A Guide to the Profession.* (2nd ed.) Alexandria, Va.: International Labor Office, 1983.

Lawson, F. *Conference, Convention, and Exhibition Facilities: A Handbook of Planning, Design, and Management.* London: Architectural Press, 1981.

Lee, C. "Training at Southland Corp." *Training: The Magazine of Human Resource Development,* 1984, *21* (12), 29–41.

Levitan, S. A., and Johnson, C. M. *Second Thoughts on Work.* Kalamazoo, Mich.: Upjohn Institute for Employment Research, 1982.

Lippitt, G., and Hoopes, D. S. (eds.). *Helping Across Cultures.* Bethesda, Md.: International Consultants Foundation, 1978.

Lippitt, G., and Lippitt, R. *The Consulting Process in Action.* San Diego, Calif.: University Associates, 1978.

Lippitt, G., and Nadler, L. "Emerging Roles of the Training Director." *Training and Development Journal,* 1967, *21,* 2–10.

Lord, K. *The Design of the Industrial Classroom.* Reading, Mass.: Addison-Wesley, 1977.

Lumsden, G. J. "The Training Department Budget." In J. F. Harrison (ed.), *The Management of Sales Training.* Reading, Mass.: Addison-Wesley, 1977.

Lusterman, S. *Education in Industry.* New York: Conference Board, 1977.

"Lutheran General Hospital: Nonmedical Training Fulfills Part of This Hospital's Strategy for the 1980s." *Training: The Magazine of Human Resource Development,* 1983, *20* (2), 52.

Margolis, F., and Bell, C. *Managing the Learning Process.* Minneapolis, Minn.: Lakewood Books, 1985.

Miner, M. G., and Miner, J. B. *A Guide to Personnel Management.* Washington, D.C.: Bureau of National Affairs, 1973.

*Models for Excellence.* Arlington, Va.: American Society for Training and Development, 1983.

Morris, L. L., Fitz-Gibbon, C. T., and Henderson, M. *Program Evaluation Kit.* Beverley Hills, Calif.: Sage, 1978.

Morse, S. W. *Employee Educational Programs: Implications for Industry and Higher Education.* Washington, D.C.: Association for the Study of Higher Education, 1985.

Mouton, J. S., and Blake, R. R. *Synergogy: A New Strategy for Education, Training, and Development.* San Francisco: Jossey-Bass, 1984.

Nadler, L. "Developing Nonprofessional Trainers." *Journal of The American Society of Training Directors,* 1955, *9*, 23–28.

Nadler, L. "A Study of the Needs of Selected Training Directors in Pennsylvania Which Might Be Met by Professional Education Institutions." Unpublished doctoral dissertation, Teachers College, Columbia University, 1962.

Nadler, L. "Human Investment Act of 1967." *Training and Development Journal,* 1967, *21* (7), 2–8.

Nadler, L. "Has Federal Legislation Affected Your Training?" *Training in Business and Industry,* 1969a, *4* (8), 16–19.

Nadler, L. "The Organization As a Microculture." *Personnel Journal,* Dec. 1969b, *48* (12), 949–956.

Nadler, L. "Helping the Hard-Core Adjust to the World of Work." *Harvard Business Review,* Mar.-Apr. 1970, pp. 117–126.

Nadler, L. "Learning from the Effect of Economic Decline on Human Resource Development." *Training and Development Journal,* 1976, *30* (1), 3–12.

Nadler, L. *Developing Human Resources.* (2nd ed.) San Diego, Calif.: Learning Concepts/University Associates, 1979.

Nadler, L. *Corporate Human Resource Development.* New York: Van Nostrand Reinhold, 1980.

Nadler, L. *Designing Training Programs: The Critical Events Model.* Reading, Mass.: Addison-Wesley, 1982a.

Nadler, L. "Keeping Up-to-Date." *Training and Development Journal,* 1982b, *36*, 40–48.

Nadler, L. *Personal Skills for the Manager.* Homewood, Ill.: Dow Jones-Irwin, 1983.

Nadler, L. (ed.). *The Handbook of Human Resource Development.* New York: Wiley, 1984a.

Nadler, L. "What Japanese Managers Learned from the U.S." *California Management Review,* 1984b, *26* (4), 46–61.

Nadler, L. "The Organization As a Microculture." In C. Bell and L. Nadler (eds.), *Clients and Consultants: Meeting and Exceeding Expectations*. Houston, Tex.: Gulf, 1985.

Nadler, L., and Nadler, Z. *The Conference Book*. Houston, Tex.: Gulf, 1977.

Nadler, L., and Nadler, Z. "The Client-Consultant Relationship in Organizational Transition." In C. Bell and L. Nadler, *Clients and Consultants: Meeting and Exceeding Expectations*. Houston, Tex.: Gulf, 1985.

Naisbitt, J. *Megatrends: Ten New Directions Transforming Our Lives*. New York: Warner Books, 1982.

Noer, D. "Ready, Set, Turn a Profit!" *Training and Development Journal*, 1985, *39* (5), 38–39.

Odiorne, G. S. *Strategic Management of Human Resources: A Portfolio Approach*. San Francisco: Jossey-Bass, 1984.

Ouchi, W. *Theory Z: How American Business Can Meet the Japanese Challenge*. Reading, Mass.: Addison-Wesley, 1981.

Palmer, B. C., and Palmer, K. R. *The Successful Meeting Master Guide*. Englewood Cliffs, N.J.: Prentice-Hall, 1983.

Pepper, A. D. *Managing the Training and Development Function*. Hampshire, England: Gower, 1984.

Peters, T. J., and Waterman, R. H., Jr. *In Search of Excellence: Lessons From America's Best-Run Companies*. New York: Harper & Row, 1982.

Phillips, J. J. *Handbook of Training Evaluation and Measurement Methods*. Houston, Tex.: Gulf, 1983.

Reynolds, A. S. "Computer-Based Learning." In L. Nadler (ed.), *The Handbook of Human Resource Development*. New York: Wiley, 1984a.

Reynolds, A. (ed.). *Technology Transfer*. Boston: International Human Resources Development Corporation, 1984b.

Rockwell, D. M. *Educational Change and Architectural Consequences*. New York: Educational Facilities Laboratories, 1971.

Rockwell, D. M., and Sleeman, P. J. (eds.). *Designing Learning Environments*. New York: Longman, 1981.

Rosen, L. S. (ed.). *Topics in Managerial Accounting*. (2nd ed.) New York: McGraw-Hill, 1974.

Schein, E. H. *Career Dynamics: Matching Individual and Organizational Needs.* Reading, Mass.: Addison-Wesley, 1978.

Schein, E. H. *Organizational Culture and Leadership: A Dynamic View.* San Francisco: Jossey-Bass, 1985.

Schumacher, E. F. *Small Is Beautiful: Economics As If People Mattered.* New York: Harper & Row, 1975.

Scobel, D. N. *Creative Worklife.* Houston, Tex.: Gulf, 1981.

Shea, G. F. *The New Employee.* Reading, Mass.: Addison-Wesley, 1981.

Shipp, T. (ed.). *Creative Financing and Budgeting.* New Directions for Continuing Education, no. 16. San Francisco: Jossey-Bass, 1982.

Sisson, G. R. "Development of Training for a New Manufacturing Process." *Training and Development Journal,* 1972, *26,* 22–31.

Spector, A. K. "Identification and Analysis of Human Resource Development Policy in Selected U.S. Corporations." Unpublished doctoral dissertation, School of Education and Human Development, George Washington University, 1985.

Steele, F. *The Role of the Internal Consultant.* Boston: CBI Publishing, 1982.

Theodore, T. K. "The Reality of the Nadler HRD Role Model." Unpublished doctoral dissertation, School of Education, Temple University, 1977.

Tough, A. *The Adult's Learning Projects.* Ontario, Canada: Ontario Institute for Studies in Education, 1971.

Tracey, W. R. *Managing Training and Development Systems.* New York: AMACOM, 1978.

Tracey, W. R. *Human Resource Development Standards.* New York: AMACOM, 1981.

Tracey, W. R. (ed.). *Human Resources Management and Development Handbook.* New York: AMACOM, 1984.

*The Trainer's Resource.* Amherst, Mass.: HRD Press, 1985.

*Webster's New World Dictionary of the American Language.* (2nd ed.) New York: Simon & Schuster, 1982.

Wiggs, G. "Development of a Conceptual Model for Achieving Professionalization of an Occupation, As Applied to the ASTD and to Other HRD Organizations." Unpublished doctoral dissertation, School of Education, George Washington University, 1971.

Zemke, R. "Industry-Education Cooperation: Old Phrase, New Meaning." *Training: The Magazine of Human Resources Development,* 1985, *22* (7), 20-24.

Zey, M. G. *The Mentor Connection.* Homewood, Ill.: Dow Jones-Irwin, 1984.

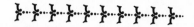

# Index